Medicolegal Library 3

Edited by A. Carmi

Disability

Edited by
A. Carmi E. Chigier S. Schneider

With Contributions by
H. Ariel P. J. Blommestijn A. Carmi E. Chigier
B. Fishel D. W. Florence J. K. M. Gevers
B. L. Gonzales D. Greenberg N. S. Greenberg
A. F. Halmosh A. Kjønstad U. Lowental
J. E. Magnet N. J. Marlett A. Mashiah T. Mashiah
G. Mendelson S. Moskowitz S. Navon M. Neumann
A. Ohry B. Posner J. Rattock H. S. Rollmann-Branch
J. Rubin S. Schneider L. Seda-Mendoza L. Shahani
M. Sigal H. Schünemann R. Stolberg-Acosta
H. Stoll J. B. Varcoe M. Yaron

With 5 Figures and 20 Tables

Springer-Verlag
Berlin Heidelberg New York Tokyo 1984

Judge Amnon Carmi
P.O.B. 6451,
Haifa 31063, Israel

Dr. Emanuel Chigier
Medical Services, Youth Alliyah
12 Kaplan St., Tel Aviv 63474, Israel

Dr. Stanley Schneider
Summit Institute, Wurzweiler School of Social Work,
Yeshiva University Michlala, College for Women,
P.O.B. 7446, Jerusalem, Israel

The Institution for National Insurance in Israel assisted with the editorial preparation.

ISBN 3-540-13421-2 Springer-Verlag Berlin Heidelberg New York Tokyo
ISBN 0-387-13421-2 Springer-Verlag New York Heidelberg Berlin Tokyo

Library of Congress Cataloging in Publication Data. Main entry under title: Disability. (Medicolegal Library; 3). Includes bibliographies and index.
1. Handicapped – Legal status, laws, etc. 2. Handicapped. I. Carmi, Amnon. II. Chigier, E. III. Schneider, S. (Stanley). VI. Ariel, H. V. Series.
[DNLM: 1. Handicapped. 2. Handicapped – legislation. HV 3011 D6105]
K637.D57 1984 346.01'3 84-5459

Typesetting and binding: G. Appl, Wemding, printing: aprinta, Wemding
2119/3140-5 4 3 2 1 0

Foreword

The Medicolegal Library is the first and only series of its kind. Its importance is self-evident. During the last decade, science, especially medical practice, has become an increasingly complex undertaking. Recent dramatic developments in medicine have given rise to both theoretical controversies and practical dilemmas. Society is struggling with new scientific, economic, cultural, and legal issues. The establishment of a series such as this appears vital for lawyers and physicians, for sociologists and psychologists, and for the public at large.

The editorial board of the Medicolegal Library consists of distinguished scientists from many different countries and disciplines. Judge Amnon Carmi acts as principal series editor. Judge Carmi is the author of many books and articles on medical law, and is Editor-in-Chief of *Medicine and Law: An International Journal.*

The Medicolegal Library will issue two books each year. The first four books, soon to be published, will deal with child abuse, euthanasia, disability, and nursing, laws and ethics.

It is the wish and intention of Springer-Verlag that the Medicolegal Library play an important role throughout the world in the study and understanding of the field of medicine and law, for the benefit of both professions and of mankind at large.

Contents

I. Introduction

Speech Before the International Convention on the Medicolegal Aspects of Disability
L. Shahani 3

What Is Medical and what Is Legal About Disability?
E. Chigier 5

II. Disability and Law

On the Realization of the Rights of Invalids According to the Israeli National Insurance Law
H. Ariel 11

Issues of Competence and the Dependent Adults Act
N. J. Marlett 16

Employment Opportunities for the Handicapped in the United States
S. Moskowitz 41

Implementing Legal Mandates Regarding the Disabled in Educational Institutions in the USA
N. S. Greenberg and D. Greenberg 50

Learning Disabilities and the Court
J. B. Varcoe 58

Judicial Self-awareness and Psychoanalytic Countertransference
H. S. Rollmann-Branch 63

The Disabled Person as a Witness in Court
A. Carmi 70

Economic Constraints on the Effectiveness of Litigation and Legislation for the Disabled
J. Rubin 75

Assessment of Disability
A. Kjønstad 84

Chronic Pain in the Medicolegal Aspects of Workers' Compensation Cases
D. W. Florence 106

III. Disability and Medicine

Psychosocial Aspects of Disability
M. Neumann 115

Psychosocial Factors in Successful Rehabilitation
U. Lowental 125

Liability of Medical Malpractice in German Law
H. Stoll 128

The Family and the Invalid: Who Needs Whom?
A. F. Halmosh 141

Self-concept of Rheumatoid Arthritis Patients
S. Navon, B. Fishel, and M. Yaron 147

Definitions of Rehabilitation in Legislation
P. J. Blommestijn 159

Medicolegal Considerations in the Care of Severely Disabled Newborn in Canada
J. E. Magnet 181

Rehabilitation of Heroin Addicts with Methadone Maintenance: A Five-Year Clinical Experience
R. Stolberg-Acosta and L. Seda-Mendoza 187

Rehabilitation of Traumatic Brain-injured Patients
A. Ohry and J. Rattok 191

Prostheses for Disabled Elderly Amputees
T. Mashiah and A. Mashiah 193

The Effect of Legal Settlement on Work Disability Following Compensable Injury
G. Mendelson 198

IV. Medicolegal Aspects

Medicolegal Criteria for Post-traumatic Psycho Syndrome
M. Sigal 209

Informed Consent by Mentally Disabled Persons
H. Schünemann 215

Confidentiality: The Moral/Legal/Treatment Conflict
S. Schneider 222

Disability, Medical Intervention, and Individual Freedom
J. K. M. Gevers 230

Medicolegal Aspects of Sterilization for Mentally Disabled Persons
B. L. Gonzales 238

V. Epilogue

The Eighties: Decade of Handicapped People
B. Posner 247

Subject Index 252

29 [illegible]

List of Contributors

Judge H. Ariel
Hanna Street 16, Haifa 31999, Israel

Dr. P. J. Blommestijn
Head, General Department of Old Age Welfare Policy and Social Rehabilitation, Netherlands Ministry of Culture, Recreation and Social Welfare

Judge A. Carmi
P.O.B. 6451, Haifa 31063, Israel

Dr. E. Chigier
Medical Services, Youth Alliyah, 12 Kaplan St., Tel Aviv 63474, Israel

Dr. B. Fishel
Department of Rheumatology and Physical Medicine, Tel Aviv Medical Center, Tel Aviv University Medical School, Tel Aviv 63474, Israel

Dr. D. A. Florence
205 South Rhode Island Avenue, Minneapolis, MN 55426, USA

Dr. J. K. M. Gevers
Institute of Social Medicine, University of Amsterdam
Herrengracht 520, 1017 CC Amsterdam, The Netherlands

Dr. B. L. Gonzales
Deputy Director of National Program, Association for Voluntary Sterilization, Inc., 708 Third Avenue, New York, NY 10017, USA

Dr. David Greenberg
Fiorello H. La Guardia Community College, The City University of New York, 31-10 Thomson Avenue, Long Island City, NY 11101, USA

Prof. N. S. Greenberg
Fiorello H. La Guardia Community College, The City University of New York, 31-10 Thomson Avenue, Long Island City, NY 11101, USA

Dr. A. F. Halmosh
Psychiatric Community Service, Soroka Medical Center, Faculty of Health Sciences, Ben-Gurion University of the Negev, P.O.B. 2016, Beer-Sheba 84120, Israel

Prof. A. Kjønstad
Professor of Law, University of Oslo, Oslo, Norway

Dr. U. Lowental
Eshkol Boulevard 22, Apt. 3, Jerusalem 92-585, Israel

Dr. J. E. Magnet
Faculty of Law, University of Ottawa, Ottawa, Canada

Dr. N. J. Marlett
Faculty of Education, Department of Educational Psychology, The University of Calgary 2500 University Drive, N. W. Calgary, Alberta T2N IN4, Canada

Dr. A. Mashiah
Vascular Surgery Unit, Kaplan Hospital, Rehovot, Israel

Dr. T. Mashiah
Geriatric Medicine Department, Harzfeld Hospital, Gedera, Israel

Dr. G. Mendelson
Department of Psychological Medicine, Monash University, Prince Henry's Hospital, 30 Queens Road, Melbourne 3004, Australia

Prof. Dr. S. Moskowitz
19 Connstock Hill Road, Norwalk, CN 06850, USA

Dr. S. Navon
Department of Rheumatology and Physical Medicine, Tel Aviv Medical Center, Tel Aviv University Medical School, Ichilov Hospital, Tel Aviv 62239, Israel

Dr. M. Neumann
Shalvata Mental Health Center, Tel Aviv University Medical School, P.O.B. 94, Hod Hasharon, Israel

Dr. A. Ohry
Neurological Rehabilitation Department, Chaim Sheba Medical Center, Tel Hashomer, Israel

Dr. B. Posner
Washington, DC 20067, USA

Dr. J. Rattock
Head Trauma Program, Institute of Rehabilitation Medicine, New York University, Medical Center, New York City, NY 10017, USA

Prof. H. S. Rollmann-Branch
University of Southern California, Law Center and Medical School, Los Angeles, CA 90033, USA

Prof. Dr. J. Rubin
Department of Economics, Rutgers University, New Brunswick, NJ 08903, USA

Prof. L. Seda-Mendoza
Department of Psychiatry, School of Medicine, University of Puerto Rico P.O.B. 5067, San Juan 00936, Puerto Rico

L. Shahani
Assistant Secretary General, Center for Social Development and Humanitarian Affairs United Nations, Postfach 500, 1400 Vienna, Austria

Dr. M. Sigal
Pardessia Government Hospital, Sackler School of Medicine, Tel Aviv University, P.O.B. 2167, Netanya 42121, Israel

Dr. S. Schneider
Summit Institute, Wurzweiler School of Social Work, Yeshiva University Michlala, College for Women, P.O.B. 7446, Jerusalem, Israel

Dr. H. Schünemann
Institut für Pharmazie und medizinischem Recht an der Universität Göttingen, Gosslerstraße 19, 3400 Göttingen, FRG

Prof. R. Stolberg-Acosta
Department of Psychiatry, School of Medicine, University of Puerto Rico, P.O.B. 5067, San Juan 00936, Puerto Rico

Prof. H. Stoll
Universität Freiburg, 7800 Freiburg, FRG

Dr. J. B. Varcoe
Judge of the Provincial Court of British Columbia, 22460 Dewdney Trunk Road, Maple Ridge, British Columbia, Canada

Dr. M. Yaron
Department of Rheumatology and Physical Medicine, Tel Aviv Medical Center, Tel Aviv University Medical School, Tel Aviv 63474, Israel

I. Introduction

Speech Before the International Convention on the Medicolegal Aspects of Disability

L. Shahani

Within the past decade, the General Assembly of the United Nations has sought to deal with the problems of disabled persons within the framework of a unified approach to development. The central aims of the United Nations in its policies and programs on behalf of disabled persons have been to ensure the rights of these people and to facilitate their integration into society. The overarching purpose of these aims is to enable physically and mentally disabled persons to contribute effectively to the development process and to derive appropriate benefits from their efforts.

In 1971, consistent with these aims, the General Assembly adopted resolution 2856 containing the Declaration on the Rights of Mentally Retarded Persons. In 1975, resolution 3447 followed, containing the Declaration on the Rights of Disabled Persons, and on December 16, 1979, resolution 31/123 was adopted proclaiming 1981 International Year of Disabled Persons (IYDP) with the theme "self-participation."

These, in rather summary form, were the steps taken by the Assembly leading to its adoption in 1979 of resolution 34/154. In it, the Assembly set forth the broad principles and policy objectives of the IYDP and approved the recommendations of the Advisory Committee, which had been set up under an earlier Assembly resolution. These recommendations were adopted by the Assembly as the Plan of Action of the IYDP.

It is at the national level, of course, that the most meaningful and enduring work can be done in support of IYDP objectives. Mindful of this, the IYDP Plan of Action invited member states to establish machinery "to plan, coordinate, and execute, or encourage the execution of activities in support of the objectives of the Year at the local and national levels". Already, over 100 countries have created national committees to do just this.

The importance of the work to be done at the national level cannot be sufficiently emphasized. Each country knows best how to deal with its disabled persons within its own cultural traditions and developmental priorities. Clearly, in certain developing countries it would be most judicious to emphasize prevention of disability over treatment. In parts of Africa, for example, a sanitation program that could stamp out the causes of river blindness or prevent polio through a simple vaccination would prove far more beneficial than dealing with the consequences of such diseases. On the other hand, in certain developed countries there is a growing interest in helping disabled persons pursue independent life-styles within the community.

Despite different approaches there are commonly shared philosophies in dealing with the disabled. One such philosophy that is gaining acceptance is to promote the integration of disabled persons into the larger society. Except for the severely disabled, who require continuing and specialized treatment, it is no longer to the benefit of disabled persons nor in the interest of society to isolate them or place them in institutions. Under such confining conditions these people cannot achieve a maximum of individual self-expression or participate in a meaningful way in society. Promoting their acceptance and integration into the larger community has already become a central concern to many governments. What forms should integration take, and how can they be carried out? Integration should become a reality in the work place – in the factory, the office, and the rural areas – so that disabled persons can contribute to their own development. In this way, they become valued and productive members of society. Integration should also take place within a community's educational, social, cultural, and political institutions so that disabled persons have opportunities to contribute to community growth and development. Instead of isolation and dependence, the disabled person is afforded the chance to interact with society as an independent being.

In achieving these goals government, private organizations, and people at large have important roles to play. Government must create the appropriate psychological and material conditions for integration to become a reality rather than remain an elusive goal. In concert with private organizations, government can help change negative public attitudes so that society will become accepting of disabled persons. This involves educating people in ways that can break down long-standing misapprehensions and prejudices about the physically and mentally handicapped. Government must also do everything it can to remove man-made and natural barriers that limit access of disabled persons to the physical, social, and cultural environment. And it also has to make available within the community appropriate supportive social, medical, and vocational services so that disabled persons can secure the services they need, and that they have a right to expect.

The task of helping disabled persons is an enormous one. One person in ten, or about 450 million people in the world have physical or mental handicaps. All too often we curse the disabled by despising, or worse, ignoring them, and we place stumbling blocks in their path by institutionalizing them and excluding them from our midst. Every one of us should remember the guiding principle for the integration of disabled persons, which comes from the Old Testament, Leviticus 19: 14: "Thou shalt not curse the deaf, nor put a stumbling block before the blind . . ." This should be our motto in helping the disabled.

What Is Medical and what Is Legal About Disability?

E. Chigier

Although disabled people have been part of the community since the beginning of mankind, the organized scientific approach known as rehabilitative medicine is very new, having only become recognized as a special area of medicine after the Second World War. Renowned physicians such as Drs. Rusk and Kessler in the United States and Dr. Guttman in the United Kingdom began to develop intensive, activated techniques aimed at restoring the disabled patient to maximal capacity as soon as possible after the onset of illness or organic damage. Rehabilitation was described as the "third arm of medicine," after preventive and curative medicine. This concept has recently been challenged by many rehabilitative physicians who regard certain conditions such as spinal cord injury as requiring immediate and continuing care in a special rehabilitation department from the beginning, and not, as often happens, transfer ("dumping") to a rehabilitation department from the acute wards of a hospital when nothing more can be done for the patient.

In recent years, Rehabilitation International and other agencies concerned with the handicapped in society have begun to pay attention to preventive rehabilitation, and to indicate that it is up to rehabilitation workers, who are daily challenged by the consequences of severe disability, to be more involved in the prevention of disability caused by accidents, overeating, lack of immunization procedures, etc.

As a medical discipline, rehabilitative medicine was linked with physical medicine, and medical care was focused on those people with a locomotor disability – paralysis, cerebral palsy, amputation – known as cripples. As a matter of fact, Rehabilitation International, which in 1982 celebrated 60 years of activity, was initially called "The International Society for Cripples." However, over the years it became clear that a rehabilitative approach was necessary in the care of people with chronic medical conditions such as diabetes, renal disease, arthritis, cardiac disease, neurological disorder, epilepsy, cancer, mental retardation, emotional illness, drug dependency, and facial disfigurement. In recent years, the concept of disability, or the need for a rehabilitative approach, has been extended by some workers to include people of very short stature, or with a chronic dermatological disorder such as psoriasis; some geriatricians talk of rehabilitation of the dying patient.

It is clear, therefore, that involvement in disability has become extended to almost every medical discipline, arousing questions as to what role is to be played by the primary care physician, by the medical specialist, and by the rehabilitative physician in dealing with the increased number and range of people who are disabled. With increasing longevity in industrialized countries and diminished hospitalization for acute illnesses, estimates of the percentage of patients who are discharged from a general hospital with a disability range from 25% to 40%, so that medical involvement in prevention, care, aftercare, and maintenance of function with regard to disability is a growing but somewhat amorphous process.

At the other end of the scale, with better medical care and rehabilitation procedures, the life expectancy of many disabled people is much longer than before, and they may reach a static situation where there is no further deterioration, and even function well within the limits of the disability. Can a person with paraplegia who plays wheelchair basketball, a person with diabetes who runs a large corporation, a woman dancer who has had a mastectomy for breast breast cancer, a retarded person working in open industry, or an artist who has been hospitalized for schizophrenia be regarded as ill, or as healthy despite the presence of disability? The fact that it is possible to become disabled and remain a healthy person has obvious medicolegal implications.

When rehabilitative medicine became organized, the medical aspect of rehabilitation became established and dominant, with its doctors, nurses, physical, speech and occupational therapists, with its emphasis on finding a clear-cut etiology, a structured therapeutic approach, and a defined end point with regard to provision of services. But with time it became clear that the medical model alone would not work, and that psychosocial factors were equally important. Without attention to such factors through the intervention of psychologists and social workers, some amputees complained of inadequacies of prosthesis, the disabled did not go back to work to the extent that their condition allowed, people with epilepsy or diabetes were irregular in maintaining their medical regime, people who had experienced cardiac infarction did not resume sexual intercourse, aged people with stroke became depressed and deteriorated rapidly. So rehabilitation became a multidisciplinary approach, with difficulties in defining and coordinating the respective functions of the medical and psychosocial professionals, and in linking hospital care to care at home and within the family. Problems of fragmentation and duplication of services, financing of rehabilitation services at the centralized, local, voluntary, or personal level, training of personnel to provide special services – all these and other problems have come about with the realization of disability as a multifactorial and dynamic situation that must be tackled on many fronts.

But that is not the end of the story. Once the medical and psychosocial models of rehabilitation began functioning, it became apparent that what goes on among the nondisabled sector of the community is also of major importance in determining the success or failure of the rehabilitative process. If disabled persons succeed in overcoming physical and psychosocial difficulties, but are prevented from utilizing their human potential because of physical barriers to transport and lack of accessibility to places of work, public buildings, theaters and restaurants, and because of the negative attitudes of employers, neighbors, and the general public, what is the use of putting so much effort into the rehabilitation of the disabled person per se? A Canadian poster for the general public states, "Your attitude to the disabled person may be the biggest handicap of all." The "societal" or "community" factor has thus also entered the awareness of those concerned with the advancement of disabled persons. This has been characterized by recognition of the rights of the disabled person on an international and a national basis, a turning to the legislature and to the courts to ensure better, nondiscriminatory opportunities for disabled persons. There has been research into attitudinal barriers in society and how to overcome them, a burgeoning of books, newspaper articles, plays, and movies dealing with the human issues of disability, and the growth of a consumer approach and activist community organizations of disabled people. A coalition of organizations of disabled people in the United States, Canada, Sweden, Denmark, Israel, and elsewhere has been established, as well as an international organization called Disabled Peoples International (DPI), and Mobility International, which concerns itself with travel and tourist possibilities for disabled persons. Another very recent, and as yet embryonic, trend is the exploration of successful techniques in providing education about disability to the nondisabled at the school level, before discriminatory and prejudicial opinions become stratified and established to the extent that change is very difficult in adulthood. Finally, the acknowledgement of the need to tackle the problem on a global basis has brought about the program of the International Year of Disabled Persons in 1981, declared by the United Nations.

What is "legal" about disability? It is acknowledged that where there are people, there are problems, and where there are problems there are lawyers, judges, courts, and legislators. So it is, too, with regard to the 10% or so of the population who have a disability, who require help or financial assistance, seek compensation or redress for what has happened to them. The involvement of social security programs in providing financial assistance for disabled persons, the increase in the number of disabled people demanding compensation as victims of the activities of others, the legal issues that arise when disabled people move about in open society or demand the right to do so, all have involved not only lawmakers but also judges and lawyers more and more in the rehabilitation process. In many instances this has been to the benefit of disabled people, but in some cases there has been the feeling that intervention by the legal profession has placed a burden upon rehabilitation services, may have helped to reduce incentive toward full rehabilitation, and thus sometimes works to the ultimate disadvantage of the disabled person and his family. There is nothing "legal" or "illegal" about disability, but it would seem that the time has come for those from the legal profession to meet with rehabilitation workers and with disabled persons to discuss these issues, and to learn and benefit from each other's experience.

I think it is advisable to look at several definitions recently formulated by the World Health Organization and published in 1980, which can be very useful for those involved in the field of rehabilitation [1]. They deal with three terms – "impairment", "disability" and "handicap" – which are defined as follows:

1. An *impairment* is any loss or abnormality of psychological, physiological or anatomical structure or function.
2. A *disability* is any restriction or lack of ability to perform an activity in the manner or within the range considered normal for a human being (resulting from an impairment).
3. A *handicap* is a disadvantage for a given individual, resulting from an impairment or disability, that limits or prevents the fulfillment of a role that is normal (depending upon age, sex and social and cultural factors) for that individual.

It is our common cause and purpose to do our best to ensure that those who have a congenital or acquired impairment leading to a disability be handicapped as little as possible, as the result of our combined efforts at rehabilitation.

Reference

World Health Organization (1980) International classification of impairments, disabilities and handicaps: A manual of classification relating to the consequences of diseases. Geneva

II. Disability and Law

On the Realization of the Rights of Invalids According to the Israeli National Insurance Law

H. Ariel

1 Qualifying for Disability Pension

Three major conditions must be met by the invalid applying for a monthly pension under the chapter on disability insurance in the National Insurance Law (consolidated version) of 1968:

1. He must be incapable of earning a living, or his capacity to earn a living by any employment or occupation must have been reduced in consequence of his disability by at least 50%.
2. His medical disability must be at least 35%.
3. His functional disability must be at least 50%.

Without going into the specific details relating to housewives, it should be pointed out that they, too, are insured under the disability chapter, even if they are not employees or self-employed workers. In these cases, of course, the test of functional disability will not be the capacity to earn a living, but the capacity at a given age to perform the work involved in running a household.

Special tests have been evolved in order to examine the capacity of a housewife to perform the work that is typically required in households. The principal difference between the requirements for the housewife and those for other insured persons is that the medical disability of the former be at least 50% (if it stems from one defect) or 60% (if it stems from more than one defect), before she is entitled to a monthly pension.

1.1 Incapacity to Earn a Living

The first condition relates to the actual incapacity of an individual to earn a salary as an employee, or an income as a self-employed person.

This fact is fundamental to the consideration of whether the person involved qualifies as an invalid under the law; if he does not meet the requirements he does not qualify, and further conditions need not be examined. This condition is a prerequisite which is determined by the National Insurance Institute by means of a "claims officer", and not by a medical or professional board.

However, the applicant has the right to appeal directly to the Regional Labour Tribunal if his claim for recognition as an invalid is rejected under this condition. The Tribunal will decide in such an appeal on the basis of the evidence, and both parties may adduce medical opinions if necessary. The Tribunal may also take the initiative and appoint a medical expert to clarify the issues before it.

In effect, the Tribunal's taks is to decide on the basis of the evidence whether or not the applicant suffers from a physical or mental defect, and whether he earns an income at all, or earns an income reduced by 50% in comparison with his earnings before he became afflicted.

At this stage the parties to such litigation, or the Tribunal, rarely enter into an examination of the relationship between the defect and the capacity to earn an income, though the causal relationship is indeed a basic consideration. If the existence of these two basic facts is proven, i.e., the physical or mental defect and the loss of income following closely upon appearance of the defect, it becomes a matter of logical deduction to assume a causal relationship between them.

Accordingly, the National Insurance Institute will find it difficult to disprove the existence of such a causal relationship, and success will depend on whether the Institute can show clearly that despite the defect, the reason for a loss of income or for a sharply reduced income lies elsewhere, for example in the shutting down of a factory, or lack of work, or wrongful behavior of the applicant. Both parties have the right to appeal a decision of the Regional Labour Tribunal before the National Labour Tribunal.

1.2 Medical Disability

The second condition mentioned above is that the invalid's medical disability be at least 35%. This disability is determined by a board of one or more medical experts. The board reaches its decision by evaluating the physical and mental defects that afflict the invalid, according to regulations that determine the relative degree of disability relating to each defect, disregarding the question of functional or nonfunctional infirmities. The sum total of disabilities arising from each of several defects represents the final disability of the insured. This decision may be of a final or a temporary nature.

Both sides, the insured and the Institute, are entitled to appeal the decision of a medical board to a board of appeal, composed of three medical experts. It may confirm the appealed decision, set it aside, or amend it.

Further appeals can be lodged directly with the National Labour Tribunal, but are limited to points of law only. Since the medical board is a quasi-judicial body, issues that can be reviewed by the Tribunal include the questions of whethter it proceeded according to the rules of "natural justice" and whether it exceeded its authority. The Tribunal pays special attention to whether the board gives reasonable decisions and examines all the evidence brought before it by the experts of both parties.

The National Labour Tribunal has interpreted its autority of review broadly, and it is not unusual for the Tribunal to examine whether the decision of the board regarding the degree of disability does indeed correspond to the defects of the invalid.

The Tribunal relies on medical opinions submitted to it by the invalid, who may claim that the degree of disability he is entitled to is higher than the one determined by the board. Should the Tribunal agree with such a plea, it will set aside the decision and return the case to the board for renewed consideration, but the Tribunal will not determine the degree of disability.

1.3 Functional Disability

Having overcome the obstacle of showing that he suffers from 35% physical or mental disability, the insured has to measure up to the third condition, which is the degree to which his disability limits his earning capacity; this functional disability must be at least 50%.

The invalid is examined by a board of two or three specialists in the fields of medicine, occupation, and rehabilitation, and their decision may also be of a temporary or permanent nature. This decision can be appealed before a board of three experts, one from each of the above fields of specialization. The board of appeal may confirm the decision of the lower board, set it aside, or amend it.

As in the determination of medical disability, the insured is entitled to take the decision of the board of appeal to the National Labour Tribunal on an issue of "law" only. The Tribunal may overrule the decision of the board of appeal, similar to the way it handles appeals regarding medical disability.

However, if the Tribunal takes a broad view of its powers of review on appeals regarding medical disability, it does so to an even greater extent with appeals regarding functional disability, and extends its authority to overrule the decision of the board of appeal several steps further. Its reasons for doing so are based principally on the fact that the issue of functional disability as a cause of diminished earning capacity is closely linked to the correct interpretation of the law and the correct evaluation of the evidence of experts. Since an appeal before the Tribunal brings the case for the first time before jurists, there is a greater tendency to overrule the board on matters relating to the interpretation of the law and the evaluation of the functional capacity or incapacity of the insured.

The most important directive that the National Labour Tribunal has issued as a guide line to the boards is to assess the functional incapacity of the insured, not in the abstract but as it is in effect. The board has not done its job by giving a general evaluation that the insured is capable of full-time or part-time work, according to his defects, unless it can point concretely to a place of work where the insured can find such full-time or part-time employment. In the absence of such a finding, the insured will be entitled to the monthly pension.

Obviously, this directive places a heavy burden on the shoulders of the National Insurance Institute, which must now adduce proof before the board, through its rehabilitation workers, that there is indeed a place of work for the insured, giving him full-time or part-time employment, according to his limitations.

2 Summary

It can readily be seen that the intervention by the various boards and instances of appeal, and the evaluations they make of the given conditions, may complicate matters and actually obstruct the realization of the invalid's rights. There is no doubt that the number of boards and instances of appeal dealing with the conditions vital to the recognition of the invalid's rights should be restricted, and the National Insurance Institute, itself, is aware of this.

In summarizing the above, we are of the opinion that the entire process could be simplified, with all findings and decisions regarding the right of the invalid to a monthly pension vested in one board, composed of experts in the fields of medicine, occupation, and rehabilitation, which would decide on all the relevant issues.

There may be a certain amount of redundancy in the appointment of experts in the fields of occupation and rehabilitation to this board, since the insured may fail to pass the very first test, i. e., the loss of earning capacity; however, we believe that this waste of manpower would be more than balanced by the shortening of the long and arduous road the invalid presently has to travel.

Naturally, we do not recommend abolishing the right to appeal against decisions of this board, but consideration should be given to the proposal that there be only one board of experts as a tribunal of the first instance, with a right to appeal on issues of law only to the National Labour Tribunal. A jurist or legal advisor could also be made available to the board, upon its request, to help in drafting its decisions – an innovation that might limit the number of appeals to the National Labour Tribunal.

In this connection it may be worthwhile to consider the establishment of Center for Occupation and Rehabilitation, with branches in the various districts, where occupational incapacity due to physical or mental defects would be determined – not only for the purpose of this law, but for various kinds of litigation, for example over work-related accidents, traffic accidents, or injuries incurred in the Army or as a result of terrorist activity.

The decisions of experts in the fields of medicine, rehabilitation, and occupation would be final under this proposal, and would be binding on all courts and tribunals in litigation concerning the payment of monthly pensions or damages to injured persons.

It should be pointed out that when the invalid is entitled to damages under any law other than the National Insurance Law, these damages will generally be reduced by the amount of money the invalid is entitled to receive under the National Insurance Law, so that these damages only amount to the difference between these two sums.

The National Insurance Institute has a right of subrogation to be compensated for any amount it has paid or is paying to the invalid by the person responsible for the invalid's incapacity. In this connection, it might be preferable to present the invalid with the alternative of suing either the party responsible for the injury or the National Insurance Institute, that is, of choosing between the two – particularly since the sums paid under this chapter of the National Insurance Law are generally less than what the invalid would be entitled to under any other law.

However, it is true that the damages paid to the invalid under other laws are lump sums, whereas under the National Insurance Law pensions are paid on a monthly basis, with the possibility of revision due to an improvement or worsening of the invalid's health or of his rehabilitation status. The opinion of the experts is divided as to which system is preferable.

Presenting the invalid with a choice, as suggested above, gives him the final decision on the mode of payment.

Whatever the relevancy of our suggestions, the stand taken by the National Insurance Institute in realizing the rights and the rehabilitation of invalids, together with that of the National Labour Tribunal as a guardian of rights of the invalid under this insurance (which was actually introduced only a few years ago), ensures that the lot of the invalid will gradually improve.

Issues of Competence and the Dependent Adults Act*

N. J. Marlett

1 Introduction

This is a nontechnical report of a research study – *Issues of Competence and the Dependent Adults Act* – which was commissioned by the Public Guardian's Office of the Department of Social Services and Community Health (Alberta). The study had three purposes:

1. To investigate operational definitions of competence that have meaning both to rehabilitation services and to the judicial system
2. To provide informal comparative information for parents and other potential guardians about the proposed dependent adult's relative competence
3. To investigate methods of obtaining indicators of competence

The study was considered necessary because the Dependent Adults Act (Alberta 1976) [1] is a dramatic departure from existing guardianship legislation in which the need for guardianship was synonymous with diagnostic classifications such as mentally retarded, senile, idiot, etc. These classifications were replaced with functional statements, e.g., "unable to care for himself," "unable to make reasonable judgements in respect to all or any matters relating to his person," and "in need of a guardian." These statements, while reflecting a positive trend away from traditional labels, are subjective, open to interpretation, and have potential application to a much broader spectrum of persons than was originally intended. Thus, the Dependent Adults Act, conceived as human rights legislation and designed to ensure the dependent adult's rights to treatment, service, and legal support has the potential to become a vehicle for denying persons who are undesirable rather than incompetent the right to self-determination.

The study attempted to identify some safeguards against overinclusion or underinclusion by studying the Act in light of historical developments, current research, and legal precedents. It also investigated skills and abilities that could be of use in assessing a person's ability to make decisions and participate in community life.

Section 1 presents a historical perspective of guardianship, competence and the legal rights most relevant to guardianship. Section 2 describes the Dependent Adults Act as an alternative to historical concepts of guardianship. Section 3 briefly

---

* Funding provided to the Vocational and Rehabilitation Research Institute through a research contract under the auspices of the Public Guardian's Office (Alberta) and the Department of Social Services and Community Health (Alberta)

describes the study and the major findings. Section 4 presents a number of proposals to strengthen the human rights orientation of the Act. The Appendices, in a separate volume, present a summary of results, definitions of competence from other sources, and article reviews related to guardianship.

2 Guardianship, Competence, and Legal Rights

2.1 Changing Perspectives of Guardianship

The following is a very brief historical perspective of the key developments of guardianship legislation. One is referred to *Guardianship of the Person* by Paul McLaughlin [19] for a detailed account of the historical and sociological aspects of guardianship.

"Trusteeship" was the first declared in Roman law (5 BC), which made extensive provisions for the protection of property of the mentally disabled, but none for personal protection. In medieval England, guardianship (called tutorship) was applied to both the person and the property of the "insane" to protect the person's assets for subsequent heirs.

In the English statute, *De Prerogativa Regis* (approximately 1300), the assets of mentally retarded persons (considered potentially curable) were held by the King until the return of lucidity. Later, amendments initiated incompetency hearings and "committees" who administered estates and had custody of "committed" persons.

The Lunacy Act of 1890 amended *De Prerogativa Regis,* facilitated disposal of land and dispensed the formal hearing, allowing a judge to declare incompetence based on affidavit evidence.

The Ontario Lunacy Act of 1909 was essentially the same as *The Lunacy Act* of England and has formed the basis for most Canadian guardianship legislation. The name of the Act was changed to *The Mental Incompetency Act* in 1937 and a new definition of the "mentally incompetent person" was added: "mentally incompetent person" refers to a person,

(a) in whom there is such a condition of arrested or incomplete development of mind, whether arising from inherent causes or induced by disease or injury, or
(b) who is suffering from such a disorder of the mind, that he requires care, supervision and control for his protection and the protection of his property.

In most provinces, county and district courts have jurisdiction to declare a person mentally incompetent. Appeal options are to the Supreme Court.

In Canada, there are two procedures for establishing the mental incompetence of the person. Incompetency may be declared through affidavit evidence without oral testimony. If there is any doubt about incompetency, the allegedly incompetent person is usually given a court hearing. While the person subject to the application may demand trial by jury, this can be overridden by the court if the judge is satisfied as a result of personal examination that the person is not competent to express the wish for trial by jury.

Generally, evidence is required of two medical practitioners, including at least one specialist, setting out the facts that lead them to the conclusion that the person is mentally incompetent as defined by the appropriate law, and of a layperson who knows the alleged mentally incompetent person and can testify that he is mentally incompetent as defined by the law.

Most provinces have a government official who serves as "statutory committee." This official serves as trustee in conserving and protecting the mentally incompetent person's assets while he is in a mental health facility, and sometimes beyond that point. Only Newfoundland and Nova Scotia do not maintain offices of the statutory committee.

The civil rights movement and normalization – a philosophy affirming the rights of devalued people to live and to be accepted in their own communities – have had a dramatic impact on the acceptance of the legal rights of less able people. As attitudes have changed, new approaches to the question of guardianship of the mentally handicapped have been formulated.

In 1972, the Ohio legislature passed the "Protective Services" law as an alternative to traditional legal guardianship for the mentally retarded or developmentally disabled persons [12]. Three categories of protective service were established under the aegis of the Division of Mental Retardation: guardianship, trusteeship, and "protector" to provide "guidance, services, and encouragement in the development of maximum self-reliance."

This Act is significant in three respects: first, it recognizes different degrees of guardianship; second, it removes the majority of guardianship cases from the court system to what McLaughlin calls a Social Welfare System [19]; and third, it recognizes the rights of the mentally retarded person to be involved in selecting a guardian and in terminating guardianship.

A comprehensive evaluation of the person is mandatory, and written reviews must be completed yearly. In cases where guardianship is terminated by the client but the guardian feels that there is a continued need for guardianship, the guardian may file an application with Probate Court for legal declaration of guardianship.

The first Canadian Act to reflect the changing view of guardianship is the Alberta Dependent Adults Act (1976). It deals with the issue of selectivity in guardianship by establishing not degrees of support, but rather full guardianship in specific contexts, e.g., where to live, licenses, medical consent, social activities.

A guardian is instructed to exercise his power and authority:
„(a) in the best interests of the dependent adult, and
(b) in such a way as to encourage the dependent adult to become capable of caring for himself and of making reasonable judgements in respect of matters relating to his person." (Section 11)

The guardianship order must be reviewed at least every 2 years. The dependent adult or any interested person can, at any time, request the court to review the guardianship order.

2.2 *Changing Perspectives of Competence*

Before the 1950s mental retardation was synonymous with incompetence. Clarke and Clarke [5] summarized perceptions of the mentally retarded in scientific literature as follows:

"incapable of adapting themselves to anything out of the ordinary"; "only capable of simplest routine tasks under constant supervision." This perspective of permanent incapacity changed in the 1950s, when research showed that, when learning principles were systematically applied, the mentally retarded were capable of learning and performed manual tasks close to "normal" expectations [6]. Not only were the retarded able to perform complex manual tasks, but their intellectual growth also followed the same development stages as that of the normal child, albeit at a slower pace (Woodward, in Stevens [24]).

The acceptance of the principle of normalization and the subsequent development of service delivery alternatives – family support, small residences, integrated schooling, workshops, and protected employment – have provided many opportunities for the mentally retarded to learn new skills. The development of specialized vocational rehabilitation methods have shown that competitive vocational skills are within the range of not just the mildly and moderately handicapped, but also the severely handicapped [3, 4, 10, 18]. Significant advances have also been made in residential and recreational domains [2, 16, 28].

Similar trends can be noted with the aged. Decreasing competence has been seen as an inevitable result of aging, and institutionalization was considered the only alternative to providing care. Unfortunately, institutionalization usually accelerates the loss of independence. Recent trends in in-home services and support are proving to be superior to institutionalization in maintaining independence.

As persons who have been isolated are allowed greater opportuntities to become involved in the full spectrum of community life, new challenges arise. While training technologies have provided the means to teach many skills for living and working within society, the mentally handicapped are increasingly exposed to subtle and often ambiguous situations within the community that they have not been trained to handle. Decision making, assertion, and social discrimination are just now being addressed as targets for training [8, 21, 23, 25].

2.3 *Competence and Legal Rights*

If one is committed to developing methods of teaching the handicapped to handle the complexities of modern life, one must also take steps to establish and protect the legal rights of those who may become politically vulnerable. The following legal rights and the legal definitions of competence are particularly important to issues of guardianship.

2.3.1 The Right to Give Informed Consent

"Consent" protects the right of self-determination to undergo or forego treatment (medication, health care, aversive therapies, etc.). It also provides legal coverage for those offering the services.

The need to validate a person's ability to give informed consent, or failing this, to provide alternative mechanisms to informed consent has been a major impetus for enactment of guardianship legislation. Roth et al. [22], as part of a major research study into legal and medical issues of consent, deal with the following legal/medical tests of competency:

1. Evidencing a choice: This test is set at a very low level and is most respectful of the autonomy of patient decision making. Criteria of competence relate to the presence or absence of choice – not the quality of the choice. This test of competence is the easiest to measure.
2. "Reasonable" outcome of choice: This test entails evaluating the patient's capacity to reach the "responsible" decision, i.e., the emphasis is on outcome, not on the decision or how it was reached. This is the test used most often when clear guidelines are not available. Because criteria for evaluation often depend on the values of the evaluators, inconsistencies can arise.
3. Choice based on "rational" reasons: This test relates to the quality of the patient's thinking – is his decision due to, or the product of, mental illness? Roth et al. advocate against the use of this test because it is conceptually and legally not sound, and it can too easily become a global indictment of the competence of mentally disabled persons.
4. Ability to understand: The ability to understand the risks, benefits and alternatives is the test that is most consistent with the law of informed consent, and is basically the definition adopted by McLaughlin [19]. Decision making need not be rational in either process or outcome, but the person must evidence sufficient ability to understand the information. A major problem with this test has been the reliance on unobservable and inferential mental processes rather than on concrete and observable elements of behavior.

2.3.2 The Right to Use the Courts

Rights and privileges are meaningless unless they are complemented by an ability to enforce these rights. In order to be considered capable of standing trial, the person must have "sufficient present ability to consult with his lawyer with a reasonable degree of rational understanding and a rational as well as factual understanding of the proceedings against him" [22].

In order to be considered capable of bringing suit to recover damages, the mentally handicapped person must be able to explain the nature of his injuries and the facts surrounding the incident, and must be able to withstand cross-examination in court.

Tests of capacity to stand trial, initiate action, secure defense, or bring evidence are determined within the context of the case except in situations where, by reasons of insanity, the individual is considered mentally incompetent in all matters.

2.3.3 *The Right to Contract*

A contract, a legally binding promise, is an essential part of commercial and financial transactions – agreements to purchase, to lease, to provide service, etc. Anyone may enter a contract if he or she has the capacity to "understand the nature of the promise made and the obligations arising out of it." Mentally handicapped persons are not, by law, considered incapable of contracting but the Unfair Practices Act does specify that an unfair trade practice has occurred when:

(a) the consumer's ability was such that he was not reasonably able to understand the character or nature of that transaction;
(b) that the supplier took unfair advantage of that consumer's inability to understand the character or nature of that consumer transaction (Section 4(1)).

There are no rules or precedents to use in determining when the courts will set aside a contract on the basis of contractual incapacity. Instead, courts generally weigh all of the facts of the particular case and will support a contract even if the person is mentally deficient, if he had sufficient capacity to comprehend the nature and consequences of the particular agreement.

Each of the above rights have exclusion clauses based on the competence of the person in the particular context. If the mentally retarded are to gain permanent access to these and other important legal rights, it is important that there continue to be a positive assumption of the competence of the mentally retarded, the aged, etc. When there are reasonable doubts as to competence, there should be clear, objective guidelines as to how to assess competence in that context.

Predetermination of competence prior to the event presents serious problems. Ability to give informed consent, to give evidence, or to contract is determined largely by the individual's experience or exposure to that situation; thus, until the situation arises, it is almost impossible to determine whether the individual, given the circumstances and adequate training, could be considered competent or incompetent.

3 "Competence" and the Dependent Adults Act

The Dependent Adults Act has gone a long way towards affirming the presumption of competence by formalizing the principle of selectivity of incompetence, i.e., a person can be incompetent in one context but not in others. Guardianship may be granted in one to ten areas of everyday living in which an adult is expected to take care of himself and make reasonable judgements. These areas are:

1. Where to live
2. With whom to live
3. Social activities
4. Work
5. Education/training
6. Licenses/permits
7. Legal action

8. Health care
9. Diet and dress
10. Other decisions as can be made by a father in respect of a child under 14 years of age

Thus, information must be gathered on the adult's ability to take care of himself and to make reasonable judgements within each of the above significant aspects. This negates global measures such as intelligence quotients and diagnostic categories, which cannot provide specific information.

The principle of "due process" is embodied within the Act. This means that no person is to be denied a right enjoyed by other citizens unless, through an unbiased legal hearing, it is determined that the person is unable to exercise that right reasonably and in his best interest. The Act also supports the concept of "least restrictive alternatives," in that guardianship is viewed as the course of last resort. This principle implies that partial guardianship is preferable to plenary guardianship, and that provisions other than guardianship are preferable to partial guardianship. The question then becomes: "Could this person exercise his rights in these situations without guardianship, as long as supports such as advocacy or professional guidance are available?"

Section 11 of the Act requires the guardian to use his powers and authority in ways to increase the dependent adult's ability to care for himself and to make reasonable judgements. In addition, the establishment of periodic reviews and the option of time-limited guardianship suggest that persons may outgrow their need for guardianship. The review process and the assumption of growth opens possibilities for including expectations or goals in the guardianship order. In order to monitor the achievement of these goals, evaluation processes which are specific to the improvements expected will have to be developed.

The following is a detailed description of each of the significant personal matters listed within the Act.

Section A: The Right to Decide Where the Dependent Adult Is to Live, Whether Permanently or Temporarily

Indicators of Need for Guardianship

1. Lack of basic personal routines, housekeeping skills, or community awareness
2. Unable to evaluate present situation, unaware of the alternatives and supports needed
3. Family neglect, abuse, or overprotection; self-neglect

Possible Actions of a Guradian

1. Support in gaining access to residential training, group homes, etc.
2. Signing a lease
3. Involvement in involuntary institutionalization

Legal Precedents

Legal reviews have dealt extensively with involuntary commitment to mental health and mental retardation facilities [20, 22, 27]. Although many statutes grant the guardian permission to control his ward's environment, recent court actions in the United States seriously question a guardian's decision to commit a person to an institution as equivalent to the consent of the person.

Measurement of Competence

One must not overlook the impact of environmental influences – the mentally retarded young adult living in a very protective environment is similar to the aged person in a nursing home, in that many of the skills considered necessary to appear competent may not be actively encouraged and, in fact, may be discouraged. Thus, when the environment is restrictive, measurement of competence should take the environment into consideration. Where possible, the proposed dependent adult should be seen in an environment that can assess whether he can be taught the skills necessary to be considered competent.

In order to be competent to decide where to live, it is not necessary that the individual be capable of being totally independent. Other research related to success in residential alternatives suggests that control over personal routines, community awareness, and a working knowledge of time and basic money concepts are central to success [16].

Section B: To Decide with Whom the Dependent Adult Is to Live and with Whom the Dependent Adult Is to Consort

Indicators of Need for Guardianship

1. Unable to recognize potential dangers in social situations
2. Does not assert personal choice
3. In situation of danger due to exploitation

Possible Actions of a Guardian

1. Discouraging questionable friendship choices
2. Deciding who the individual should associate with or have as companions
3. Attempting to remove ward from a living arrangement which is deemed unsuitable by the guardian because of undue influence exerted on the ward by the other persons in the living arrangement

Legal Precedents

Although it is generally recognized in related literature that some mentally retarded or senior citizens might be subject to victimization because of compliance or lack of assertion, no known legislation or law review has proposed legal intervention. In addition, it is doubtful whether the guardian could enforce his personal choice if the ward refused to be persuaded.

Measurement of Competence
Measurement of competence to decide on one's friends must be guided by the principles of rights to personal choice in life-style. Ability to indicate friendship choice, behavior consistent with personal standards, and assertion would appear to be central to competence in this section [15, 21]. Adherence to a specific set of values should not be used as a determinant of competence to make choices related to friendships.

Section C: To Decide Whether the Dependent Adult Should, or Should be Permitted to Engage in Social Activities, and if so, the Nature and Extent Thereof and Matters Related Thereto

This section is closely related to Section b) above. The wording of the section implies facilitation of social activities rather than the prevention of social activities.

Indicators of Need for Guardianship
1. In situations where social activities are not available

Possible Actions of a Guardian
1. Involvement in increasing the availability of social activities in an institutional setting
2. Imposing restrictions on social activities that the guardian feels are inappropriate because of religious or moral beliefs, e.g., social drinking

Legal Precedents
Again, none of the legislation or the law reviews studied relate to modifying social activity, although general descriptions of guardianship have some applicability here, in that most support the right of the ward to as much personal choice and freedom in life-style as is possible.

Measurement of Competence
Expression of personal choice of social activities depends on personal desires, previous experience, and existing situational constraints.

Section D: To Decide Whether The Dependent Adult Should, or Should be Permitted to, Work and if so, the Nature or Type of Work, for Whom He Is to work, and Matters Related Thereto

Indicators of Need for Guardianship
1. Unable to evaluate present situation or alternatives
2. Does not understand concepts of wages, insurance, etc.
3. In exploitive situation but unable to remedy situation

Interpretation of this section again relates to facilitation of employment rather than to prevention of the individual being involved with work or work activity programs.

However, a client who has the ability to secure a job could not usually be considered incompetent enough to need a guardian in this aspect; therefore the majority of actions would likely relate to the guardian's involvement in work activity programs, such as sheltered workshops, group employment, etc.

Possible Actions of a Guardian
1. Facilitating alternatives for work activity or employment
2. Involvement in restricting the individual from certain aspects of a program which he feels are detrimental to the individual
3. Speaking on behalf of the client in negotiating salary, working conditions, etc.
4. Ongoing review of the individual's performance within a work activity setting when other follow-up mechanisms are not in place
5. Ensuring that the ward is covered in terms of unemployment insurance and worker's compensation when no other agent is available

Legal Precedents
Legal discussions relate to the inconsistencies of labeling a prospective employee incapable of handling his own affairs yet capable of being competitively employed and to the ethical dilemma – abilitiy to earn wages vs. the right to spend wages. For detailed discussions of work-related issues, the Alberta Law Review papers, Kindred et al. [14], and Swadron and Sullivan [26] are recommended.

Measurement of Competence
Although exhaustive research has been conducted to find a way to predict potential for success, no definitive measures have yet been found. Nevertheless, Cobb [7] supports the notion that success in one phase of vocational continuum tends to predict success in the next phase. Research done at the Vocational and Rehabilitation Research Institute under a National Health and Welfare grant (unpublished) also indicates that improvement as measured by behavioral ratings (Adaptive Functioning Index Vocational Checklist) and retests on practical tasks offer some potential as predictors of ability to take advantage of further training. Whether this should be used as a measure of competence related to this section is debatable, for the issue is not whether the adult will be successful, but whether he should be allowed to decide details of work or other activity.

Section E: To Decide Whether the Dependent Adult Should, or Should be Permitted to, take or Participate in any Educational, Vocational, or Other Training and if so, the Nature and Extent Thereof and Matters Related Thereto

The intent of this clause is to facilitate, rather than exclude or prevent, the ward from taking part in activities.

Indicators of Need for Guardianship
1. Unable to evaluate present situation or alternatives
2. Does not understand purpose of training/treatment or possible result
3. Unable to gain access to education/treatment

Possible Actions of a Guardian

1. Giving consent to behavioral training/treatment
2. Advocating for the development of, or the inclusion of the ward in, existing educational programs, e. g., securing access to a school program
3. Extending or shortening the length of training proposed by the training facility

Legal Precedents

Although little has been written on education or training as issues of consent, there has been detailed discussion on the need for consent to psychological treatment. Friedman [9] offers an extensive discussion of behavior management and consent.

Measurement of Competence

There are few sources that relate even indirectly to measurement of competence in educational decisions.

Section F: To Decide Whether the Dependent Adult Should Apply or Should be Permitted to Apply for any License, Permit, Approval or Other Consent or Authorization Required by Law

Possible Actions of a Guardian

1. Obtaining a license to fish, carry firearms, receive liquor permits, etc.
2. Involvement in securing a marriage license

Legal Precedents

Legal reviews generally consider that the right to marry, the right to vote, and the right to make a will are so private, personal, and fundamental that they cannot be exercised through a substitute decision-maker [14]. Most reviews consider that a guardian should not be empowered to vote, dispose of property, or sign a marriage license on behalf of his ward. At present, existing legal rights of the mentally retarded to vote have not been called into question. It may be that establishment of a guardian could be considered tantamount to removal of these rights. The granting of most other licenses ultimately rests within the granting power of the statute governing the license itself. For further information on this, one is referred to Kindred's review [14] or the Alberta Law Review on marriage and contracts.

Section G: To Commence any Legal Action that Does not Relate to the Estate of the Dependent Adult

Indicators of Need for Guardianship

1. Does not recognize when he has been wronged
2. Cannot instruct legal counsel, give evidence, etc.
3. Charged and unable to inform counsel or, if wronged, unable to seek redress

Possible Actions of a Guardian
1. Securing defense counsel
2. Initiating court procedures when the ward has been wronged

Legal Precedents
This section refers to the rights of the guardian to make substitute decisions with regard to contracts, civil litigation, and criminal action. With few exceptions, contracts of mentally incompetent persons are considered voidable rather than void, and only in fairly limited circumstances would the guardian be seen as the legal personality of the ward for purposes of making contracts. In the area of civil litigation, there are precedents for someone speaking on behalf of an unable person – amicus litum. There is a debate within the legal reviews as to the legal responsibility of the guardian in circumstances where he could be considered liable for negligence in controlling the ward in the case of injury to another person.

Measurement of Competence
Issues in assessing competence in this area must be tempered by the realization that the general public is, by and large, unaware of the role of lawyers and how to make use of legal services. Assessment should therefore relate more to a knowledge of when one has been wronged and potential sources of advice as opposed to the ways to secure specific redress.

Section H: To Consent to any Health Care that Is in the Best Interests of the Dependent Adult

The Act further designates health care to include:
(a) any examination, diagnosis, procedure or treatment undertaken to prevent disease or ailment;
(b) any procedure untertaken for the purpose of preventing pregnancy;
(c) any procedure untertaken for the purpose of an examination or a diagnosis;
(d) any medical, surgical, obstetrical or dental treatment, and
(e) anything done that is ancillary to any procedure, treatment, examination or diagnosis.

Indicators of Need for Guardianship
1. Lack of basic health care routines – in either performing routines or instructing others who provide the care
2. Unable to give informed consent to health care
3. Consistently refuses to give consent

Legal Precedents
To be considered valid, consent must be voluntary, knowledgeable, and "competent" [13, 27, 29]. Voluntary consent assumes an exercise of free will and clearly precludes the existence of overt coercion and force. More difficult is determination of the voluntary nature of consent of persons where such coercion is implied because of the dependent situation of the individual. A landmark decision in ruling that implied coercion overruled a written consent made the following general statement:

> Involuntarily confined mental patients live in an inherently coercive environment where indirect and subtle psychological coercion has profound effects upon the patient population. They are not able to give voluntarily informed consent because of the inherent inequity of their position [13].

The same question of voluntariness of consent also applies to other institutional situations, situations where extensive control is maintained by behavioral means or situations where the person has no realistic alternatives. Thus, determination of capacity to give consent must include both the individual's capacity and the situation in which consent is required.

Measurement of Competence

In measuring competence in the area of health care, one must determine whether the individual has an awareness of his own health and the health care precautions that are necessary to promote or maintain health. It is difficult to measure comprehension of potential health care. Most normal people do not know the implications of various health care procedures until they have experienced them. They rely instead on a trusted physician to give them information and advice needed. Health care experience is a major factor in awareness of health care options; those who have been healthy have had less opportunity to learn abouth health care than those who have had extensive problems.

Section I: The Right to Make Normal Day-to-Day Decisions on Behalf of the Dependent Adult, Including the Diet and Dress of the Dependent Adult

Indicators of Need for Guardianship

1. Lack of basic personal routines
2. Unable to evidence a choice or initiative in diet/dress
3. Unaware of surroundings and needs to the extent of potential danger to self
4. Unable to use day-to-day services
5. Dependent entirely on established routines

Possible Actions of a Guardian

1. Securing adequate and specialized diets required in institutional settings
2. Ensuring that appropriate clothing for current weather conditions is available to the individual

Legal Precedents

No reviews have dealt specifically with this topic although the concepts would relate to plenary guardianship.

Measurement of Competence

As with Section A, the measurement of ability to make decisions related to diet and dress must be done within a setting where such decisions are encouraged. Given this, self-care skills and an understanding of basic nutrition would likely provide some guidelines in this respect.

Section J: To Make such Other Decisions as Can be Made by the Father in Respect of a Child Under 14 Years of Age and that Are Not Specified or Referred to in this Subsection

This section is only applicable within considerations of plenary guardianship, and represents blanket coverage allowing the guardian to make any decisions that are not specified. Such situations might refer to withdrawing life support systems in the case of a terminal illness. Blanket coverage as is evident under the provisions for plenary guardianship is evident in most of the guardianship or conservatorship legislation prior to the 1970s. However, there is a consistent movement away from unlimited guardianship orders.

Measurement of Competence
Inability to understand information, to make needs known, or to relate to others at a profound level might be considered appropriate tests in this regard.

The Research Study

This study was designed to identify skills and abilities which could be useful in defining competence in "caring for oneself" and in "making reasonable judgements" in those areas identified within the Dependent Adults Act. Unfortunately, the preliminary survey of existing literature and legal precedents yielded little in the way of concrete indicators of competence, apart from general definitions such as "unable to manage or take care of his property or himself without assistance", "likely to be imposed upon by artful and designing persons", "lacks sufficient central judgement and discretion", etc.

Instead, the definitions within the Act were used to generate theoretical models of skills inherent in "unable to care for oneself" and "unable to make reasonable judgements." Once the models were approved by the Advisory Committee, they were translated into test formats and these were pretested. The resulting interviews and assessment items were used to assess the performance of persons considered to be in need of differing degrees of guardianship. The responses of these persons were then used to test the initial models. Questionnaires and interview formats were developed from those items which were reliable and which discriminated between persons in need and those not in need of assistance in making decisions.

Six groups of subjects (25 persons in each) were selected and interviewed.

4.1 Young Adult Groups

Group 1. Individuals were chosen from among persons identified by agencies as definitely in need of assistance in making decisions. The following are examples of three persons within this group:

1. . . . appears a very immature woman who has problems in self-care, communication and social maturity. She has made slow progress in her residential training

program and does not have acceptable community standards of cleanliness and appearance. Although she was generally cooperative with testing, her auditory reception and verbal expression were very poor.
2. . . . still lives at home with his parents. He is well motivated and has made attempts to overcome some problems of his handicap. However, he has some unrealistic views of himself and his functioning in the community. He tends to seek support from his parents for many things, e. g., providing a living situation, making medical appointments, transportation.
3. . . . works half-time in a vocational program and half-time in a pre-vocational program. She lives in an institutional setting and has limited self-care skills. She has very immature speech and is difficult to understand.

Group 2. Individuals were randomly selected from persons presently enrolled in rehabilitation agencies. As a contrast group, they represented rehabilitation clients not necessarily in need of assistance in making decisions. The following are examples of three persons within this group:

1. . . . is a young trainee at a rehabilitation center, where she went after graduating from a school for the trainable mentally handicapped. She has excellent work skills but is still "young and inexperienced" in most areas. She is living at home but showing some interest in moving out on her own, with a friend.
2. . . . is a 23-year-old man who is employed in a sheltered workshop. He lives at home with his parents. He has a very pleasant disposition but limited social skills – barely able to write his name and address.
3. . . . is a pleasant 26-year-old woman employed in a sheltered rehabilitation center. She has had short-term jobs but has been unsuccessful in them. She is presently living at home but is anxious to move out where she and her friends, particularly her boyfriend, can have privacy. She has both hearing and visual problems.

Group 3. Individuals were randomly selected from among graduates of rehabilitation programs. They were competitively employed and were living either on their own or in a group-home setting. The following are examples of three persons within this group:

1. . . . is a graduate of a vocational rehabilitation program. He has speech and hearing handicaps, but is able to make himself understood most of the time. He is working for a bottling company and shares an apartment with another graduate. He has some follow-up contact with the agency.
2. . . . is a graduate from a vocational rehabilitation program and presents herself as a fairly competent individual. She was working for a linen-supply company until her recent gall stone operation. She has been employed in various jobs over the past few months: babysitting and temporary part-time work. She rents an upstairs suite and plans to do some upgrading at Alberta Vocational Centre this year.
3. . . . is a graduate of both a vocational and a residential program. He is fairly intelligent but has speech and hearing handicaps which make communication very difficult. He shares an apartment with another graduate and works at a manufacturing plant. He has a driver's license and a car.

Group 4. Individuals were selected from among persons who were marginally employed or on public assistance but had not been seen by rehabilitation agencies. Below are three examples from this group:

1. ... has lived in Calgary for 2.5 years and has worked in a warehouse and as a cook's helper. He resides at a hotel where he has been for 3 months.
2. ... is a 47-year-old man who has been doing casual labor for a number of years. Health restrictions (bad heart, stomach problems, ulcer) and a lack of education have prevented him from doing heavier or more skilled labor.
3. ... is a 24-year-old man who drives a bus. He has taken a variety of jobs from time to time.

4.2 Senior Citizens Groups

Because of the large number of persons over the age of 65 being referred for guardianship, two groups of senior citizens were added to the initial study.

Group 5. Individuals were over 65 and considered in need of assistance in making decisions by their care facility or by community workers. These persons were fairly easy to locate but hard to test because of their lack of interest and ability.

1. ... seemed very disoriented. He described himself as about 65, and a farmer. He could not describe his transition from his farm to his present location. He could not read or write.
2. ... is an elderly woman confined to a wheelchair. She appears to have very little voluntary movement. She made eye contact with the tester only twice in 10 minutes and did not respond to any questions or show any recognition of the testing situation other than the tester's physical presence.
3. ... is the 85-year-old son of a famous pioneering rancher in Alberta. He shares a small cottage (which he calls a "shack") with two dogs. He does his own cooking, cleaning, and personal care. He accepts help with yard work. An elderly lady friend does his banking and grocery shopping. His bad back prevents him from going on extended outings.

Group 6. Individuals were over age 65, living in extended-care facilities or in the community, but considered not in need of a guardian. These persons were difficult to locate and were generally apprehensive of the testing.

1. ... is a proper and neat 78-year-old woman who lives with her husband in their own home. She had a cancer operation in April and has come to rely on some program supports, V.O.N., and a weekly housekeeper during her recovery period. She appears very alert and artistic.
2. ... is a 75-year-old gentleman who was very smartly dressed in a suit. He shares a house with his wife. He is semi-retired and is a fourth partner in a manufacturing business. He attends a day program twice a week for physiotherapy, as he is recovering from several minor strokes.
3. ... is a neatly dressed, friendly, and outgoing widow of 75. She was concerned that her poor memory would affect the validity of the test and was afraid she would not be of much help. She was devoted most of her life to helping others,

e.g., orphans, children from broken homes, older people. She has a self-confessed weakness for lending money (up to $ 1500) without an IOU or interest. She feels that as long as she has food, a house, and a little spending money, it is her Christian duty to help others.

4.3 Methods

Information was gathered during the study through interviews with subjects and with persons familiar with the subjects. There were three general categories:

1. *Skills relating to "unable to care for himself":* This was further defined for the purposes of the study to be demonstrated underfunctioning in those skills necessary to participate in society at an adult level. The Adaptive Functioning Index (AFI) was chosen as a skill base and the most relevant items from the test were selected by a wide range of parents and staff (community workers, agency staff, Public Guardian's staff, nurses). Four new domains were added to cover concerns expressed by parents and staff. The resulting skills or behaviors were compiled into a short functional checklist which was then marked by a person familiar with the subject and/or by the subject himself. The skills covered were:

Self-care	Communication
Health care	Consideration
Time management	Handling problems
Housekeeping	Home management
Transportation	Difficulties in memory
Shopping	Difficulties in health care
Budgeting	Difficulties in handling problems

2. *Skills relating to "unable to make reasonable judgements":* This was defined as the demonstrated lack of ability to process information and the inability to make choices and decisions based on that information and previous experience. The tests developed in this section evolved from a hpyothetical model which identified four processes in making reasonable judgements.

Temporal Anchoring: The person's understanding of his existence in time, i.e., ability to use past information for present and future decisions

a) Short-term working memory or memory capacity – the number of pieces of information that can be manipulated in memory at one time
b) Intermediate (5–10 min) recall of familiar sounds and instructions
c) General memory (long-term) – the awareness of a useful past:
   1. Personal and current information and orientation – Where are you now?, general information
   2. Logical memory – recall and comprehension of stories
   3. Insights to memory – knowledge of what memory is and how to use/improve memory
   4. Sequential memory – knowledge that events happen in a reliable manner

Information Processing: The ability to perform simple functional tasks (putting together a flashlight) and perform an unfamiliar task with instruction and demonstration

Communication: The ability to make needs known and to understand and use language. This was measured according to the subject's ability to express himself (nonverbally and verbally) throughout the test situation. The subject's degree of assertion was tested in a document-signing situation.

Social Judgement: Understanding of social consequences; this was measured in a number of ways:

a) The subject's ability to plan for the immediate and distant future
b) The subject's knowledge of the community as measured by response to pictures of community situations
c) The subject's response to hypothetical situations that reflect possible events within Section 9 of the Act
d) The subject's response to a locus-of-control questionnaire – the extent to which the subject "chose" the alternative action which reflected accepting responsibility for his own actions

3. *Subject Information:* This was collected from the person identified as most familiar with the subject. Standardized forms were used as much as possible to facilitate coding of the data. Information covered:
a) Level of handicap in five major areas: supervision and care, mobility, communication/socialization, developmental skills, and behavior
b) Description of the type of residential, vocational, and leisure programs that the subject was involved in. Of primary concern was the degree of independence allowed and the types of training being received.
c) Clinical impressions of the need for guardianship in specific sections of the Act were recorded by the interviewer based on the impressions gained from the interview and the functional data.

Many of the measurements used in the study proved highly successful in discriminating between the groups considered in need and those not in need of assistance in making decisions. The majority of subjects enjoyed the interview process and the interviewers were able to learn the interview process easily. There was good reliability in most of the measures, i.e., there was similarity between raters and stability over time (when the interview was redone between 2 weeks and 3 months later).

4.4 General Findings

Age was the most consistent and powerful predictor of performance in the young-adult groups. As the developmentally handicapped young adult is exposed to training and new challenges, he gains skills and is more able to integrate into the community, and is therefore less in need of a guardian. Consequently, there should be a strong note of caution attached to assigning a guardian to a young handicapped person. Granting guardianship could, in some cases, provide a deterrent to growth, because the implied label of incompetence could reduce expectations. Limited-term guardianship would be an asset in these cases.

The impact of environment on skills acquisition was quite marked. When one compares the skills of graduates (group 3) and the skills of marginally employed persons (group 4), there are differences in auditory and visual memory, and planning for the future (cognitive skills), but there was little difference in skills such as awareness of personal living situation, free time, legal consequences, sexual exploitation, and performance of vocational tasks. The training situation was able to diminish the differences between these two groups.

When the results of all the subjects are subjected to analyses which reveal differences due to environment, the impact of a program is particularly noticeable in the following skills areas:

Community costs
Health care
Housekeeping
Shopping
Home management
Awareness of medical situations
Awareness of free time options
Handling financial situations
Awareness of living situation and alternatives

Where one lives has a bearing on whether these skills are encouraged or even possible.

While the structured interview was effective and easily administered with the young-adult group (even with nonverbal subjects), it had limitations with the older groups. Many of the more frail, elderly people became noticeably fatigued, while others were apprehensive about "tests." It took less than 1 hour to complete the testing with the young adults, but it sometimes took several days to complete the test with geriatric persons. Thus, the interview should probably be altered if used with senior citizens.

4.5 The Nature of Competence

One of the primary reasons for conducting the study was to gain some understanding of what factors were important in "competence." The model presented within the Act looks at incompetence as one's being "unable to care for oneself" and "unable to make reasonable judgements in respect of all or any matters relating to his person." The research model further defined incompetence as "demonstrated underfunctioning in those skills necessary to participate in society at an adult level" in:

Self-care
Health care
Time management
Housekeeping
Transportation
Shopping
Budgeting
Communication
Consideration
Handling problems
Home management
Difficulties in memory
Difficulties in health care
Difficulties in handling problems

and "demonstrated lack of ability to process information and the inability to make choices and decisions based on that information and previous experience" in:

Temporal anchoring (understanding of existence in time)
Information processing
Communication
Social judgement

The model which emerged as a result of the research (using statistical analyses which detected groupings among large numbers of test results), suggests an interesting compromise between the legislative and research models. The model has three components, as shown in Fig. 1.

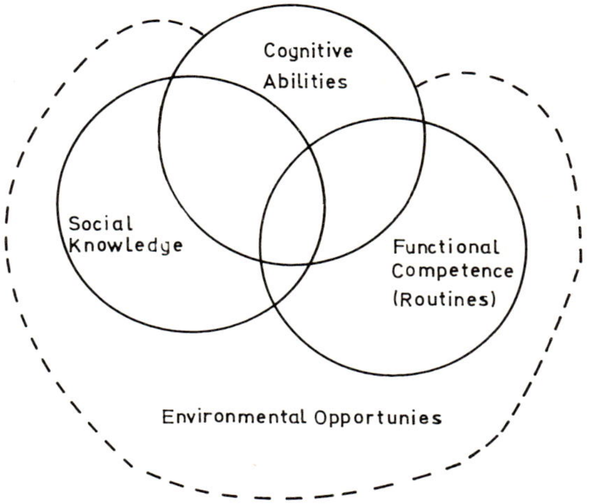

Fig. 1. Nature of competence to make decisions

Cognitive skills underlie information processing and decision making. These come close to the concept of applied intelligence as per the Social Education test of the Adaptive Functioning Index. The items which best reflect this factor are:

Temporal Anchoring	Level of handicap:
Digits Backward	socialization/communication
AFI Reading, Short Form	Functional assessment budgeting
AFI Money, Short Form	Functional assessment home management

The first four were standardized tests, while the last three were based on observations made by someone familiar with the person.

Social knowledge is knowledge of how to handle everyday situations. This factor seems related to the subject's life experience, and to his or her ability to understand information and make decisions. Thus, these skills encompass the statement "unable to make reasonable judgements" found in the definition within the Act.

The structured interview which discussed personal situation and presented hypothetical situations was an effective measure of this construct, as were the AFI

Community Awareness and the functional assessments of home management and handling problems.

Functional Competence is the ability to perform personal and community routines. This factor is closest to "unable to care for oneself" within the legislative model. Apart from three or four skills, there was little overlap between this functional skills factor and the other two major factors. This could be because even the most handicapped can learn routine skills, but the routines may be being carried out without much ability to make related decisions. In addition, the functional assessment was based on third-party observation, i.e., a person familiar with the subject rated the subject's ability. Such observations can be affected by subjectivity and by the environment that the person is in. The items which best reflected this factor were:

Self-care	Budgeting
Health care	Communication
Time management	Consideration
Housekeeping	Handling problems
Shopping	Home management

4.6 Best Predictors Between the Groups

By pooling several different methods of analysis (t-tests, Anovas, Discriminant Analyses and Multiple Regression Analyses), the following measures emerged as the best all-round predictors of the differences between those in need of assistance in making decisions and those not in need. Listed in order of effectiveness, they are:

Temporal Anchoring – awareness of the present, past and future
Housekeeping – functional assessment by checklist
AFI Money Short Form – money-handling skills
Level of Handicap: Supervision – amount of nursing care needed
Social Consequences: Medical – answering questions about medical situations
Time Management – functional assessment by checklist
Awareness of Medical Situation – awareness of present medical situation
Digits Forward – short-term auditory memory
Awareness of Legal Action – handling a document-signing situation
Residential Placement – present location
Home Management II – functional assessment by checklist
Awareness of Personal Situation – awareness of residential situation
Need of Assistance (Living) – recognition of amount of help needed in making day-to-day decisions
Health Care – functional assessment by checklist
Concept Attainment – test of basic concepts such as size and shape
Visual Memory – memory for visual stimulation
Communication – functional asssessment by checklist
Recall of Verbal Material – recall of a legal document
AFI Writing Short Form – writing personal information
AFI Reading Short Form – reading legal document
Level of Handicap: Motor Control – degree of mobility

Transportation – ability to get around the community
Social Knowledge – total of appropriate responses given to daily living decisions
AFI Community Awareness – knowledge of community resources
Home Management – functional assessment by checklist
Digits Backward – working memory
Comprehension of Verbal Material – related to reading

It is interesting to note that the three factors, cognitive skills, social knowledge and functional competence, are equally represented in the top 15 predictors, indicating that although the functional assessment may be subjective, it is nevertheless meaningful for detecting differences in the need for guardianship.

5 Application of Research Findings

The research findings have been used to develop a process of gathering information. Three evaluative processes are recommended:

1. The basic information form (form A) is to be filled out by the person applying to be a private guardian. The same form could be filled out by agencies and other relevant contacts who have knowledge of the proposed dependent adult. The research provided a useful means of selecting the best items (i.e., those which best discriminated between groups and were also reliable items) from the functional checklist within each of the main sections of the Act – where to live, social relationships, etc. Some items were added in sections with too few. These checklist items were combined with a standardized form, requesting information about the present situation and environmental factors which might indicate the need for guardianship. Form A thus represents factor 3, functional ability, and factor 2, social knowledge.
2. Form B is the documentation by a physician, psychologist, or therapist, as specified under Section 2.2 of the Dependent Adults Act. Factor 1 – Cognitive Skills – is represented by a Level of Handicap grid, the memory test, and temporal anchoring. These were selected because (a) they were among the most concrete, easily measured items in the research study, and (b) they resembled most closely the items usually measured in mental status/competence.
3. Form C is a report to be completed by an independent evaluator. The items measuring awareness and social knowledge are best assessed by an objective third party, using standardized methods. The proposed assessment report also calls for a full functional assessment which can be used in planning goals and recommending steps to reach those goals. When a full functional assessment is not feasible, Form A can be used as back-up information.

5.1 Proposed Process of Guardianship

Figure 2 is an overview of the process which was suggested by the research, the literature review, and interviews with parents, lawyers, judges, staff in agencies, and the Public Guardian's representatives. This process is intended to provide:

Step 1
Initial contact and information re: Guardianship →

Step 2
1) Send Form A to person making application and other parties able to provide information.
2) Send Form B (Section 2.2) to physician, psychologist, and/or therapist.

Step 3
Compilation of information and decision:
1) *To initiate external evaluation* (Form C and AFI) –
   - If the client is between ages 18 and 25 and in a situation where independence is not being taught
   - Where there are serious inconsistencies in the information
   - Where the proposed dependent adult is making progress towards independence
   - Where client is not allowed to make decisions and shows some potential for doing so
2) *To proceed with application:*
   - If the information is complete, consistent, and indicates clearly the inability of the dependent adult to care for himself and make decisions in his present situation
3) *Not to proceed:*
   - If the proposed dependent adult shows ability to make his own decisions and care for himself within his present situation

↓ *Decision to proceed* with application with individual program plan

↓ *Decision to proceed* with regular application

↓ *Decision not to proceed* and letter to applicant outlining reasons for not proceeding with alternatives/ suggestions, e.g., advocate referral to support agency

Fig. 2. Proposed Process for Application for guardianship

1. Consistent information systems to allow better comparison between sources (family, agencies, etc.). This should help identify areas of inconsistency that can be further checked by the Public Guardian's staff. The forms have been designed to facilitate the completion of the formal application to the court for guardianship
2. Efficient information gathering. Because the forms have been tested for ease of administration, they should mean more rapid return rate of reports.
3. More detailed information from physicians, psychologists or therapists, because of the standardized nature of the forms
4. The standardization of the decision process at each stage of the application process. Alternative actions are proposed at each step.
5. The introduction of an independent evaluation component when indicated
6. Direct involvement of the proposed dependent adult in the application process (at the level of independent evaluation)
7. Means to introduce individual programm plans along with guardianship in those cases where it appears warranted
8. Consistent data for information storage and retrieval for purposes of evaluating the effectiveness of the Public Guardian process

5.2 Concerns Raised During the Study

1. The lack of legal representation on behalf of the proposed dependent adult: The process does not have to acknowledge or involve the proposed dependent adult in the court case. Most lawyers and civil rights persons surveyed felt that the court should appoint someone to speak on behalf of the proposed dependent adult.
2. The tendency to link guardianship with other services such as trusteeship, Assured Income for the Severely Handicapped programs, compulsory care: This could lead to situations where persons not needing guardianship would require a guardian in order to gain access to other services.
3. The court process is often perfunctory in granting guardianship with real decisions being made by the Public Guardian's staff before the court date. It had been suggested that family court might be a more realistic alternative to Queen's Bench.
4. Two of the areas identified in Sections 9 and 10 of the Act were supported neither by the legal reviews nor by the research. These sections are:
   (c) to decide whether the dependent adult should, or should be permitted to, engage in social activities and if so the nature and extent thereof and matters related thereto
   (f) to decide whether the dependent adult should apply or should be permitted to apply for any license, permit, approval or other consent or authorization required by law

   These sections could likely be dropped from the Act, making the Act less restrictive and more concise.

6 Conclusion

It is hoped that the initiative shown by the Public Guardian's Office in its study of the concepts underlying the Act will be continued as society continues to strive for human rights legislation to protect the rights of less able citizens in the least restrictive manner.

References

1. Alberta Health and Social Development (1974) The Dependent Adults Act. Queen's Printer
2. Beck V, Possberg E, Brown RI (1977) Recreation and leisure time as an integral part of rehabilitation programming for the mentally handicapped adult. REAP 3: 153–168
3. Bellamy GT, Peterson L, Close D (1975) Habilitation of the severely and profoundly retarded: illustrations of competence. Education and training of the mentally retarded.
4. Brown RI, Hughson EA (1975) Prevocational training for the severely retarded adolescent. Presented to the 53rd Annual International Council for Exceptional Children Convention, April 1975.
5. Clarke ADB, Clarke AM (1954) Cognitive changes in the feebleminded. Br J Psychology 45: 173–179
6. Clarke ADB, Hermelin BF (1955) Adult imbeciles, their abilities and training ability, Lancet II: 337–339

7. Cobb HV (1972) Forecast of fulfillment. Teachers College Press, New York
8. Feuerstein R (1979) The dynamic assessment of retarded performers. In: The learning potential assessment device, theory, instruments, and techniques. University Park Press
9. Friedman P (1975) Legal regulation of applied behavior analysis in mental institutions and prisons. Arizona Law Review, Vol. 17
10. Gold M (1973) Research on the vocational habilitation of the retarded: the present, the future. In: Ellis N (ed) International review of research in mental retardation, vol. 6. Academic Press, New York
11. Hardisty JH (1973) Mental illness: A legal fiction. Wash Law Review 48: 735–762
12. Helsel ED (1972) A proposed protective service system for Ohio's developmentally disabled. Delivery at the AAMD Annual Conference, Minneapolis, Minnesota
13. *Kaimowitz* vs. *Michigan Department of Mental Health, Civil Action 73* – 19434 – *A W.* (Wayne County, Mich. Cir., Ct. 1973).
14. Kindred M, Cohen J, Penrod D, Shaffer T (eds) (1976) The mentally retarded citizen and the law. In: Guardianship and limitations upon capacity, chap 3. The Free Press, New York
15. Marlett NJ (1972) Effects of discharging adults from Alberta institutions for the retarded to community living situations. On request from: Services for the Handicapped, Calgary (unpublished)
16. Marlett NJ, Incentive for independence in residential training for the developmentally handicapped. J Pract Appr Developm Handicap 3:
17. Marlett NJ (1978) Normalization, integration, and socialization. In: Das JP, Baine D (eds) Mental retardation for special educators. Charles C. Thomas, Springfield
18. Martin A, Flexer R (1976) Three studies on training work skills and work adjustment, Monograph No. 5). Texas Tech University, Research and Training Center in Mental Retardation, Lubbock
19. McLaughlin P (1979) Guardianship of the person. National Institute on Mental Retardation, Toronto
20. Meisel A, Roth LH, Lidz CW (1977) Toward a model of the legal doctrine of informed consent. Am J Psychiatry 134: 285–289
21. Rosen M, Kivitz MS (1973) Beyond normalization: psychological adjustment. Br J Subnormality 19: 64–70
22. Roth L, Meisel A, Lidz C (1977) Tests of competency to consent to treatment. Am J Psychiatry 134: 3
23. Ryba K (1976) An evaluation of personal adjustment training for mentally retarded adults. Master's thesis, University of Calgary
24. Stevens B (1971) Teaching the developmentally young. Day, New York
25. Stott DH (1972) Behavioral aspects of learning disabilities. Paper presented at the Annual Convention of the Council for Exceptional Children, Washington, D.C.
26. Swadron B, Sullivan DR (1976) Mental retardation – the law – guardianship. National Institute on Mental Retardation, Toronto
27. Turnbull JR III (1977) Consent handbook. AAMD Special Publication No. 3
28. Wehmann P, Blankenship N, Edwards J, Karan O, R Renzaglia A, Schutz R (1976) Leisure skills and recreation for severely/profoundly handicapped adolescents and adults. Paper presented at the meeting of AAESPH, Kansas City
29. *Wyatt* v. *Anderholt*, 368 F Supp. 383, 1385 (MD Ala. 1974)

Employment Opportunities for the Handicapped in the United States

S. Moskowitz*

1 Background and Historical Overview of the Problem

Five years ago, a historic declaration by the General Assembly of the United Nations enunciated the fundamental rights of disabled persons [1]. Central to that document is the concept that every disabled person has the same rights as his fellow citizens, including the right to enjoy a decent life, as socially integrated and as normal as possible [2]. Included in the specific rights enumerated in that Declaration was the following:

Disabled persons have the right to economic and social security and to a decent level of living. They have the right, according to their capabilities, to secure and retain employment or to engage in a useful, productive and renumerative occupation and to join trade unions [3].

The association of work and a normalized life style was not coincidental. In almost all societies, work affords the individual the opportunity to assert his individuality and worth as a person. Through productive work most people achieve social recognition and the pride of self-reliance. Beyond these intangibles, work provides economic subsistence and independence. The combination of a mental and/or physical handicap with a lack of employment and income makes a normalized existence almost impossible.

Statistics from the United States concerning the poverty of the vast majority of handicapped individuals and their inability to secure employment present a stark and melancholy portrait of the social and economic status of that portion of the population. The handicapped have the highest unemployment rate of any group in the United States [4]. Among adults, approximately two-thirds of the blind, more than one-half of all paraplegics, and over three-quarters of persons with epilepsy are unemployed [5]. Those with cerebral palsy fare even worse [6]. Even handicapped veterans of the armed forces find employment possibilities almost nonexistent [7]. Most of us active in the field can testify to the fact that those who do manage to secure jobs are generally permitted to fill only unskilled and low-paying positions

* There has been, in recent years, some discussion and controversy concerning terminology, i. e., the use of "disabled" persons vs. "handicapped" persons. I have chosen to use these terms interchangeably. However, in some parts of the paper, the term "handicapped" persons predominates, because the focus here is on public policy in the United States as that is enunciated in federal statutes, regulations, and court decisions and these almost invariably use the term "handicapped" persons

[8]. Shut out of the work place, handicapped persons are consigned to a life of social segregation and economic deprivation. For masses of the disabled their handicaps mean a life of poverty as well.

The link between handicapping conditions, lack of employment, and poverty is centuries old. In medieval Europe, the "Hospital" was in reality an almshouse or poorhouse, caring not only for the sick but for all the destitute [9]. The physically handicapped were in fact granted special legal status as "legitimate" beggars, with license to solicit donations from the public since it was assumed they could not work [10]. In the colonial period, and in the period following American independence, the "mentally distracted," the retarded, the sick poor, and others were publicly "sold" to the lowest bidder willing to take responsibility for them at the lowest amount of public support [11]. During the nineteenth and early twentieth centuries, a bewildering variety of so-called defectives or degenerates were confined in American poorhouses; these included "the chronic insane, the epileptic, the paralytic, the imbecile and idiot ... prostitutes ... the shiftless poor ...," and so forth [12]. And the United States Census, beginning in 1880, combined "defectives, dependents, and delinquents" into one category, thus making explicit the connection between disability, poverty, and antisocial behavior [13].

While our terminology and social theories have changed dramatically, the economic condition of handicapped persons in the United States today remains deplorable. As noted earlier, the handicapped have the highest unemployment rate of any group in society. This lack of employment is even more ironic in light of the employability and capability of vast numbers of the handicapped. Despite the stereotype of lack of ability, Department of Labor studies show that handicapped workers have a slightly higher productivity rate and a better safety record than their non-handicapped peers [14]. Despite the fear of irregular attendance, handicapped workers are absent from the job about the same number of days per year as non-handicapped workers [15]. Actual experience indicates that employers' fears of higher insurance rates because of handicapped workers are vastly exaggerated [16]. It is thus public misconceptions and employer resistance which deter the entry of the handicapped into the work force.

We need to understand the magnitude of this problems. The United States Congress estimated the number of persons with handicapping conditions in the United States at between 11 and 35 million [17]. The number of employable workers in this group is unknown, but between 7 and 14 million is a conservative estimate [18]. The number of handicapped persons actually working is likewise unknown; some years ago, Congress estimated that only 800000 were employed [19]. Calculated in economic terms alone, the cost to society for financial assistance ("welfare") provided and the loss of productive capacity and tax revenues from the handicapped are enormous. The social cost to both the individuals involved and society as a whole dwarfs this, of course.

Dr. Howard Rusk, one of the pioneers and legends of American rehabilitative medicine, has noted that the overall goal of rehabilitation is the restoration of "the individual to the highest possible level of economic, social, and emotional self-sufficiency" [20]. Public policy can be the determinative factor in that endeavor. Recent legislative and regulatory enactments on the federal level in the United States contain the potential for making positive and dramatic improvements in the employment status of the handicapped. The enactements are the result of significant social change. The handicapped are no longer invisible. Following the lead of other minorities, self-help groups have lobbied in Congress and before administrative agencies, litigated in the courts, and dramatized their struggle for equality and economic independence by demonstrations, both quiet and raucous.

The purpose of this paper is to focus on public policy at the federal level regarding employment opportunity for the handicapped. At the outset, I should like to briefly survey that policy prior to the 1973 Rehabilitation Act. The 1973 statute and its implementing regulations will then be analyzed in some detail, for I believe they provide us with the power and the direction to make important gains in jobs, income, and social integration for the handicapped in the United States. The Act can also serve as a model for other countries facing similar problems.

2 Federal Policy Toward the Handicapped Prior to 1973

Federal efforts to improve the employment opportunities for handicapped persons are at least 60 years old and evidence a long-standing policy of encouraging employment and integration. Until recently, however, these efforts were channeled almost exclusively into assistance to generally weak state rehabilitation programs, and did not harness the enormous legal and economic power of the federal government itself.

As early as 1920, Congress enacted legislation to assist state programs for training, counseling, and placing physically handicapped persons [21]. Financial assistance and other federal support for state programs was later expanded to include the mentally impaired [22], and gradually increased in scope [23]. The 1965 Rehabilitation Act amendment explicitly set out the federal pulicy of assisting states "in rehabilitating handicapped individuals so that they may prepare for and engage in gainful employment to the extent of their capabilities" [24].

This federal policy was likewise evident in federal assistance to state-operated public assistance ("welfare") programs [25]. Here again, the federal role was to provide money and technical assistance. The Social Security Act, which formed the basis for these welfare programs, declared that "self-support" of the individual assisted by welfare was one of the purposes of such assistance [26]. The Act also provided services to help "recipients attain or retain capability for self-support or self-care" [27], and utilized the device of exempting wages in calculating the recipient's grant as an incentive for employment [28].

Taken as a whole, these efforts show both a consistent policy in favor of employment and integration and very limited use of the considerable powers of the federal government. Beginning in the 1960s, federal legislation drew upon those powers to pursue equal employment opportunity more aggressively. Discrimination against the handicapped in federal agency position was banned [29]. A series of laws mandated the "accessibility" of public buildings [30] and mass transportation facilities to the physically handicapped [31]. Statutes also required the inclusion of handicapped children in local school systems so that they might receive the education and training necessary to work in our increasingly technological and automated economy. The Education for All Handicapped Children Act of 1975 [32] seeks to assure that "all handicapped children have available to them ... a free appropriate public education which emphasizies special education and related services designed to meet their unique needs ..." [33], and provides procedural due process protection whenever a change in educational placement is proposed, requested, or refused [34].

With this brief background of policy, with respect to both substantive provisions and the willingness to use federal power directly, we can now turn to the most significant federal legislative effort to date, the 1973 Rehabilitation Act, which exhibits both the potential and the actual operation of those powers.

3 The Rehabilitation Act of 1973

The Rehabilitation Act of 1973 [35] marks a watershed in federal public policy, utilizing federal power direcly to alleviate the problems of the handicapped through their integration into the mainstream of American society [36]. The Act was the culmination of a long struggle to place the federal government in a leadership role in this area. There was intense resistance to this concept and to specific provisions of the Act. Before final adoption, two earlier bills passed by Congress were nullified by vetoes of President Nixon, and aministrative regulations implementing the Act were not issued for years, until lawsuits and public demonstrations by groups of handicapped persons forced their promulgation [37].

The Act provides federal coordination and fiscal assistance to state rehabilitation programs, encourages research, and establishes several new federal programs. Its most profound effect, however, is in the economic sphere. One of the declared purposes of the Act is to "promote and expand employment opportunities in the public and private sectors for handicapped individuals and to place such individuals in employment" [38]. Title V is a comprehensive attempt to effect that purpose. § 501 prohibits discrimination against, and mandates affirmative action for, handicapped persons employed by or seeking jobs with federal agencies [39]. § 504 bans discrimination in the myriad programs receiving federal financial assistance [40]. The growth in the number of federal grants and in the areas they cover has been phenominal in the recent past. Examples of the reach of § 504 include recipients of federal grants in employment, housing, transportation, education, and health services [41].

Title V of the Rehabilitation Acts goes even further, however, and reaches into the private sector of the American economy by placing a series of requirements on employers holding contracts with the government of the United States or its agencies [42]. The Act here utilizes the power of the government to determine those with whom it will deal, and upon what terms and conditions it will purchase needed goods and services [43]. The potential strength of this power may be gauged by the fact that commentators estimate that approximately one-half of all businesses in the United States, including almost every major corporation, are thus bound to initiate affirmative efforts on behalf of the handicapped.

Section 503 requires that government contracts over $ 2500 contain a promise not to discriminate against employees or applicants because of their handicaps and to take "affirmative action" in hiring, promoting, training, etc. [44]. Such affirmative action includes dispensing information to handicapped workers, special efforts in recruitment and promotions to reach handicapped individuals, making reasonable efforts to accommodate the limitations of handicapped employees, and reviewing and changing job qualifications which screen out qualified handicapped individuals [45]. In addition, every government contractor or subcontractor holding a contract for $ 50000 or more and having 50 or more employees is required to prepare and maintain a written affirmative action plan implementing the requirements of the Act, and to make it available for inspection and review by the government or employees [46]. Given the far reaching implications of § 503, let us examine this section in greater detail.

The Act defines a handicapped individual as any person who (a) has a physical or mental impariment which substantially limits one or more of such person's major life activities, (b) has a record of such an impairment, or (c) is regarded as having such an impairment [47]. The Department of Labor, which has the responsibility for enforcing § 503 [48], has promulgated detailed regulations clarifying each clause of this definition [49]. It should be apparent that the Act here protects not only individuals with severely handicapping conditions, such as blindness and paralysis, but also those with more minor disabilities, since a person is "substantially limited" in a "major life activity" if he is likely to experience difficult in securing, retaining, or advancing in employment because of that disability [50]. Indeed, as part 3 of the definition allows, even those who have recovered from a disability or have no disability at all are covered by the Act if they are "regarded as being handicapped." The Act here protects persons such as cured cancer or heart patients, and individuals with controlled conditions such as epilepsy or diabetes. Such legislative protection is important, because among the major blocks to jobs are employer misconceptions and stereotyped thinking regarding the functioning of such individuals [51].

Of course, a "handicapped" individual must also be "qualified" in order to take advantage of the protections of § 503. A qualified individual is one "capable of performing a particular job with reasonable accommodation to his or her handicap" [52]. Accommodation by the employer is required unless it would impose "undue hardship" on the contractor's business. Factors relevant to a determination of whether the particular accommodation is required include "business necessity and financial cost" [53]. What do these legal standards mean in practice for our clients and patients?

Some of the answers to this questions are evident, while others are not. For example, handicapped persons screened out of jobs because of non-job-related factors are clearly protected. Examples here might include overly broad medical standards [54], or testing. On the other hand, the precise amount of accommodation required of an employer toward a handicapped employee or applicant is, as yet, unclear. For example, is job restructuring or modification by the employer required [55]? Accessibility of the work site is likewise a major issue; does this mean the entire plant or office building, or simply the specific work area of the handicapped employee? Judicial interpretation of these and related issues has yet to begin [56].

Rights without corresponding practical remedies are symbolic only. How, then, is this body of legislation protecting the handicapped to be enforced? There are two potential avenues of redress. The first is through the administrative process. The Federal Department of Labor's Office of Federal Contract Compliance Programs

(OFCCP) is charged with the responsibility for the enforcement of § 503 [57]. As an aside, I should note that the OFCCP also enforces Executive Order 11246 mandating equal opportunity by federal contractors without regard to race, color, religion, sex, or national origin [58], and § 402 of the Vietnam Era Veterans Readjustment Act which requires affirmative action for qualified veterans [59]. Although the OFCCP's enforcement of the handicap provisions was originally confined to responding to individual complaints of discrimination, more recently the Agency has opted to review contractors' Affirmative Action Programs to determine whether "systemic" discrimination against the handicapped is being practiced. To pursue these administrative remedies the aggrieved individual files a complaint with the OFCCP [60]. The agency is then to investigate, make a determination of fact, and fashion a remedy if a violation has occurred. Conciliation and persuasion are the preferred models [61]. If these fail, a range of remedial possibilities exist including the withholding of payments, termination of the contract, initiation of court action, or even debarment of the contractor from eligibility for future government contracts [62].

Despite this impressive scheme, the effectiveness of the administrative process in this area is extremely suspect. Lack of speed in processing complaints has been a major problem. Fewer than one-half of the complaints received are resolved within a year [63]. Congressional hearings to oversee implementation of the Rehabilitation Act demonstrated that little headway had been made in the hiring and promotion of handicapped persons by federal contractors and by the federal government itself because of inadequate enforcement of the Act by the OFCCP and the Department of Health, Education, and Welfare [64]. More specifically, a review of 300 federal contractors across the United States in the summer of 1978 found that 90% of those reviewed did not comply [65]. My own personal experience with a number of extremely large federal contracting firms in the Chicago area indicated that § 503 was largely ignored by the contractor and unenforced by the OFCCP.

If the administrative remedies abailable are ineffectual or unenforced, may individuals and groups bring their own lawsuits against the offending contractor or even against the federal agency? Whether such litigation is permitted by § 503, i.e., whether the Act provides for a private right of action, is presently being fought out through the lower federal courts and awaits final determination by the United States Supreme Court [66]. Quite apart from the technical legal questions involved, I suggest that other basic issues are likewise implicated. Allowing handicapped individuals to initiate and control their own legal action is part of the issue of independence and self-reliance. The right to sue is an attribute of full citizenship, of equality of persons. Administrators come and go, their priorities and agendas change. We are presently witnessing the dismantling of a host of human service programs in the United States and the abolition of long-standing administrative regulations of benefit to poor people [67]. Thus, while administrative remedies are often useful, they are ever in danger of change. One of the historic functions of the federal courts is to protect civil rights and minorities, and to be placed outside the jurisdiction of those courts is to lose a significant legal and political weapon.

4 Conclusion

The challenge before us in the international Year of the Disabled and for the forseeable future is to realize the potential benefits which recent legislative and regulatory enactments have provided for our clients and patients. In short, it is to translate abstract legal rules into the reality of people's lives. Through aggressive implementation of federal policies of integration and normalization we affirm the complete citizenship and equality of handicapped individuals. Economic independence is a key element in effectuating those values.

The government's contract power is a powerful tool toward these ends. This is true of the United States and of other countries where industrial development and military spending have placed the government in a pivotal economic position. Where such a tool is present, it should be grasped and used. The history of the Rehabilitation Act illustrates creative modern solutions to age-old problems. Our responsibility is to see that potential solutions are realized.

References

1. Declaration on the Rights of Disabled Persons, General Assembly Resolution 3447 (XXX), adopted 9 December 1975
2. Ibid., see paragraphs 2, 3, 4, 6
3. Ibid., paragraph 7
4. Address of Dr. A. Adams, U.S. Commissioner of Rehabilitation Services, Dept. of Health, Education & Welfare, May 10, 1976, quoted in J Rehabil (May–June 1976) 18
5. 118 Cong. Record 3321 (1972)
6. Ibid
7. 118 Cong. Record 2998 (1972) (remarks of Congressman Vanik)
8. 118 Cong. Record 3321 (1972)
9. Tierney B (1959) Medieval poor law. University of California Press, Berkely pp 85–89
10. Ten Broek J, Matson F (1964) The disabled and the law of welfare. Calif L Rev 54: 809–810
11. Deutsch A (1949) The mentally ill in America: A history of their care and treatment from colonial times, 2nd edn. Columbia University Press, New York
12. Wolfensberger W (1972) The principle of normalization in human services. National Institute of Mental Retardation, Toronto, p 15
13. Ibid., p 15
14. Bureau of Labor Standards (1961) Workmen's compensation and the physically handicapped worker, Bulletin 234. US Department of Labor, Washington, D.C. pp 6–8
15. De Lury B (1975) Equal opportunity for the handicapped means positive thinking and positive action. Labor Law J 26: 679–685
16. See, e.g., Herlick S (1975) Rehabilitation of industrially injured workers. Workmen's Compensation L Rev 2: 495
17. Senate Rep. No. 1297, 93rd Cong., 2nd. Sess., 34 (1974) reprinted in US Code Cong and Admin News (1974) 6373–6421
18. See ibid., p 265; 118 Cong. Rec. 3321 (1972) (remarks of Sen. Williams). Parenthetically, it should be pointed out that the very vagueness of these numbers is itself significant. As the Senate Committee noted, "There is no more devastating comment on the nature of our public policy or the lives of these (handicapped individuals) than society's inability to provide accurate and current figures on how many individuals are handicapped, what forms of disability they have, and what kind of services they receive or need." Senate Rep No 1297, supra. Note 17 p 28
19. Senate Rep No 319, 93rd Cong. 1st Sess. (1973) 118 Cong. Rec. 3321 (1972) remarks of Senator Williams)
20. Rusk H (1972) Rehabilitation Medicine p 251 (C.V. Mosby, St. Louis)

21. Smith-Fess Act, 41 Stat. 735 (1920) (repealed 1973)
22. Vocational Rehabilitation Amendments to the Social Security Act, 57 Stat. 374 (1943) (repealed 1973)
23. See, e.g., 68 Stat. 652 (1954)
24. 79 Stat. 1282, 29 U.S.C. § 31 (repealed 1973)
25. The federal government later took responsibility for funding and administering programs for the elderly, blind, and disabled in the Supplemental Security Income (SSI) program. 42 U.S.C § 1381 et. seq. (1981)
26. 42 U.S.C. § 1201 (the blind); 42 U.S.C. § 1351 (the disabled)
27. Id
28. 42 U.S.C. § 1202 (a) (8) (1974)
29. 5 U.S.C. 633 (2) (a) (1964)
30. See, e.g., Architectural Barriers Act of 1968, 42 U.S.C. § 4151–57, and its implementing regulations 41 C.F.R. §§ 101–19.6 et seq
31. See, e.g., Urban Mass Transportation Act of 1964 49 U.S.C. 1612 (a) (as amended 1970)
32. 20 U.S.C. § 1401 et seq. (1976)
33. 20 U.S.C. § 1401 (16) (18) (19) (1976)
34. See, e.g., 20 U.S.C. § 1415 (1976)
35. 29 U.S.C. § 701–794 (1976)
36. See Senate Rep 93–318, 93rd Congress 2nd Session (1973) reprinted in US Code Cong and Admin News (1973) pp 2076 ff.
37. See, e.G. *Cherry* v. *Mathews*, 419 F. Supp. 992 (D.D.C. 1976)
38. 29 U.S.C. § 791 (1976)
39. 29 U.S.C. § 791 (1976)
40. 29 U.S.C. § 794 (1976) provides "No otherwise qualified handicapped individual in the United States ... shall solely by reason of his handicap, be excluded from the participation in, be denied the benefits of, or be subjected to discrimination under any program or activity receiving federal financial assistance."
41. See, e.g., educational grantees, *Southeastern Community College* v. *Davis* 99 S.Ct. 2361 (1979); *Frederick L.* vs. *Thomas* 557 F. 2d 373 (3rd Cir 1977); *Lloyd* v. *Regional Transportation Autohority* 548 F 2d 1277 (7th Cir 1977) (transportation); *Duran* v. *City of Tampa* 430 F. Supp. 75 (M.D. Fla. 1977) (public employment)
42. 29 U.S.C. § 793 (1976)
43. *Perkins* v. *Lukens Steel Co.* 310 U.S. 113, 127 (1940) (interpreting the Public Contract Act of 1936, 41 U.S.C. § 35–45, which requires government contractors to pay prevailing minimum wages)
44. 29 U.S.C. § 793 (1976). The precise contractual language required is found at 41 C.F.R. § 60–741.4 (1977):
    (a) The contractor will not discriminate against any employee or applicant for employment because of physical or mental handicap in regard to any position for which the employee or applicant for employment is qualified. The contractor agrees to take affirmative action to employ, advance in employment and otherwise treat qualified handicapped individuals without discrimination based upon their physical or mental handicap in all employment practices such as the following: employment, upgrading, demotion or transfer, recruitment, advertising, layoff or termination, rates of pay or other forms of compensation, and selection for training, including apprenticeship
45. 41 C.F.R. § 60–741.6 (1977)
46. 41 C.F.R. §§ 60–741.5 & 60–741.6
47. 29 U.S.C. 706(6) (1976) This definition reflects a 1974 amendment to Title V, which originally defined a handicapped person as one who, "(A) has a physical or mental disability which for such individual constitutes or results in a substantial handicap to employment, and (B) can reasonably be expected to benefit in terms of employability from vocational rehabilitation services ..." Id. The new definition obviously includes many more individuals
48. 29 U.S.C. § 793 (b) (1976)
49. 41 C.F.R. § 60–741.2 (1977) and Appendix A
50. 41 C.F.R. § 60–741.2 (1977)
51. See Notes 14–16 and accompanying text

52. 41 C. F. R. § 60–741.1 (1977). This clause is textually similar to § 701 (j) of Title VII of the 1964 Civil Rights Act, 42 U. S. C. § 2000 e (j), requiring employers to accommodate the religious practices of their employees. Interpretation of the religious accommodation section (see, e. g., *Trans World Airlines* v. *Hardison* 432 U. S. 61 (1977) is not necessarily applicable to the handicap accommodation provisions because of the potentially grave First Amendment "Establishment" clause problems of the former
53. 41 C. F. R. § 60–741.6 (d) (1977)
54. See, e. g., *Gurmankin* v. *Costanzo* 556 F 2d 184 (3rd Cir. 1977) (blind person automatically disqualified from teaching by school board regulations; note, however, this case involved Constitutional and Section 540 issues); *Duran* v. *City of Tampa*, 430 F. Supp. 75 (M. D. Fla. 1977) (epileptics barred from police position; both § 503 and § 504 involved)
55. While the Section 503 regulations are silent on this point, Section 504 regulations set out specific examples of the kinds of actions that would satisfy the employer's duty of reasonable accommodation. These include making facilities accessible, job restructuring, part-time or modified work schedules, acquisition or modification of equipment, the provision of readers to interpreters, etc. 45 C. F. R. § 84.12 (b) (1978). But see *Southeastern Community College* v. *Davis*, 99 S. Ct. 2361 (1979) (hearing-impaired woman not an "otherwise qualified" handicapped individual within the coverage of § 504). See also the recent final regulations implementing § 504, 45 Fed. Reg. 66706 (1980)
56. See, e. g. *E. E. Black Ltd.* v. *Marshall*, 23 F. E. P. Cases 1253 (D. Hawaii 1980) the first judicial determination of who is a "handicapped individual" for the purposes of § 503
57. 41 C. F. R. § 60–741.25 (1977)
58. 30 Fed. Reg. 12319 (1965)
59. 38 U. S. C. § 2012 (1976)
60. 29 U. S. C. § 793 (b) (1977)
61. 41 C. F. R. § 60–741.26 (1977)
62. 41 C. F. R. § 60–741.28 (b) (c) (d) (e) (1977)
63. E. g., during 1975 OFCCP received 331 complaints but only 97 were resolved. *63 U. S. Dept. of Labor Ann. Rep. Fiscal Year 1975* 33 (1976)
64. Oversight Hearings on Rehabilitation of the Handicapped Programs and the Implementation of the Same by Agencies Under the Rehabilitation Act of 1973 Before the Subcommittee on the Handicapped of the Senate Comm. on Labor and Public Welfare, 94th Cong. 2nd Session 321–322
65. Milk L (1979) The handicapped contractor: Rights and obligations. Public Contracts LJ 11: 143. Violations included use of medical criteria unrelated to job performance and failure to implement Affirmative Action programs
66. See, e. g., *Rogers* v. *Frito-Lay Inc.*, 22 F. E. P., Cases 16 (5th Cir. 1980) (§ 503 provides no private cause of action); *contra*, *Hart* v. *County of Alameda* 21 F. E. P., Cases 233 (N. D. Cal. 1979)
67. E. g., Federal rules mandating local school systems to provide bilingual eduacation were recently withdrawn by the new Secretary of Education, N. Y. Times Feb. 8, 1981

Implementing Legal Mandates Regarding the Disabled in Educational Institutions in the USA

N. S. Greenberg and D. Greenberg

In the United States of America recent federal and local laws have changed the educational environment of the disabled in universities and have mandated equal education for all children in elementary and secondary schools.

1 Public Law 94–142

In October 1979 the Education for All Handicapped Children Act of 1975 went into effect in all 50 of the United States. Public Law 94–142, as it is known, offers funding aid to any state that makes free appropriate education accessible to all handicapped children. The law originally covered all handicapped children aged 3–18 years, and it has been expanded recently to include those up to age 21.

When the law was drafted in 1975, the government estimated that 5.5–5.8 million youngsters would qualify, or approximately one in eight of the school population. The study also found that half the estimated number of handicapped children were already receiving appropriate educational services, but 1 million had been completely excluded from the educational system. Those who did receive special help often received it in inadequate facilities and via inferior instruction. Public Law 94–142 guarantees several things to handicapped children.

1.1 Identification

The school must seek out handicapped children and provide free testing and evaluative procedures to identify the special educational needs of each child. The criteria for judging a child handicapped are mental retardation, hardness of hearing, deafness, speech impairment, deafness and blindness together, visual handicaps, serious emotional disturbance, orthopedic impariment, multiple handicaps, and specific learning disabilities.

1.2 Program Placement

A handicapped child must be placed in a program in the "least restrictive environment" [1] that suits his or her special needs. In other words, a program as close as possible to that for a nonhandicapped child must be provided. The popular term for integrating handicapped children into regular school activities is "mainstreaming"

[2]. This does not mean placing youngsters universally back into regular classrooms, but rather providing a continuum of programs through the schools. In many schools consultations take place between the special education teacher and the regular teacher before and during placement, to determine whether the pupil was and is able to function in a regular classroom. Some special education pupils might attend just one regular class, while others who are thought to be ready might attend all.

1.3 Individual Planning

A detailed Individualized Educational Program (IEP) must be written for each child who is identified as handicapped. Parents, guardians, teachers, psychologists, speech therapists, and other relevant support personnel are required to join in the preparation of an IEP. For example, the IEP of a child with a learning disability might state: "John can perceive letters and some words, but has difficulty decoding sentences. By the year's end he should be able to read and write simple sentencens."

1.4 Due Process Rights

For parents who do not agree with the handicap designation, their child's classroom placement, the IEP, or the educational approach, the law provides appeal and hearing procedures about which parents must be informed. Appeals can start informally, and can reach the level of a state court. Most of the court cases related to Public Law 94–142 have begun as a result of appeals brought by parents through lay advocacy groups, which thought they had merit and subsequently introduced them as class-action suits. A school, school system, or state that does not adhere to the law will lose its government educational funding.

2 Court Cases

2.1 Lora v. the NYC Board of Education

In June 1975, at the same time that Public Law 94–142 was passed by the federal government, a number of New York City parents filed a civil rights class-action suit on behalf of all black and Hispanic children assigned to special day schools for the emotionally handicapped. The case was *Lora* v. *the NYC Board of Education*. The parents claimed that:

1. The special school had become intentionally segregated because minority pupils were not informed about heir rights to private education
2. The criteria for referring pupils to these schools were vague and subjective
3. The schools were not equipped to handle the particular type of pupil
4. There was no due process

Four years later, in July 1979, a settlement was agreed upon, which called for:

1. Evaluating or reevaluating pupils in these special schools
2. Establishing procedures for informing parents of their rights
3. Developing a new plan for finding, assessing, and providing needed services for children, to satisfy all laws of the state and federal governments
4. Providing adequate staff training so that a supportive environment may be maintained for all children

As a result of the staff-training edict, each school in the city had to send a representative to a course on how to train school personnel in all aspects of the law. The representatives established programs in their own schools to teach faculty and staff in group sessions, not only the letter of the law and its implementation on the local school and classroom levels, but an awareness of the handicapping conditions as well.

Sensory training experiences were utilized at Sarah Hale High School in Brooklyn. Teachers were introduced to mazes and perceptual tasks in order to experience the frustrations and difficulties the pupils might encounter. Devices and techniques which simulated loss of sensation, visual distortions and limitations, and delayed feedback in hearing and reception were utilized as well. These exercises increased awareness and stimulated interaction on the topic.

Some of the goals that the staff discussed in their training sessions included:

1. Teacher expectation – the need to avoid racial, ethnic, or cultural bias in evaluation
2. Discipline – the need to avoid stereotyping that may influence the handling of disruptive behavior
3. Referral – the need to recognize equal rights and opportunities when considering referrals
4. Parental involvement – to be based on nondiscriminatory practices

2.2 Jose P. v. Ambach

In December 1979 the federal court issued an order based on a class-action suit brought by parents of children who claimed that the NYC Board of Education had failed to evaluate and place handicapped children in a timely manner *(Jose P.* v. *Ambach);* it sometimes took years to get a child placed in an appropriate facility. The court ordered that:

1. An annual census be conducted of present and former pupils to determine their need for special education
2. School-based support teams be established to evaluate children in their own environment
3. Services be provided for all handicapped children in regular schools as close to their homes as possible
4. Appropriate staff, i.e., physical therapists, occupational therapists, etc., be hired where indicated
5. Due process be provided in dual languages

2.3 Intelligence Quotient

In July 1980 a federal court judge ruled that an IQ score above 75 does not automatically eliminate a child from being considered handicapped. If the pupil meets other criteria, he or she may be eligible for placement.

3 Practice

Implementation of the law regarding handicapped children is costly for New York City. In the 1980–1981 NYC Board of Education budget of 2.5 billion dollars, 290 million – or 12 cents for every dollar – was allotted for special education. In 1970 there were 27000 children who were identified as handicapped; in 1980 there were 90000 – a threefold increase. The implementation of the courts' orders has just begun. Each year more and more children will be entering the program. The cost works out to over $3000 per pupil per year for mandatory elementary and high school education.

4 Higher Education

When the student who is disabled chooses to continue his or her education at the optional university level, discrimination and architectural barriers are often encountered. Under Public Law 90–480, the U.S. Department of Health, Education and Welfare (HEW) required all projects receiving HEW funding to comply with the American National Standard "Specifications for Making Buildings and Facilities Accessible to and Usable by the Physically Handicapped." The revised HEW Barrier-free Specifications, dated August 1978, define the physically handicapped and present the minimum mandatory requirements for accessibility. Areas covered include walks, ramps, entrances, doors, floors, stairs, elevators, toilet facilities, drinking fountains, controls and identification, and warning signs and signals.

Architectural barriers are not the only concern; discriminatory practices must be addressed as well. Section 504 of the Rehabilitation Act of 1973 states: "No qualified handicapped person ... shall, on the basis of handicap be excluded from participation in, be denied the benefits of, or be subjected to discrimination under any educational program or activity receiving federal financial assistance ...."

4.1 Implementation

La Guardia Community College in Long Island City is an example of implementation of Section 504. In 1978, as part of the compliance requirements, the college conducted an extensive self-evaluation. Joint faculty-student committees were established to study the needs of the disabled, and a consulting architect was engaged. Each department was visited, and faculty members themselves participated in inspecting their facilities. Observations and recommendations were recorded. The self-study was chaired administratively by the Dean of Student Services.

The self-study focused on student admissions, activities, and financial assistance; employment practices and procedures for both instructional and support staff; grievance procedures under Section 504; and the physical accessibility of programs at the college. Upon completion of the self-evaluation, a copy was placed in the library for review and comment by the entire college community. Subsequently – again with input from both faculty and students – a Transition Plan was prepared.

The Transition Plan divided potential areas of modification or alteration into three categories:

1. Program accessibility, whereby the college committed itself to enabling the physically disabled to have access to any academic program of their choice by rescheduling classes or programs, or by altering facilities to permit access
2. Architectural barriers
3. Maintenance items, comfort or convenience items

The Committee on the Needs of the Disabled, as well as the Affirmative Action Committee, monitored college-wide efforts on an ongoing basis to assure compliance. A subcommittee, also comprised of students and faculty, on the Removal of Architectural Barriers of the College Community played an active role in the drafting and reviewing of proposals. Notifications of intention of compliance were placed on bulletin boards throughout the college, and steps were taken by Student Services counselors to inform visually impaired students of the policy of nondiscrimination on the basis of handicap.

Perhaps partially as a result of these visible notices, the student newspaper became involved. An occupational-therapy student's open letter to the president received prominent coverage. It identified areas not yet suitable for the disabled. The president's reply that progress was being made was displayed in a subsequent issue. Thus, a continuing dialogue on discrimination and accessibility involving both students and faculty was seen by the college community with the commitment of the editor. The newspaper in this manner was used as a forum for receiving suggestions, as well as for providing relevant information on the needs of the disabled.

Disabled students accepted invitations to speak to occupational therapy and other health career students in their classes about the difficulties they encountered and the solutions they found most beneficial.

Disabled students were encouraged to identify themselves as such on the admissions application, so that the college could be aware of individual student needs prior to registration, and arrange for special services where appropriate. Each student was contacted for a preadmission interview, at which time he or she was informed of support services available to the disabled. The counselor likewise evaluated the kind of educational resources and assistance which might be required by the student for maximal participation in the college program.

The college also developed a continuing education program to help both deaf and physically handicapped adults to develop skills needed to cope with the academic, social, and physical adaptation problems related to college experience. Through individual counseling, workshops, seminars, and special course work, the program emphasized career planning and educational development for entry into college, skills training programs, or immediate employment. Student tutors offered special assistance to students in this program through the college's Adult Learning

Center. The long-range goal was to make the college's antire array of services and academic offerings accessible to deaf and physically handicapped persons. Sign language interpreters were assigned on a one-to-one basis in special classes where needed, and were present at all general functions, including graduation and professional staff meetings.

Perhaps the most exciting and innovative activities were introduced in 1980, after the Transition Plan was underway with its designated priorities. First, an all-day conference was scheduled on Helen Keller Day, to which agency representatives, students, potential students, parents, and faculty and staff were invited. One of the highlights was an all-disabled panel of both current and former students, presenting their experiences both within the classroom and on the job. Questions from the audience led to active discussions on the rights of the disabled, on the abuses or nonfulfillment of legal mandates, and on the avenues open to the disabled to insure equal opportunity beyond the supportive environment of La Guardia Community College. Potential and current students were particularly interested in the job satisfaction that former students had been able to obtain after graduation. One deaf former health career student told of her current exciting work with deaf-blind children as an occupational therapy assistant. The work-study program offered to students through the college's Cooperative Education Department had enabled her to be placed while still a student, thereby demonstrating her capabilities and leading to her being hired upon graduation.

The second of these special workshops was entitled "Faculty Awareness."Attendance was required of all professional staff. The first half of the workshop featured a panel presentation on the topic "Disabled Students in the College." A deaf student spoke through an interpreter about how normal she looked, felt, and acted when enabled to do so. A deaf counselor spoke directly, with labored speech, about his own achievements and those of the college. But the most impressive speaker was a blind counselor who addressed the audience about her own difficulties in obtaining a PhD. She was the first in her family to go to college, and she believed that if she were not blind she would not have sought higher education. She spoke of failing biology because the instructor would not allow another student to describe for her what could be seen in the microscope so that she could then identify it.

This was a perfect introduction to the second part of the program, in which the audience of faculty members was divided into small groups, each given a description of a series of actual classroom situations to discuss. The groups were asked to generate solutions to a problem, including the handling of the interpersonal dimension of the situation, the teaching strategies, and the equipment and support services to be suggested. There was tremendous excitement about the task, with much controversy about how various instructors would accept changes in their classroom routines.

The most significant outcome of the workshop, however, was true faculty awareness of the individual differences and needs of each disabled person. One example of contrary agendas among the disabled themselves was that of street crossing. Modifying a sidewalk curb from a 5-in. step to a graded ramp will enable the wheelchair-bound student to independently manage street crossing; however, that same modification may hinder the blind individual, who counts on the step of the curb to know that the street has been reached.

Such issues, as well as those of the classroom integration of the disabled, may have varying solutions. Yet, the dialogue has been started and true faculty awareness introduced.

References

1. University of Minnesota (1977) Least restrictive educational environment. University of Minnesota, Minneapolis
2. Anonymous (1975) What mainstreaming is and is not. In: Thomas MA (ed) Exceptional Children Nov: 174

Additional Reading

American Standards Association (1961) American national standard specifications for making buildings and facilities accessible to and usable by the physically handicapped. American National Standards Institute, New York

Ashford N, Bell WG (1978) Mobility for the elderly and the handicapped. Loughborough University of Technology, Cambridge, England

Biehl GR (1978) Guidelines for the section 504 self-evaluation. Business Officer March: 12–17

CEC Delegate Assembly (1973) The organization and administration of special education and education of the gifted. Council for Exceptional Children, p 2

Center on Human Policy (1972) Handbook for parents, children with special needs, and New York State education laws. Syracuse University, Devision of Special Education and Rehabilitation

Denos E (1971) Strategies for improvement of educational opportunities for handicapped Children. In: Reynolds MC, Davis MD (eds) Exceptional children in regular classrooms. University of Minnesota, Minneapolis

Department of ConsumerAffairs (1976) Consumer rights for disabled citizens. City of New York, New York

Division of Educational Facilities Planning (1975) Comprehensive long range plan for educational facilities. New York State Education Department, Albany

Division of Educational Facilities Planning (1975) Educational specifications for the erection, enlargement or remodeling of educational facilities, in compliance with Section 155.1 of the regulations of the Commissioner of Education. New York State Education Department, Albany

Division of Educational Planning and Support (1978) Creating least restrictive learning environments: a guide for mainstreaming. Board of Education City of New York, New York

Educational Research Services (1963) Program of requirements for a school for severely physically handicapped. Human Resources, Albertson, NY

Hepner, PJ (1980) Update: *Lora* v. *The Board of Education*. The Advocate April: 6–7

Institute for Research and Development in Occupational Education (1969) Barrier free checklist. City University of New York, New York

Kaufman MJ et al. (1975) Mainstreaming: Toward an explanation of the construct. Intramural Research Program, Bureau of Education for the Handicapped, U. S. Office of Education, Washington, DC

La Guardia Community College (1978) Self assessment study. City University of New York, Long Island City Sect 504

La Guardia Community College (1978) The self evaluation plan. City University of New York, Long Island City

La Guardia Community College (1979) Transition plan. City University of New York, Long Island City

Lora Decree Staff Development Program (1980) Planning for school staff development. City of New York, New York

National Research Council (1965) Building standards for the handicapped. National Research Council, Ottawa

New York Junior League (1981) Accessibility guide for the disabled to Manhattan. New York Junior League, New York

Nyquist E (1973) Mainstreaming: idea and actuality. New York State Education Department, Albany

Office of the Superintendent of Public Instruction (1961) Guide for administrators establishing classrooms for physically handicapped children. State of Illinois, Springfield

Precht CE (1980) Education inequality. The Advocate: April: 14–15

Project on Classification of Exceptional Children (1975) The futures of children: categories, labels and their consequences: highlights: a summary and recommendations from the final report. Vanderbilt University, Nashville

Schoenbohm WB (1962) Planning and operating facilities for crippled children. Thomas, Springfield

State University Construction Fund (1967) Making facilities accessible to the physically handicapped. (Checklist/Addendum 1969) State Univ. Construction Fund, New York

Steinfeld E (1975) Barrier-free design for the elderly and disabled. Syracuse University All-University Center on Aging, Syracuse

Stern J (1980) Legal brief: *Jose P.* v. *Ambach*. The Advocate, April: 5–6

Teaching Resource Center/NEw York City Regional Resource Center (1980) Selected educational materials on legislation and court action. The Graduate School of the City University of New York, New York

Tucker WV (1964) Higher education and handicapped students. Kansas State Teachers College, Emporia

U.S. Department of Health, Education and Welfare (1975) Barrier-free. U.S. Government Printing Office, Washington, DC

U.S. Department of Health, Education and Welfare (1978) Policy Interpretations on handicapped issued. Personnelite of City University of New York, New York, 5/37

U.S. Department of Internal Revenue (1977) Rules and regulations regarding architectural and transportation barrier removal expenses. Federal Register 42 (64)

Yuker HR (1968) The modification of educational equipment and curriculum for maximum utilization by physically disabled persons. Human Resources Center, Albertson

Learning Disabilities and the Court

J. B. Varcoe

As knowledge expands, judges are becoming aware that the system of laws, courts, procedures, and traditions that has been developed does not always deal fairly with all persons who become involved as accused adults or juveniles. Justice in Canada is a verbal system dependent on language, visual perception, and memory. If these qualities are defective, then justice, truth, and fairness to the handicapped witness or accused will suffer.

It is now a widely accepted fact that 15% of all children have a learning disability. These children have average or above-average intelligence, but fail to perform satisfactorily in a classroom, and when adults, their disabilities obviously continue to affect them in their work, and in particular, in their ability to participate in a system that requires skills that are absent or inadequate. The problem is not whether learning disabilities are a contributing cause of delinquency and consequent criminal behavior, but whether the disabled person can receive fair treatment in a court of law.

Learning disabilities that are neurologically based, as opposed to learning problems that are related to personality or psychosocial symptoms, have been characterized in part as hyperactivity, short attention span, poor powers of concentration, poor school work, unpredictable emotional activity, impulsiveness, irritability, low frustration tolerance, hostility, perceptual impairment, poor coordination, and disorders of memory, thinking, speech, and hearing. Outlining the effects of these characteristics or any combination of them, Dr. Harold Levy, Professor of Pediatrics at Louisiana State University, wrote:

> Because of prejudice and misunderstanding, the learning disabled child has been the victim of mismanagement of many of those who deal with him. The hyperactive child who does not sit still in the classroom may be considered spoiled or acting out his hostilities to parental mismanagement, while the withdrawn hyperactive child is often called lazy or underachieving. His awkwardness and clumsiness are likely to make him an object of scorn and derision by his classmates so that he becomes a loner on the playground. The short attention span and distractibility are often misinterpreted as indicating the child is nervous, probably due to discord at home, while the memory difficulties are considered to indicate willful disobedience or poor study habits which require punishment or more pressure. The concept disorders and poor abstraction are often felt to indicate that the child has deep-seated emotional problems rooted in early childhood trauma, again blamed on the parents [1].

Experience has shown that the child with learning disabilities is pressured and humiliated by his teachers, punished and possibly rejected by his parents, and ridiculed by his peers. Desperate to gain recognition, this child becomes the class clown or a boastful liar, or he may resort to unlawful acts to gain recognition. The disabled child, although average or above average in intelligence, may suffer various forms of disability that may go undetected into adulthood.

There is evidence that a large percentage of persons who are involved in criminal activity suffer from some form of learning disability. The guilt or innocence of a learning-disabled adult will depend in no small measure on his ability to function before the police, in the courtroom, and if convicted, during the sentencing period. Without detailing the various forms of disability, let us consider the person who has a perceptual handicap. Such a person overlooks important details. He mishears word structures, and may be distracted by sights and sounds. In addition to perceptual problems, the person may have problems with concept formation, and hence may not be able to think abstractly or reason properly. With faulty perceptions the person will arrive at wrong conclusions, and with poor concept formations he may have difficulty in formulating the correct answer, although he knows what he wishes to say.

A court of law must exercise vigilance when faced with a witness or an accused person who has a visual perceptual difficulties and auditory perceptual impairment; it must question whether justice and truth are possible in a system of that depends on verbal skills. The court must be aware that a person with auditory and visual disabilities may have problems in instructing his lawyer, with the result that a possible line of defense is not considered and the person involved pleads guilty to an offense not committed. Such a person will have serious difficulty in giving evidence in a court of law, and to avoid continued embarrassment may be reduced to silence, which may be interpreted as lying conduct or evading tactics. Such people are easily distracted, due to their visual and auditory difficulties, and their behavior in court may be unfairly viewed as aggressive and hostile.

The child or adult who is unable to recall events, or to compute time or distances, even with a normal IQ, acts in what appears to be a primitive way. The special language of the police witness used in giving evidence in court must sound like a foreign language to the disabled person. Does the evidence of the police officer have any real relationship to the comments made by the learning-disabled person at the scene of the crime, or when first contacted by the police. Does the written statement or confession transcribed by the police officer truly reflect what the witness was trying to verbalize? Can the learning-disabled person with auditory or perceptual problems receive fair treatment?

The learning-disabled child with perceptual problems who is unable to master learning skills at school will become discouraged and angry, and without proper help will soon be dropout. This form of handicap continues as the child becomes an adult, but with proper training, the effect of perceptual difficulties can be reduced. If nothing is done, and the handicapped adult is confronted with the judicial system, designed without consideration for his special problems, his anger and frustration will increase, leading to a misunderstanding of, or even lack of respect for the concept of law and justice that exists in Canada. The learning-disabled person has difficulty succeeding in our system of justice.

Judges will recall many situations where the credibility of evidence given by a witness or accused person was questionable. When the witness claimed lack of recall of the events even after his memory was refreshed by reading a statement he had given to the police at the time, was he deliberately refusing to give evidence, or did he have a genuine failure of recall? The written statement prepared by a police officer may have read like a well-developed piece of literature, but when the witness gave oral evidence the result was exceedingly primitive. The witness may have contradicted the evidence of the police officer, saying, "That is not what I said to him; he must have misunderstood me." In such a situation, can the Court not conclude that the witness had difficulty formulating what he perceived? Although it was obvious that the witness had been at the scene of the crime, he could only recall insignificant or immaterial aspects of the event. Was he being deliberately evasive, or was he genuinely distracted by extraneous matters?

How the court assesses the witness or accused person with a learning disability determines the value of the evidence and the fate of the accused. Expecting a judge to be able to determine whether the person before him has a learning disability is asking him to be superhuman. Nevertheless, in case of doubt, he must be aware enough to consider the possibility of such a disability in order to keep fairness paramount. Judges who deal with juveniles must have an idea of how learning-disabled children function, so that they can introduce the help and assistance required when they recognize such cases.

The adult court judge, just as his juvenile court counterpart, must be aware of how adult criminal behavior relates to the progression from learning disability to dropout to juvenile delinquency. Without hoping to be an expert diagnostician, he must learn from observation that certain behavior demands further investigation; in such cases he should call upon professionals in the community who can best advise the court as to the problems of the offender, so that the disposition of the court will consider the offender's disability.

Failure to deal with a learning problem is a serious problem in rehabilitation, particularly since it appears that antisocial and criminal behavior may stem from such a handicap. It does not necessarily follow that those who have learning disabilities will commit crimes, but if the jails contain a large proportion of such handicapped persons, the problem of rehabilitation must assume a different role. If a judge suspects or is made aware that the convicted person before him, especially a young adult offender, has a learning disability, he may not wish to impose the usual form of penalty. In such a case the judge will certainly require a pre-sentence report, including an in-depth analysis of the offender, his or her school records, and a psychological assessment.

The Corrections Branch of the Ministry of the Attorney General operates the Haney Forest Camps as a correctional facility for certain offenders. One of these facilities, the Stave Lake Camp, is located 20 miles east of Maple Ridge on the foreshore of Stave Lake. The facility houses a maximum of 50 inmates and offers job placement for first and second offenders. The camp authorities recently decided to experiment with a tutoring project for those inmates who wished to receive educational training and skills from community volunteers. Two elementary school teachers with special remedial skills tested a small group of inmates. The first teacher tested four persons and reported the following results:

Four men were tested using a Standard Reading Diagnostic Test, and the overall reading levels were:
Inmate A – Grade 1
Inmate B – Grade 3
Inmate C – Grade 3½
Inmate D – Grade 9
On certain sections of the test, such as structural analysis, the results were at kindergarten level [2].

The second teacher tested and tutored then inmates, and reports as follows:

a) Three 19- and 20-year-old inmates – diagnosed "slow learners ... attended special classes in Greater Vancouver School District, level of achievement ... illiterate to Grade 2–2½ reading, writing skills.
b) One 19-year-old inmate – claimed Grade 9; level spelling skills – Grade 3 (Ottawa-area school district).
c) One 19-year-old inmate – Grade 9 (occupational) ... spell and writing skills poor ... cultural background deprived (i.e. knowledge of Canadian geography – local geography nil). Attended special classes in Greater Vancouver School District.
d) One 19-year-old inmate – achievement Grade 9 (Central B.C. school district) was recognized; advised to carry on with correspondence course.
e) One 28-year-old inmate – New pupil (Nov. 7/79) requests help in grammar, spelling ...
f) Two inmates, 19 and 20 years old – achievement Grade 8 level, but request help in English ... composition, spelling, plus mathematics [3].

What, if anything, can be learned from these findings? The project is in its infancy, but does seem to indicate that a proportion of inmates in this particular correctional facility have a very low level of ability in the elementary skills of reading, writing, and arithmetic, the basic skills necessary for survival in the current system of society. Can judges really be satisfied, knowing that a large number of persons being sentenced to jail can barely read and write? One of the tutored inmates said to his teacher, "I hope I can read before I leave, so I can read a story to my daughter." At this point, it is not known if the unskilled persons in jail are illiterate due to mental inability, lack of education, or a learning disability, but for the judge, the point is that such people seem to comprise a fair proportion of the jail population. Many research studies have been undertaken concerning learning disabilities and juvenile delinquency, without a definite connection having been established between the two, but it is a fact that a high proportion of juvenile delinquents have learning disabilities. Research with convicted adults in the Province of British Columbia is in its beginning stages but it seems obvious that some adult inmates have little or no skills in such basics as reading and writing.

A capable judge must be informed about the knowledge that is available on human behavior, and should keep abreast of new findings to ensure that an accused person, whether disabled or not, receives a fair trial. In a court truly concerned about rehabilitation, a judge who imposes sanctions or sentences a person found guilty of an offense should investigate further where there are indications that the offender may be handicapped in some way.

The court's final disposition may be affected by the apparent behavioral and emotional disorders of the offender, which have to be considered before a learning handicap can be diagnosed and treated. Judges need help to properly assess such handicaps and require from the community proper diagnostic and treatment facilities. Judges have always been aware of the serious injustice done to the innocent person who is found guilty, but they are not recognizing the need to ensure that an accused person with a learning or other form of disorder receives a fair trial, and if convicted, a proper and fitting sentence.

References

1. Levy HB (1979) Statement made by Dr. Harold B. Levy at 14th annual Neuropsychology Workshop held in Victoria, British Columbia, Canada in April 1979. Dr. Levy is a pediatrician, and author of *Square Pegs, Round Holes – The learning-disabled child in the classroom* (1973).
2. Haylow L, personal communication. Mrs. Linda Haylow, School District No. 42, British Columbia, Canada (1979).
3. Wouterloot AE, personal communication. Mrs. Agnes E. Wouterloot, Douglas College, British Columbia, Canada 1979).

Judicial Self-awareness and Psychoanalytic Countertransference

H. S. Rollmann-Branch*

1 Introduction

This article is concerned with the mental and emotional functioning of judges [1–3], those awesome authorities who inspire strong emotions, trust, and expectation of wisdom, but who also elicit fear and submission or even rebellion. To explain judges' reactions, we have to look also at those of the people who appear in court – the defendants, plaintiffs, witnesses, and to some extent the attorneys – all of whom we may term "participants".

How do judges respond to the emotions, thoughts, and actions of participants who appear before them – to their "transference"? If the judge's responses are based on his own psychic makeup rather than on an objective situation, we call these reactions "counter-transference."

We will better understand the emotional aspects of the situation of judge and court participants if we can apply what we know of the situation of psychoanalyst and patient; the latter can also be called a "participant." We already know a good deal about the psychoanalyst's emotional responses, which may be manifest or suppressed, conscious or beyond our awareness. We can take the analyst's counter-transference as our known model and enable judges to apply this thinking to their own experiences.

Before attempting to look inside the analyst or judge, let us turn to certain basic assumptions of psychoanalysis which may be familiar, but which bear brief mention to ensure that the terms "transference" and "counter-transference" are understood.

2 Some Psychoanalytic Concepts

2.1 Psychoanalysis

Psychoanalysis is best known as a method of treating emotional disturbances of various kinds, mostly long-standing disturbances which interfere with a person's occupational productivity, his enjoyment of recreation, and his social relations including his love life. Because these emotional malfunctions have been present for a long time, it also takes a long time and a thorough knowledge of the person's life from infancy on to correct them. As a by-product of the investigative collaboration between analyst and patient, psychoanalysis becomes a research tool for exploring the

* I wish to thank Professor M. Levine for his very helpful suggestions

functioning of the mind; as a matter of fact, the exploration itself leads to the therapeutic result. The more broadly useful aspect of psychoanalysis, however, is that its body of knowledge constitutes a general psychology of man. The findings of individual psychoanalysts have led to the formation of general principles about how the human mind functions, which allow us to form hypotheses regarding any given individual's mental functioning. Without that individual's corroboration, however, we cannot be certain.

2.2 *Transference*

Most of the patient's feelings toward the analyst are based not on the analyst's objectively perceived personality, but on characteristics attributed to him by the patient. These characteristics derive from the patient's feelings toward important people in his infancy or childhood: parents, siblings, grandparents, or servants as the case may be. We call these emotions "transference" because they are transferred onto the analyst from early relationships [4–6]. Such transferences do not occur exclusively with relation to the analyst. Everyone's childhood experiences predispose him to a certain attitude toward others, but the response of the others will confirm, contradict, or modify his expectation. The less neurotic the person – and no one is 100% free of neurosis – the greater his capacity to test his fantasied expectations against reality. The psychoanalyst, however, maintains a neutral, unobtrusive attitude in his professional work, expressing little of his own feelings and opinions; even his facial expressions are not perceived by the patient who lies on the couch facing away from the analyst. In order to facilitate the emergence of the patient's childhood feelings, fantasies, and memories, and the development of the "transference," the analyst does not talk about himself nor discuss his personal life. The transference is noted by the analyst, and with his help, shows the patient as well how his past still interferes with his present life. In this way, the patient will be able to make more appropriate choices in the future based on present reality.

2.3 *The Unconscious*

Our repressed memories, emotions, thoughts, sensations, observations, and reactions of childhood are harbored within our unconscious. We cannot recall this repressed material, but it nevertheless affects our adult emotions, thoughts, sensations, observations, and reactions. If they are unconscious, how do we know they exist? They appear in garbled messages in our dreams. Sometimes we can decipher them without the method of psychoanalysis. Other clues to the unconscious can be detected in faulty actions, such as slips of tongue or pen, forgetting, misplacing, and the like. Furthermore, if we are alert to them, we may also detect unconscious forces at work in our reactions to events and people, if they do not seem warranted by the circumstances. Our reactions may seem unusually strong or weak compared to our normal attitude; we may notice that without sufficient external cause we become tired, bored, impatient, angry, excited, or excessively gentle. Some people may even react with headaches, sneezing, or a stomachache when an unconscious memory has been touched; it may evoke an emotional reaction, which nevertheless does not become manifest or conscious.

2.4 Emotional Life of the Child

Another concept of psychoanalysis which explains transference and counter-transference is the strongly erotic emotional life of children: for example, the strong emotional and sexual attachment of the boy to his mother and his fear of punishment from his rival, the father. This triangle may have many variations and complications, but most frequently the father is the authority figure who punishes, to whom the boy submits, against whom he rebels. But the father also serves as a model for the boy's strivings and ambitions.

As already noted, these attitudes may persist into adult life. They become manifest on every occasion at which the person is again confronted with an authority figure: a teacher, a boss, a judge, a psychoanalyst. As long as the origins of these attitudes remain unconscious, the attitudes themselves can only be repeated; they cannot be changed. Instead of reacting appropriately to an authority figure according to the circumstances, e.g., with respect, the person will react stereotypically in the old childhood way, whether it be appropriate to the occasion and person or not.

3 "Transference" to the Judge

The participant – the patient or the litigant – feels, thinks, and acts toward the analyst – or the judge – as if the latter were a significant figure from his childhood. We say "as if" because this attitude is an unconscious equating of the analyst or judge with persons from the past. Only after this equating is realized consciously can the participant shed his image of the judge or analyst as parent and see him as the person he really is.

It is not surprising that the analyst or judge most frequently represents the father as authority in the transference. It makes no difference whether the analyst or judge be male or female. The judge/analyst equals father if seen as authority, mother if seen as protector, sibling if seen as competitor, or even grandma if seen as one who comes to the rescue and consoles the culprit. This role unconsciously given to the analyst or judge does not remain constant or static. It can change from the nurturing mother who ministers to, feeds, and indulges the infant, to the distant and rejecting mother whose interest is turned toward a sibling, father, or a job. The role can also change from the nurturing mother to the punishing and forbidding father who makes the child move out of the parental bedroom, who expects self-control and good behavior, who uses the strap, a stern glance, or a loud, angry voice to elicit obedience. This role may not fit the analyst/judge at all, but if the participant feels unconsciously guilty about something (he doesn't know what), guilty as he felt as a naughty child, he must attribute the disapproving-father role to the analyst/judge.

In psychoanalysis, the "setting" facilitates the development of transference. The analyst sits on a chair behind and slightly above the patient, who is lying on the couch with his head on a pillow. From this position, the analyst can observe the patient's body movements and most facial expressions, but the patient cannot see the analyst without an awkward turning of the head. For the patient, this setting is reminiscent of lying in bed as a child telling a parent about the triumphs and defeats of the day. The brief, almost stereotyped greeting which marks the beginning and end of the analytic session, the length of which never varies, is not unlike the judge's ritualized entrance and exit. The judge's robe and elevated bench favor the litigant's deference, reminiscent, too, of looking up to a judging parent who demands to know the truth. As children, we are convinced that our parents can read our minds and know the truth, even without our confession. The adult patient may still believe that the analyst knows his unspoken, innermost thoughts, and the accused may fear that the judge knows his guilt even without the evidence.

3.1 Guilt Feelings

The feeling of guilt may arise from nothing more than a fantasy or a wish – most often an unconscious wish. We may take an example from psychoanalysis: A patient thinks the analyst looks angry when opening the door; the patient is self-critical in a vague way and expresses fear of the analyst's criticism. After a while, the patient may remember that he saw another patient leave the analyst's office, smiling. This arouses his anger and jealousy and the wish to do away with all the analyst's other patients, to be the only one, just as he once wanted to do away with all his parents' other children and be the only child. But all these wishes to be the only one, to "liquidate" all competitors, are unconscious. Nonetheless, the unconscious guilt manifests itself in the misperception that the analyst looks angry. It is important to note that these were *wishes* only; the patient *did* nothing.

Similarly in legal situations, a guilty conscience, an unconscious expectation of or search for punishment, even the confession of a crime, do not necessarily reflect a crime committed [7]. Guilty consciences flower especially in the presence of "investigating" analysts, and more so, of course, in the presence of judges. Even judges and analysts may drive more carefully in sight of a police car, or have twinges of conscience when they hear the police siren or see flashing lights in the rearview mirror. Such twinges of conscience are usually unrelated to the speedometer. What power of observation and sanction do we ascribe to policemen; what clairvoyance do patients attribute to the analyst; what punitive power do the defendants expect from the judge? That some power and clairvoyance which the child attributed to, and partially experienced from his parents.

If even the gentlest, most benign, most empathically understanding psychoanalyst can sometimes appear as a severe and omniscent judge to his patient, it requires little imagination to surmise how real judges are seen in the psychological transference which occurs in all who appear before them. Whether a judge provokes awe, fear, mistrust, guilt – or trust in his impartiality and fairness, belief in his omnipotence – may in part depend on the judge's personality and reputation. But usually those present in his court have a variety of preconceived ideas of "the judge", which may be modified, attenuated, or reinforced by the actual judge. These preconceived ideas are part conscious expectation, part unconscious sum of childhood experiences and fantasies, part attribution to the judge of the person's own severe self-criticism.

4 "Counter-transference" by the Judge

Ideally, neither analyst nor judge should be affected by even the strongest emotions and misconceptions of those who seek his help and justice; that is to say, he should not be prone to reactions of counter-transference. The dedication of the analyst or judge to his task, and the concern for the people he encounters in fulfilling his professional aim, should be all the emotion that he contributes to these relationships. To this end, the analyst has undergone his own personal analysis as part of the preparation for his profession; his own unconscious fantasies and memories have become conscious and have been resolved in the light of adult reality. His major unconscious conflicts should have been consciously resolved and should not be reawakened by his patients. Fortunately, judge and analyst alike are protected against the arousal of their emotional conflicts by not being themselves under scrutiny; they do the scrutinizing, and their equilibrium is therefore greater than that of those whose transferences are directed at them. Nevertheless, anxiety can be aroused and there may be unconsciously motivated irrational or unwarranted responses in even the most mature and unperturbed analyst or judge [8, 9]. As far as the analyst is concerned, "When, in the patient–analyst relationship, anxiety is aroused in the analyst, with the effect that communications between the two are interfered with by some alteration in the analyst's behavior (verbal or otherwise), then counter-transference is present" [10].

This applies to a consciously experienced anxiety or discomfort, one the analyst or judge is immediately aware of. It also applies if the anxiety is out of awareness or unconscious, and the anxiety is probably replaced by an attitude meant to combat it. Another example from psychoanalysis: The analyst may conclude that the patient has made progress, in that he is able to express anger freely, or the analyst may grow sleepy or daydream of vacation plans; both may be unconscious maneuvers on his part to deny the anxiety aroused in him by the patient's angry attack.

Analyst and judge are not useful in their prime function if they have difficulties with their own responses. The stereotyped and generalized anxiety responses which constitute the patient's transference have been analyzed for the most part in the analyst. His own responses have been brought to awareness and replaced by more mature and integrated responses. As the analyst's problems are not the subject of his patient's analysis, their residue can remain dormant during the analysis of the patient's problems. But occasionally, and under certain circumstances, these sleeping anxieties may be aroused. When this occurs, the analyst's responses interfere with the desirable situation of a concerned, dedicated, calm, and understanding analyst – one who is unanxious and therefore most helpful to his anxious patient. Similarly, the judge's responses may interfere with his functioning.

4.1 Causes of Emotional Reactions

There are three main causes for the analyst's – and very likely the judge's – unhelpful reactions. The first is real occurrences in his life, such as a quarrel with his spouse, sickness, or death in the family, or worries about retirement income and the stock market. He may also be concerned with his reputation as a competent professional, especially if he is dealing with a prominent person or the relative of a colleague. The second may be his insufficiently resolved neurotic problems, such as fear of his own anger. In response to an angry participant, he may then lean over backwards and try to soothe him; or he may wish to retaliate, thereby becoming angry with the participant instead of understanding (and analyzing) his anger. Communication of the participant's anxiety to the analyst or judge, much as if it were caught from him like a contagious disease, can be a third cause.

For the analyst, susceptibility may be part of his professional sensitivity to the patient's emotions; an empathic analyst resonates with his patient and takes small, brief samplings of the patient's feelings, to try them out in himself so as to better understand them. And a judge may take samples, for instance, of a witness's emotions. But if instead of transient samplings, the analyst or judge takes a big bite and swallows the participant's anxieties and tensions so that they become his own whereby his reactions are determined by these tensions, a significant interference – actually, an interruption – in communication has occurred.

We may be manipulated into playing all kinds of roles, and are the more likely to do so the more urgent the participant's appeal or the closer our own personality and history fit into the participant's pattern. The participant's violent expression of hostile feelings can arouse in the analyst or judge fear, the angry wish to ridicule, or pacifying and reassuring behavior. Depression and suicidal thoughts in the participant may make the analyst feel worthless and useless. The participant's overvaluation of the analyst/judge may feed the latter's narcissism. The judge who hands down decisions which are rarely appealed, but have important consequences for persons before the bar, may be tempted to misinterpret the power of his office as his own omnipotence. The analyst whose clarifying interpretations promote change and are received with gratitude may risk believing himself omniscient and the master of his patient's destiny. None of these reactions is useful in performing the function of analyst, or of judge.

4.2 Dealing with Emotional Problems

Vigilant monitoring can set the engine of self-scrutiny in motion to reestablish optimal calm attention to the participant's problems. Judges, like analysts, can pay attention to their own feelings and fantasies, changes in their voices, their habits, their movements in the chair, a different manner of greeting the participant, increased or decreased frequency and length of their own verbal communications, an unusual choice of words. Sometimes a sudden flash of understanding explains and eliminates the cause for a counter-transference interference. At other times, more prolonged self-analysis is required before the next transaction with the participant. If repeated and prolonged problems arise with a particular participant, with similar aspects of several participants or even with all participants, which cannot be resolved by himself or with occasional consultation, an analyst may resume personal analysis with a colleague.

Judges may not often resort to this last remedy of personal psychoanalysis for disturbances of their optimum functioning. But we can assume that judges experience interferences in their professional tasks as analysts do, that the causes for these interferences also stem from real occurrences in their lives, from their emotional constellation, or from contagion by the attitudes of those who appear in court. Self-scrutiny and consultation are also available to the judge for his attainment and maintenance of optimal impartiality and considerate judgement.

We need not harbor the impression that inside judge and analyst alike there exists a profusion of anxieties and emotional dissonances, constantly and continuously erupting into behavior unbecoming to their professional purposes. The members of both professions desire to avoid psychological interferences in their professional efficiency and usefulness and they function effectively most of the time; one assumes that analysts and judges are relatively free from neurosis. Both analysts and judges are generally even tempered, mature, empathic but also objective, enjoying a harmonious family life, taking a recess when preoccupied with overwhelming grief or worry, and immune to contagion by patients' or litigants' anxieties.

References

1. Frank J (1930) Law and the modern mind. Coward-McCann, New York, pp 106, 338–339
2. Frank J (1949) Courts on trial: Myth and reality in American justice, chap. 11. Princeton University Press, Princeton
3. Katz J, Goldstein J, Dershowitz AM (1967) Psychoanalysis, psychiatry and law. Free Press, New York
4. Freud S (1910) Five lectures on psychoanalysis, standard edn (1957) vol 11. Hogarth Press, London, pp 3–55
5. Freud S (1912) The dynamics of the transference, standard edn (1958) vol 12. Hogarth Press, London, pp 99–108
6. Orr DW (1954) Transference and counter-transference: A historical survey. J Am Psychoanal Assoc 2: 621–670
7. Freud S (1916) Some character types met with in psychoanalytic practice: criminals from a sense of guilt, standard edn (1957) vol 14. Hogarth Press, London, pp 32–33
8. Racker H (1957) Meanings and uses of the counter-transference. Psychoanal Q 26: 354–356
9. Spitz R (1956) Counter-transference: Comments on its varying role in the analytic situation. J Am Psychoanal Assoc 4: 204–208
10. Cohen MB (1952) Counter-transference and anxiety. Psychiatry 15: 231–249

The Disabled Person as a Witness in Court

A. Carmi

In practically every disputed case, part of the proof is based upon the alleged perception and memory of some witness or witnesses, who claim to have been present at some relevant past event. There is hardly any trial of importance in which the qualities and limitations of human perception and memory should not be carefully considered [1]. For the sake of discussion we shall deal separately with perception and memory; however, the first stages in the process of remembering are a direct continuation of the process of perception [2]. Memory overlaps with perceptual and decision processes as a synthesis of diverse cognitive activity [3].

1 Perception

Perception might be described as an immediate discriminatory response of the organism to energy-activating sense organs [4]. Enormous quantities of information particles are constantly bombarding us. Our perception functions through a complicated nervous system and symbolical processes founded upon past experience. But what we see is not a mirror of the stimulus [5]. Man does not perceive objects directly; he responds or reacts to their presentation. One's own interpretation plays a major role in the mechanism of perception; testimonies reflect individual stories and subjective descriptions. People are prone to see what they want to see [6], and perception works as a selecting mechanism.

The witness's attention constitutes a prerequisite for the perception of certain events, forming in itself a screening process. His or her attention is stimulated by internal factors, such as motivation, as well as by external factors, such as the event itself. The witness's perception, too, is determined by internal factors, such as interests, needs, and values. We hear what is easier heard, we see what we are interested in seeing, we perceive that which we are prepared to perceive. Moreover, human perception may be influenced and distorted by suggestion, association, emotion, and bias. As long as the court is not aware of these internal factors, the judge will not be able to determine the accuracy of even an honest report of past events. Judges may acquire theoretical knowledge with respect to the general functioning of internal factors, but there seems to be no practical way of supplying them with specific information concerning the internal factors of the individual witness. Judicial findings based on ordinary testimonies should thus be received as defective products.

This is all the more true with regard to exceptional reports. Two issues concern the testimony of a disabled witness: Do his physical and mental conditions influence his perception? Would it be possible to localize certain "weak" points throughout his story?

Undoubtedly, disability of one kind or another may lead to some misinterpretation of reality [7]. Physical defects are more easily localized and recognized. Judges will not rely on the hearsay evidence of the deaf or on the vision of the blind. The same pertains to certain mental defects.

There are psychotic disorders in which a delusion, generally persecutory, is accepted as the essential abnormality. Paranoia is characterized by misinterpretation of reality. Even an hysterical neurosis may occasionally be accompanied by some hallucinations. Delusions and hallucinations can interfere with the process of perception and distort matters already perceived, although such an interference may be restricted to certain matters or fields only. On the face of it, there should not be a substantial difference between the schizophrenic's perception and that of an ordinary witness. However, judges will find it quite difficult to determine in a given case whether a schizophrenic has applied "normal" perception, unless assisted by a professional expert. It is doubtful whether even contemporary psychiatry can offer such help to the judiciary, however.

2 Memory

One who listens attentively to testimonies in courts of law soon comes to see that much litigation actually grows out of inaccuracies of human memory. In fact, most erroneous testimony is due to inaccuracies of memory [8]. Prior to any discussion of the memory of the disabled, it should be stated that even the so-called normal memory is defective by nature.

Memory reflects the knowledge of past events. It is a complex functional system, consisting of both the process of memorizing and the process of reproduction of the imprinted traces.

Remembering can be regarded as a gradual process resting on multidimensional systems of connections incorporating elementary (sensory), then more complex (perceptual), and finally the most complex (cognitive) components [9].

One of the most effective distorters of memory is emotion. Excitement, fear, hate, horror, or affection may so influence memory that the report of an occurrence becomes very different from the original fact [10]. A witness may have a strong bias in his conception of the justice of the case, so that in total innocence he may recall things which have never occurred, or forget important things which have [11].

Memory and memory defects have been the subject of wide scientific research. Modern physiology and neuropsychology have proved that mnemonic activity constitutes a complex system of different parts of the brain working together [12]. Several investigations have dealt with memory disturbances arising in patients with local brain lesions. Psychiatry supplies us with various explanations as well. They relate, for instance, to unconscious psychic processes, acting as unconscious screens or censors which often serve as a protection from embarrassing facts.

Amnesia constitutes a major topic when dealing with the memory of witnesses. Amnesia is a forgetting, at some later date, of events that occurred at an earlier time and which should be easily remembered under ordinary circumstances.

Amnesia may be due to various organic conditions such as tumor, heart attack, arteriosclerosis, or head trauma. It may be also caused by alcoholic disorders, drug addiction, or psychogenic factors [13]. There are several hypotheses about the nature of amnesia, as a consolidation (of memory traces), proactive interference (retrieval difficulties), or semantic coding defect [14]. However, the accurate determination of the nature of the amnesia is often difficult and occasionally impossible.

We have said that human memory is defective by nature, and that scientific research has not supplied us with the full understanding of the memory process. This is all the more true with regard to the memories of disabled persons. The influence of certain disability on memory, as well as the nature and the intensity of such an influence, should be determined prior to drawing any conclusions with regard to the testimony of a disabled witness. Here, too, it is doubtful whether science can supply the courts with the necessary direction.

3 Credibility of Testimony

How are judges then to evaluate the disabled's report in court? The credibility of a witness is determined according to his appearance and his message. The contents of the message can be more easily examined by the court, which applies criteria of logic and common knowledge.

The appearance of the witness is assessed according to external symptoms, such as blushing or paleness, changed rhythm of breathing and pulse, perspiration, dry mouth, trembling, nervous movements of the eyes, stammering, etc., which are associated with various conditions common to most people, and which indicate the witness's intentions and credibility. This assumption suits the ordinary witness, but it is of no help to the court with respect to certain disabled witnesses. Ordinarily the judge does not know them, and their appearance cannot be compared by him to any similar inner image.

Take for example schizophrenic persons. The main symptoms manifested by hebephrenic schizophrenics are inappropriate smiling and an incoherent stream of talk, while the catatonic schizophrenic may grimace curiously [15]. Judges who are not aware of these facts may wrongly interpret the appearance of such persons on the witness stand.

Psychopaths are usually regarded as pathological liars. Experiments show that even with the polygraph it is difficult to verify whether the psychopath is telling the truth or lying [16]. Judges might definitely be misled by false reports of such persons if not assisted by the testimonies of experts. On the other hand, an "ordinary" liar may be identified by nervous spasms and superfluous talking. Judges may turn down the true report of a schizophrenic due to misunderstanding and misinterpretation of his behavior on the witness stand.

On principle, the judiciary cannot function without the necessary evidence. The limited credibility which is sometimes granted to testimonies in court might bring about frustration as one recalls the true purpose of judicial litigation and the important role of testimony within this process. One of the main functions of judicial litigation is to reconcile controversies or to decide in favor of or against each of the litigants. In doing so, the court is obliged to determine the nature of some event which took place in the past. Past events are "known" to us due to the functioning of both perception and memory. "Direct" knowledge is held superior to intermediate knowledge as it dispenses with the need of applying the perception and the memory of third parties. Since judges are not allowed to apply their own direct knowledge of the case, they are expected to base their findings on others' testimonies only. This kind of evidence presents the image of the past event as it has been perceived and remembered by the witness.

The evaluation of testimonies proves to be a sophisticated process, as it depends not only on the evidence and the circumstances, but on the evaluator as well. The assumption that judges "know" a witness who appears in front of them for a few minutes is nothing but a fiction.

One writer has stated that it almost seems that the human observer cannot see clearly, cannot understand spoken words correctly, and cannot report accurately [17]. Nevertheless, judges are required to base their findings on human testimony, and they are expected to apply some super, nonexistent power to the examination and verification of it.

Society has endowed judges with awesome, almost monarchical powers, and they have occasionally been attacked for applying these powers; one American writer claimed: "Our courts are filled with desirable laws and undesirable judges" [18]. But judges could not exercise such powers unless the public at large wished them to do so. Apparently, the general law reflects some common agreement that disputes should be settled in spite of defective testimony. There seems to be no alternative for the courts but to try to fulfill their impossible mission within these limitations.

As a general rule, every person is competent to testify unless the court concludes that he or she is not capable of understanding the questions put, or of giving rational answers to those questions, owing to extreme youth, extreme old age, disease – whether of body or mind, or for any other reason. Judges apply some inner scale in order to reach this conclusion. Those who are not acquainted with disabled persons may measure their credibility according to their general criteria or tend to entirely reject their reports. A judge, like anyone else, classifies people, whether known or unknown to him, according to a limited number of types. Classifying disabled persons according to certain general types without taking into account their special background might lead to mistaken evaluations. The same rule applies where the court automatically rejects the testimony of a disabled witness owing to a basic misunderstanding of his behavior and personality. Judges, as well as many other members of our community, may be influenced by prejudice in rejecting the testimony of disabled persons. Throughout history behavior disorders, especially the various forms of mental defects, have been viewed with suspicion and aversion. This feeling is deeply embedded in human cultural tradition [19]. Until recently, mentally disordered people were hardly distinguished from criminals [20].

Modern research concerning the effect of physical appearance on the judgement of guilt may also apply to the appearance of the disabled on the witness stand [21]. The theory of cognitive dissonance suggests that judges tend to disbelieve certain disabled persons due to their own bias [22]. One may also point out that judges, like anyone else, are susceptible to aesthetic bias [23, 24]. When faced by a disabled witness in court, especially one with a mental defect or an unusual appearance, the judge is prey to the age-old prejudices of society at large.

Judges should therefore be trained to acquire wider knowledge of disabled persons, and to understand that different degrees of competency may exist in the same individual in various situations [25]. The role of medicine is to improve the administration of justice [26] by supplying the courts with the necessary training and reports. However, scientists themselves are still looking for some well-founded guidelines with respect to the credibility of witnesses. Much research should therefore be done to form such guidelines for the benefit of both the disabled person and the public at large.

References

1. Osborn A (1950) The problem of proof. Boyd, New York, p 206
2. Luria A (1976) The neuropsychology of memory. Winston, Washington, p 4
3. Kennedy A, Wilkes A (1975) Studies in long term memory. Wiley, London, p 13
4. Bartley H (1969) Principles of perception. 2nd edn. Harper, New York, p 11
5. Haber R, Hershenson M (1973) The psychology of visual perception. Holt, New York, p 157
6. Frank J (1949) Law and the modern mind. Coward-McCann, New York, p 107
7. American Psychiatric Association (1968) Diagnostic and statistical manual of mental disorders, 2nd edn. American Psychiatric Association, Washington, DC
8. Osborn A (1950) The problem of proof. p 206
9. Luria A (1976) The neuropsychology of memory. p 4
10. Osborn A (1950) The problem of proof. p 214
11. Frank J (1949) Law and the modern mind. p 107
12. Luria A (1976) The neuropsychology of memory. p 15
13. Sadoff R (1975) Forensic psychiatry. Thomas, Springfield, p 28
14. Kennedy A, Wilkes A (1975) Studies in long term memory, p 329
15. White R, Watt N (1974) The abnormal personality. 4th edn. Ronald, Kidlington, p 432
16. Lykken D (1959) The G. S. R. in the detection of guilt. J Appl Psychol 43: 385
17. Osborn A (1950) The problem of proof. p 207
18. Stein D (1974) Judging the judges. Exposition, New York, p 1
19. White R, Watt N (1974) The abnormal personality, p 48
20. White R, Watt N (1974) The abnormal personality, p 6
21. Efran M (1974) The effect of physical appearance on the judgement of guilt. J Res Personality 8: 45
22. Festinger L (1957) A theory of cognitive dissonance. Stanford University Press, Stanford
23. Homans G (1961) Social behaviour: its elementary forms. Harcourt, Brace and World, New York
24. Aronson E (1972) The social animal. Viking, New York
25. Sadoff R (1975) Forensic psychiatry. p 154
26. Szasz T (1974) Law, liberty and psychiatry. Collier, New York, p 241

Economic Constraints on the Effectiveness of Litigation and Legislation for the Disabled

J. Rubin

1 Statement of the Issue

Disability programs in the United States have come under a variety of criticisms in recent years [1, 2]. Dissatisfaction with disability policy stems from the perception that some individual programs are ineffective, inequitable, and too costly. At the same time, the entire system of disability programs can be described as confusing and inadequate [3, 4].

Although the emphasis may shift with changes in national leadership, efforts to reform the system and to resolve the problems will continue. The existence and structure of programs is affected by a great many factors. In the U.S., it is often suggested that the will of the electorate guides the actions of their democratically-elected representatives. It has also been argued that special interest groups, with well-funded lobbying activities, are influential participants in the budgetary and policy decisions made in Washington, D.C. Others attribute substantial power to bureaucrats responsible for turning often vaguely written legislation into actual, working policy [5]. Through the drafting of the required rules and regulations, bureaucrats are viewed as acting to increase the size and authority of their respective agencies.

Another, growing influence on policy formation has been the judiciary. Using constitutional principles and existing legislation, advocates for the disabled have petitioned the courts to order changes in existing programs or the creation of new programs. In going to the courts, the disabled are following a path taken by other minorities, such as blacks and women. By using the courts, advocates and public interest lawyers are able to circumvent the legislative process.

It would be difficult to classify all of the activities of the disabled and their advocates as an attempt to achieve some ideal disability policy. In fact, the approach of responding to problems by filing lawsuits is certain to produce relatively narrow solutions. This haphazard and incremental approach is partly responsible for the problems cited earlier; unfortunately, it may be hard to do much better.

Physical and mental impairments cause not one, but many difficulties. A single, universal program is not likely to be able to cope fairly and efficiently with these differences [6]. But if we are forced to live with a multitude of programs and policies, can the process of litigation and legislation just described be counted on to do the job of reforming existing programs and creating new ones? I am not convinced that these methods cannot work, but if they are to succeed, there must be a better understanding of the role of economic factors.

Stated simply, my thesis is that because of a misunderstanding or ignorance about how economic factors influence political and bureaucratic decisions, choices made by the disabled and the actions of persons involved in the delivery of services, litigation, and legislation are apt to produce unexpected and undesirable consequences. It is only in recent years that the implications of this hypothesis have come to play a significant role in the design of disability policy in the U.S.

2 An Overview of the Disability System

It is best to begin with a brief overview of the structure of public disability programs. (Private-sector assistance is so diffuse that it is impossible to accurately quantify. Much of the public-sector expenditures are for private-sector services. Of course, families may expend a great deal of time and effort to assist the disabled.) I would place programs in five distinct categories: cash transfers, medical services, nonmedical rehabilitation services, special services (generally designed to enhance independent living skills), and indirect assistance. In terms of 1977 expenditures, cash transfers is the largest category [7]. The vast majority of expenditures within the cash-transfer group are programs for the disabled poor, disabled veterans, and disabled workers covered under the Social Security Disability Insurance program. Simply put, these programs provide income (not always on the basis of how much other income is available) to the disabled. One problem associated with cash transfers (discussed in detail later) is their potential effect on an individual's decision to participate in the labor force.

Public medical assistance for the disabled in the U.S. is most often in the form of reimbursement for privately purchased medical care (veterans' programs and some workers' compensation systems are exceptions). Often, but not always, eligibility for medical coverage is contingent on eligibility for cash transfers. Again, linking eligibility for benefits to meeting certain conditions creates the potential for an individual to adjust his behavior to affect the eligibility decision.

Public nonmedical rehabilitation services generally have as their objective a return to work. Although increasing emphasis is being attached to such nonemployment objectives as independent living (an equity-based decision) there is continuing and strong support for using scarce rehabilitation dollars to help an individual return to work (an efficiency-based criterion) [8].

Independent-living services include the provision of special aids and devices, attendant care, and housing and transportation assistance. These expenditures often produce a nonmeasurable but valuable output. The decision to make such services available to more people is often based on the contention that individuals have a right to such assistance [9]. The introduction of ethically based claims to services makes this a difficult and complicated matter. Yet, with resources being limited, the decision to offer a particular service to a particular individual must be supported by arguments other than a claim to a right. Furthermore, winning rights that require the use of other people's money is more easily achieved when those who are paying agree that the rights in question, do, in fact, exist. I do not believe that consensus on this matter yet exists in the U.S., and the austerity signals coming out of Washington suggest that it may be farther away than advocates would prefer.

The final category, indirect assistance, serves partly as a catchall for programs that do not fit into one of the four previous groups. The two most significant items are research (rehabilitation and prevention) and broadly-written legislation in such areas as nondiscrimination and affirmative action.

The development of such of wide range of assistance has been incremental [10]. Some people are covered by several programs while others may fail to qualify for any assistance [11]. The problem lies in both the difficulty of defining the eligible population and the need to limit costs. Disability is often defined not as the existence of a medical condition, but in terms of the impact of the condition on the ability to perform in a social role such as work. Others who have chronic conditions but are able to work may be handicapped but not work disabled. The kind and amount of public assistance which such persons should receive is, and will remain, a debatable issue. Even when programs are created, funding restrictions require careful selection of clients and services.

3 An Economic View of Disability Policymaking

Understanding the process of making decisions about who to serve, what services to offer, and how much to spend requires some appreciation of the roles of the different parties to the process. Furthermore, the factors affecting the behavior of these persons will be an important consideration later, when we turn to the difficulties of achieving reform through litigation and legislation.

Using the economic principle of utility-maximizing behavior, I will concentrate on the actions of politicians, the disabled, and program personnel. Economists have been devoting increasing attention to developing models of how political systems actually work [12]. In the past, the efforts of economists focused on ways to identify characteristics of economic systems that would produce efficient outcomes.

Most models begin with the concept of a self-interested politician seeking to stay in office. This is not as cynical as it may sound, nor does it automatically imply that politicians will not favor the disabled. The large number of programs already in existence testify to that conclusion.

To remain in office, politicians must respond to the wishes of a majority of their constituents. The problem is complex, because citizens judge politicians according to inadequate information and over a range of issues that come up during a term in office. In constructing programs, there is often a need to balance the losses imposed on one group against the gains received by another. (Of course, it is less difficult to achieve consensus on programs that benefit all, but such programs are often hard to find.)

Much is made of the wide-ranging benefits of disability programs. For example, Disability Insurance (DI) offers insurance for all workers while paying benefits only to some. Rehabilitation promises savings in benefit payments and increased output as a way of justifying its costs.

The political process, therefore, places emphasis both on the beneficiaries and those who pay for programs. To the extent that the political system functions as a marketplace does, one can view politicians as doing the buying for taxpayers. While mistakes can occur, the threat of being voted out of office constrains political activity. Constitutional restrictions place other limits on what can and cannot be done.

The process cannot work smoothly. For any number of reasons, the political process may fail to do a good job. Small groups that may face large gains or losses can be more vocal than large groups of individuals, each of whom may have little to gain or lose, but for whom the aggregate effects are greater than and opposite to those of the vocal minority. It is this possibility that makes cutbacks in existing programs so difficult.

The disabled also behave with the objective of maximizing utility in mind. Faced with a given income potential, available programs, and cost of services, they will respond to improve their own well-being. This may involve leaving the labor force when they are still able to work [13].

Perhaps the fundamental question is simply: What should society do for the population limited by some chronic physical or mental condition? If one of the by-products of the resulting programs is withdrawal from the labor force, is that sufficient to justify abolishing or significantly changing the program? The answer lies in balancing costs and benefits. No one seriously suggests that automobiles be banned because they pollute the air or contribute to accidental injuries and deaths. But it is reasonable to identify cost-effective actions to reduce pollution and to increase safety.

In the area of disability policy, the tradeoffs are less clear-cut, but are made all the time. Part of the judgment lies in deciding on the value that we place on giving the disabled more income or increasing access to transit systems or some other policy alternative. No one has yet determined how much adequate income and access to transit is really worth, although one could view legislative and legal actions as the means to move the system toward a truer accounting of such benefits.

In the process of operating programs, we must rely on individuals to manage resources and to deliver services. As a result, a number of persons come to rely heavily on such programs as a means of employment for themselves. In addition, it is likely that those involved in programs choose to remain involved because they believe in what the program does. In such settings, change is obviously difficult to achieve.

Each of the three parties to disability programs will react to legislated and judicially ordered changes. Such changes cannot simply be put onto paper and into action. Failure to understand the reactions of these and other affected persons has made for some negative and unexpected consequences of litigation and legislation. These actions, unilaterally imposed on an existing system, often do not bring about the desired results. It has been said that "... whatever the legislated law, it does not follow that its intent will be achieved. Legislated law is overpowered by economic laws of capitalism which often nullify or pervert intended effects" [14]. The same can be said for judicial mandates. It is the laws of supply and demand that have the last word. The products of political and judicial processes may change the costs and benefits of certain actions, but we need to understand how people will respond to these changes to predict the final outcome.

4 How Disability Policies Fail

In an effort to support the arguments made in the previous sections, I will now offer two case studies, one of legislation and one of litigation, concerning U.S. policy toward the disabled. Both instances provide support for claims made earlier and suggest the difficulty of trying to reform a part of the disability system without considering the system as a whole. The cases also point to the necessity of recognizing the impact of economic considerations on behavior of the disabled, as well as on politicians and those responsible for delivering services.

The first case concerns the structure of disability benefits in the disability insurance program and the attempt to rehabilitate disability insurance recipients [15]. In the United States, the large majority of the work force is covered under the public Social Security system that includes disability insurance in addition to old age and survivors benefits. To qualify for benefits under this program, an individual must be unable to perform substantial gainful activity, often tested in terms of ability to earn a given monthly income. The eligibility test can be satisfied purely by meeting medically established standards. In addition, the United States Congress has passed legislation providing for the expenditure of a maximum of 1.5% of the benefits paid in the previous year to be used for rehabilitation services. Faced with concern that the existing rehabilitation programs were not providing adequate resources to the more severely disabled DI recipients, the legislature attempted to establish rehabilitation programs financed 100% from the Social Security Disability Insurance trust fund, based on the notion that savings could be generated for the trust fund as a result of individuals returning to the labor market. While the rehabilitation program has grown quite dramatically in the past 10 years, except for some very recent reductions in real expenditures, the DI program has also been exploding. Numerous explanations have been put forward to explain this growth, including the easing of disability criteria and higher relative benefits [16]. Our concern here is the effectiveness of the rehabilitation program and the contradictions inherent in making cash transfers to the disabled while trying to encourage rehabilitation.

In the U.S. program, average cash benefits have increased rapidly as has the availability of other forms of benefits to individuals who are disabled. In particular, those on the disability rolls for 2 years qualify for eligibility under the federally financed Medicare program, which provides coverage for most medical bills with some minor deductibles and coinsurance. Another important feature that should be mentioned is the structure of DI benefits in the U.S. program. Because of the method by which benefits were calculated until recently, many younger workers could receive benefits that were 80% or more of their predisability earnings [17]. Of course, the purpose of these benefit levels is to insure that the disabled do not suffer deprivation as a result of their disability.

When Congress first legislated the introduction of the rehabilitation program, some confusion was evident in the objectives established for it. Congress referred to both saving the trust fund money and maximizing the number of people rehabilitated. These objectives can be contradictory. The rehabilitation of some people would involve more costs than benefits, thereby losing money for the trust fund while increasing the absolute number of people rehabilitated.

The reason for discussing this program in the context of the views presented earlier is that the attempt to initiate and effectively achieve rehabilitation is likely to be stymied by the disincentives posed by higher cash-benefit levels and the availability of other noncash benefits [18]. With the potential loss in income following a return to work being quite severe, it is reasonable to expect many individuals receiving disability benefits either to try to avoid rehabilitation programs or to somehow maintain their benefit level. There is a failure to recognize that the disabled who are eligible for disability benefits often consist of a group of individuals capable of choosing some degree of participation in the labor force, but who choose to remain disabled because of benefit levels. The lack of success for which this rehabilitation program has been criticized recently is perhaps more attributable to the structure of the disability insurance programs than to the rehabilitation program itself. Yet Congress has moved to cut back rehabilitation expenditures on the grounds that the program was failing to achieve its stated objectives.

There is a general problem to be recognized in terms of how Congress interpreted the results of benefit-cost studies, but that is a separate topic for discussion. While the disabled were faced with decisions about employment, the counselors responsible for providing the services were themselves faced with an incentive system that offered little motivation to rehabilitate the disabled at wages sufficient to get them off of disability benefits. Rehabilitation programs generally rewarded counselors on the basis of rehabilitation, and not on the basis of whether or not a client ultimately left the DI rolls. Counselors did not have sufficient incentive to close cases at the highest wage rates possible.

In recognition of this problem, recent legislative changes have restructured the financing system of the beneficiary rehabilitation program. The distribution of funds of the states is now based on the proportion of rehabilitations that occur at a given wage rate. Ultimately, the test will be whether or not such incentives get passed down to the counselors, and whether or not it is possible to achieve more rehabilitations at higher wages.

Other actions under consideration are experiments, similar to welfare-reform experiments tried in the U.S., to determine what the costs and benefits to the DI program would be of gradual reductions in disability benefits as individuals move into the labor market. There has always been a fear of instituting this sort of program in DI because the opportunity to earn some income and collect partial disability benefits might attract a great many new applicants. The result might be more costs than savings, but this cannot be foretold without the kind of information offered by the experiments now being considered.

In sum, the problems faced by a system which attempts to rehabilitate DI recipients show that for programs to be effective, the disabled and the rehabilitation counselors need to be viewed as rational decision-makers. When programs are structured to include the correct incentives for going back to work, it is much more likely that the ultimate policy ends will be met.

The second example that I would like to use to point up some of the problems of making a successful change in disability programs concerns the relatively recent activity in the U.S. directed at improving the quality of institutional care for the mentally ill and mentally retarded, and at speeding up the deinstitutionalization of such persons. The United States, along with many other countries, has embraced normalization as the desired policy for the mentally retarded and mentally ill. The development of drug therapies and new knowledge about mental conditions have enabled society to offer more care in the community. The process and the speed with which this occurred was unsatisfactory for many advocates of the mentally disabled in the United States. As a result, a number of legal actions were brought, seeking to have the judiciary step in, affirm the rights of these individuals, and order changes in the structure of state policies [19].

Most significant among these actions was the ruling in 1972 by Judge Johnson in *Wyatt* v. *Stickney* in Alabama. It established that involuntarily institutionalized mental patients had a constitutional right to treatment. The strategy underlying the lawsuit was really twofold: to force states to upgrade institutional care, but at the same time, to point out that increased institutional costs would hopefully lead to deemphasis on institutions.

Much has been written and said about the impact of these court cases. It is very difficult to assess empirically their separate effects. In one instance, I myself attempted to document how the proportion of total state spending used for mental institutions has been affected by the court cases [20]. I found that the proportion of total state expenditures going to mental institutions was higher in 1978 than it otherwise would have been, as a result of the court rulings. The implication, of course, is that a great many more dollars were going into institutions than would otherwise have been the case. One might question whether that was a reasonable objective, given the shift of clients to the community. Patient populations were declining, and states were under various kinds of judicial orders to place clients in the least restrictive setting. The deinstitutionalization movement has resulted in a rapid growth of what might be called psychiatric ghettos. An entire industry built around the use of older houses as boarding homes, group homes, and halfway houses has been encouraged. The development has been haphazard and has been criticized because of the lack of organization of the necessary services in the community. In one state (New Jersey), a serious side effect has been a number of boarding home fires resulting in many deaths.

As might be expected, there has also been a great deal of community opposition to these efforts to deinstitutionalize mental patients, and strong resistance to the establishment of halfway houses in many communities. The political decision-makers are clearly acting in a manner designed to implement the court order, while enabling them to provide services and meet their legal obligations without imposing substantial financial burdens on the community. At the same time, these legislators are now faced with criticism from the community for providing unsupervised and inadequate care and encouraging the development of the psychiatric ghettos. In some cases, even the parents of the mentally retarded have tried to force states to move in the opposite direction and maintain the institutions, but to improve them to the point where the parents would prefer that their offspring remain.

There is no way for us to determine the net impact of these court orders. Although I have highlighted some of the negative consequences, I think it only fair to point out that many programs have succeeded, and that many people have remained out of institutions and avoided some of the deterioration in their condition that often accompanies long-term institutionalization. It may not be possible to reach a conclusion as to whether or not the costs of these policies outweigh the benefits. It does seem that forming policies through indirect judicial intervention in the budgetary process has the disadvantage of emphasizing or focusing on parts of the system, without considering the potential reactions to changes. This lack of a broader view results in some of the problems mentioned earlier.

I believe that both of these examples illustrate some of the difficulties of formulating disability policies. They reflect the continuing trade-offs that exist in terms of work and adequate benefits and in terms of patients' rights, the rights of the community, and the costs of care.

5 Some Concluding Comments

Although the tone of my remarks has been somewhat critical of recent legislative and judicial activity, I believe these avenues of change can be effective instruments in the development of disability policy. It is probably true that a satisfactory result can only be achieved after incremental and piecemeal reforms have solved some problems and created new ones. Building a new system from scratch is not feasible, partly for political reasons, but mostly because a large, entrenched system already exists. Attacking it with a barrage of lawsuits and legislation seems the logical strategy. Understanding the economic motivations involved should help to improve the selection and design of the legal actions. Although it may be possible to avoid some of the deleterious consequences resulting from past actions, not all problems can be foreseen. Litigation and legislation are imperfect instruments of change, but the imperfections should not blind us to the great good that can be done through well-designed changes in the existing system for dealing with disability.

References

1. Rubin J (ed) (1981) Alternatives in rehabilitating the handicapped: a policy analysis. Human Sciences Press, New York
2. U.S. General Accounting Office (1976) Improvements needed in rehabilitating social security disability insurance beneficiaries. US GAO, Washington, DC
3. Rubin J, Dolan R (1980) The work disabled in poverty: an assessment of the effectiveness of public transfer programs. Rutgers, The State University of New Jersey, New Brunswick
4. Wolfe B (1979) Impacts of disability and some policy implications. Institute for Research on Poverty, University of Wisconsin, Madison
5. Gifford A jr, Santoni GJ (1979) Public economics: politicians, property rights, and exchange. Dreyden Hinsdale, Illinois
6. Berkowitz M, Rubin J (1980) Disability pension issues: a report to the president's commission in pension policy
7. Berkowitz M (1981) Social policy and the disabled: the main issues. Conference on the implications for social security of research on invalidity, Vienna, Austria, April 1–3
8. Levitan S, Taggart R (1981) Rehabilitation, employment, and the disabled. In: Rubin J (ed) Alternatives in rehabilitating the handicapped: a policy analysis. Human Sciences Press, New York
9. Purtilo RB (1981) Justice, liberty, compassion – analysis of and implications for "humane" health care and rehabilitation in the U.S.: some lessons from Sweden. World Rehabilitation Fund, New York
10. Berkowitz ED (1979) The American disability system in historical perspective. In: Berkowitz ED (ed) Disability policies and government programs. Praeger, New York
11. Johnson W (1979) Disability, income support, and social insurance. In: Berkowitz ED (ed) Disability policies and government programs. Praeger, New York
12. Browning EK, Browning JM (1979) Public finance and the price system. Macmillan, New York
13. Berkowitz M; Johnson WG; Murphy EH (1976) Public policy toward disability. Praeger, New York
14. Alchian AH (1977) Economic laws and political legislation. In: Siegan BH (ed) The interaction of economics and the law. Heath, Lexington
15. Berkowitz M, Horning M, McConnell S, Rubin J, Worrall JD (1981) An economic evaluation of the beneficiary rehabilitation program. In: Rubin J (ed) Alternatives in rehabilitating the handicapped: a policy analysis. Human Sciences, New York

16. Schobel BD (1980) Experience of disabled-worker benefits under OASDI, 1974–78. Actuarial Study No. 81, SSA Publication No. 11-11528
17. Muller LS, Lando M (1980) Replacement of earnings of the disabled under social security: levels and trends 1969–75. Research Report No. 53, SSA Publication No. 13-11809. Department of Health and Human Services, Washington, DC
18. Berkowitz M (1980) Work disincentives. Institute for Information Studies, 200 Little Falls Street, Suite 104, Falls Church, Virginia 22046
19. Rubin J (1978) Economics, mental health, and the law. Heath, Lexington
20. Rubin J (1980) Judicial standards and the financing of mental health services. Inquiry 17 (2)

Assessment of Disability

A. Kjønstad

1 Introduction

A primary goal of any society should be to offer handicapped people treatment and rehabilitation in order to improve their ability to function as much as possible. Places of work and social conditions should be adapted so as to enable them to make optimal use of their resources. However, this is not always done, and quite often it is difficult or impossible for handicapped people to undertake the tasks carried out by most other members of society. Therefore, in a society with a money economy, the question arises whether they should be financially compensated.

During the twentieth century the industrialized countries have seen the emergence of a number of public compensation systems. Handicapped people may be granted various forms of aid under a public social security system, they may benefit from private insurance plans, and/or the conventional law of torts may warrant payments of compensation.

As a rule the amount of compensation depends on the severity and inconvenience of the individual's handicap. A disability degree is fixed, and is an important factor in computing compensation. Other factors frequently taken into account are the individual's age and sex, his or her previous income, the current interest rate, and statutory or agreed maximum amounts.

This paper describes the principles underlying the assessment of the degree of disability. It is a systematic survey of the concepts of disability applied in Norwegian legislation and in juridical and medical literature.

We are now on the border line between law and medicine, specifically social medicine, rehabilitative medicine and insurance medicine. I use as a basis the work of the most prominent Norwegian physicians in this field. I have not examined medical literature outside of Norway. The model and the general ideas which follow are formulated with a view to attracting international interest.

2 A Model for Comprehension of the Concept of Disability

2.1 General Comments

The concept of disability tells us something about how the individual manages or does not manage to carry out the tasks with which life confronts him, that is to say, how the individual functions. It is a measure of a person's ability or disability to function. The assessment is nearly always followed by the stipulation of a degree of disability, normally given as a percentage, so that total disability is said to equal 100%.

Assessment in connection with disability concepts is done as a rule because of accident, injury, sickness, defect or similar events and conditions. So what we are interested in is a reduction of the ability to function due to a health condition.

The terms "invalid", "handicapped", "disabled", and "crippled" are usually interchangeable. "Handicapped" is the broadest of these terms, and "crippled" the narrowest.

The task of lawyers is to define the contents of the disability concepts applied in legislation. An assessment of disability is made on the basis of certain rules and norms. Most of the statutory provisions in our legal system are aimed at the regulation of behavior. They are rules (directives) prohibiting certain actions, ordering the undertaking of certain actions, or permitting certain actions.

The provisions on disability and handicaps tell us something about how to measure the individual's capacity for social adjustment, for instance as regards the demands of working life. They detail the conditions for classification of a person at a definite degree of disability, i.e., norms of qualification [1, 2].

2.2 *The Resources of the Individual*

The individual's ability to function depends on a number of circumstances. Since we are primarily interested in the reduced ability to function caused by a health condition, it might be natural to begin with the WHO definition of health: "Health is a state of complete physical, mental and social well-being and not merely the absence of disease or infirmity" [3].

This definition has been criticised, particularly regarding the claim for complete well-being, but it is not necessary to go into detail about that here. What is most important in this connection is that there are three main components of health – physical, mental, and social. The circumstances having a bearing on the individual's ability to function may thus be divided into three groups.

The importance of the physical (bodily or somatic) state for the ability to function is clear. Injuries to and the loss of limbs and other parts of the body constitute the classical disabling events. To this group belong also the losses of sight, hearing, and other senses. Nor should we forget pathologies of the internal organs, such as the impaired function of heart or lung.

There should be no need for deliberating on the fact that mental suffering (psychoses, mental retardation, psychopathy, and neuroses) may involve a reduced ability to function. In the course of this century there has been a substantial increase in the number of people disabled because of mental illness. Nearly one-third of the total number of people receiving disability pension under Chapter 8 of the National Insurance Act are suffering from some kind of mental disease [4].

Social conditions that may affect the ability to function include housing, whether or not a person receives support and encouragement from his family and others, and whether the handicap in question is generally accepted by society or is looked down upon, e.g. alcoholism. So far, negligible weight has been attached to such social circumstances in the assessment of disability.

2.3 The Tasks of the Individual

Measuring the ability to function should be done in relation to the tasks which the individual is supposed to undertake [5, 6]. Rougly, it may be said that adults have three main types of tasks to fulfill:

1. *Work* occupies about one-third of the time we are awake (assuming a 40-hour workweek and deducting for legal holidays and 4 weeks' vacation every year). The terms handicap and disability are often used to measure the capacity to carry out work (working capacity).
2. *Leisure activities* for most people also occupy about one-third of the time we are awake, time which is spent on sports, outdoor life, reading, watching TV, playing games, being with family and friends, traveling, etc. So far, concepts of disability have not been used for measuring the ability to function in these respects.
3. *Personal affairs* probably also occupy about one-third of our time, such as personal hygiene (washing, bathing, haircutting), preparation of food, eating, shopping, laundry, housework, etc. Disability concepts have been used to measure functional ability in some of these fields.

2.4 Schematic Survey of the Model

It is quite clear that disability is not a uniform concept. A physically disabled person, for instance, may be 50% disabled where work is concerned, 90% disabled as regards leisure time activities and 10% disabled when it comes to managing personal affairs. However, a mentally disabled person may be 100% disabled where work is concerned, 10% disabled in respect of leisure time activities and only 1% disabled as regards personal affairs.

An indefinite number of disability concepts may be imagined. What is decisive to the substance of each disability concept is which quantity claims one's interest on the "resources" side and which quantity engages one on the "task" side. One may, of course, envisage more detailed or rougher breakdowns than are given here. However, the following section is confined to an account of the various concepts of disability used in legislation and insurance conditions, and of the theoretical definitions given.

3 Grading of Tabular Disability

3.1 Explanation of the Concepts

The degree of disability or invalidism which is linked to injuries to various parts of the body or to the senses is laid down in general provisions. There are authorized lists and tables in which the different senses, limbs, and organs are asssessed in percentages.

The tabular assessment of disability takes into consideration only physical disability to function. As a rule one does not take into account that a certain reduced ability to function, for instance the amputation of a leg, may have a varying impact on various individuals. Such an amputation will be a much greater strain on an old, heavy person than on a younger person in good physical shape.

One may also have separate tabular rates where age, weight, and a number of other individual circumstances are included in the description of the various injuries. Some such individual circumstances have been incorporated in some tables, for instance whether the artificial limb or organ is functioning well or badly, and whether a person is left-handed or right-handed.

In the case of tabular grading of disability the reduced ability to function is not related to definite tasks. The injury is viewed separately. However, when definite injuries in the table have been linked to definite values (percentages), it is because experience has shown that these injuries lead to a definite restriction of the capacity to solve the large register of tasks life consists of.

The stipulation of the individual's degree of disability is based solely on "objectively ostensible clinical symptoms"; doctors have regarded this as the central feature of tabular disability [7, 8, 9]. When such symptoms are the only ones to be taken into account, no one but a doctor is qualified to assess the disability. The specialists within the various branches of medicine become experts in assessing injuries and diseases within their own sphere. The ophtalmologist assesses eye injuries, and the lung specialist assesses reduced lung function.

Briefly, one may say that the tabular assessment of disability is general (abstract) in a twofold sense. Consideration is given neither to the person's individual faculties nor to the areas where his functioning capacity is reduced.

3.2 Accident Insurance

Probably the first disability tables were worked out by German private insurance companies in the last century. Accident insurance was the field where compensation was fixed on that basis. Public accident insurance for factory workers was greatly influenced by methods adopted in private insurance.

To start with, the degree of disability was fixed according to an assessment of the impact of the injury on the person's wage-earning ability. Gradually, however, certain rates developed for injuries to arms, legs, eyes, etc. One important reason for the introduction of such rates was the establishment of appeal boards and insurance tribunals. Decisions by these were considered as precedents. They were entered into registers, and in Germany these registers were called "Kompassammlungen" [10].

The accident insurance offered by Norwegian insurance companies today is based on tabular assessment of disability. The insurance conditions contain a table stating the percentage of disability for various injuries. According to the conditions "no consideration shall be given to profession, individual faculties or social position" when assessing the degree of disability.

It may seem unreasonable not to take into account the specific nature of each case. But accident insurance is a mass product which the companies want to market. The insured person buys certain benefits in case he should be injured in an accident. If the disability were to be assessed on the basis of a grading in which a number of individual circumstances were to be taken into account, conflicts might easily arise as to the degree of disability, and the companies' product would become more expensive [11].

3.3 Industrial Injury Benefit [12]: Sect. 11.8 of the National Insurance Act

The first public insurance scheme to be introduced in Norway was the accident insurance for factory workers by an act passed in 1894. After an industrial accident the injured person was awarded compensation for the disability that resulted.

Tabular determination of disability came into use about the turn of the century. The system worked for more than 50 years without meeting with any serious objections. The injured persons constituted a homogeneous group as far as the kind of work was concerned. When a worker in the building trade lost an arm the consequences were about the same as when another worker in the same trade lost his arm.

However, as the number of workers in industry gradually came to constitute a decreasing part of the population, and with the steadily growing differentiation in trade and industry, tabular grading became an inadequate yardstick for stipulating compensation for the loss of wage-earning ability. One and the same injury might have varying consequences for the wage-earning ability of an office clerk and that of an industrial worker.

By amendments in Norway in the 1950s it was decided that, when determining the degree of disability, due consideration should be given to the nature and extent of the injury as well as to the injured person's income from work before and after the injury occurred. The year 1970 saw the introduction of a system in two parts under which disability compensation now consists of two components, the pension and an industrial injury benefit. The economic loss resulting from a reduced income is determined on the basis of an assessment of the disability in the light of the person's occupation. The noneconomic loss stemming from drawbacks caused by the injury is fixed on the basis of a tabular/medical assessment. The other Scandinavian countries (Sweden and Denmark) have adopted a similar two-part system.

The industrial injury benefit is aimed at providing economic compensation for the loss of physical and mental fitness. It compensates a reduced capacity to enjoy the opportunities offered or for the aggravation of one's life situation. The industrial injury benefit compensates for reduced mobility, a limited capacity to enjoy outdoor life, to pursue hobbies and activities, dancing, entertainment, etc., the loss of the sense of smell or taste, chronic pains (e.g., headache), scars and other forms of disfigurement.

The industrial injury benefit also provides compensation for the injury itself. The intention is that to enable the injured person to "buy" things and other benefits to replace those lost because of the injury. A person who has had to amputate a leg and therefore cannot go walking in the mountains, may for instance be able to go more often to the theatre or to the cinema than he could otherwise have afforded.

The fact that we have an industrial injury benefit in Norway is, I believe, primarily due to the historical background, with the transition from tabular assessment of disability to an assessment based on economic capacity. There are probably other cases as well. First, people have more leisure time, longer holidays, and enhanced possibilities of "enjoying life". Such advantages are valued on a par with economic advantages. Second, the general social insurance system now covers practically all economic losses due to sickness and injury. It was quite natural that at the beginning the insurance was aimed at covering the loss of income and expenses. And, having solved this task, taking care of other consequences of sickness and injury would seem the right track to follow. Here as elsewhere in the history of social insurance, the industrial injury plan has paved the way.

The industrial injury benefit is a sociopolitical measure that promotes high priority goals in modern social politics. It is now considered essential that the individual be given the opportunity of self-realization. Social politics should not only be aimed at an increase of the economic standard of living, but should also work towards improving the individual's total life situation. Welfare in the classic sense of the term is no longer sufficient; the welfare concept is being extended to cover a more comprehensive concept of standard of living and a general standard of life.

The central question in cases of industrial injury benefit is the determination of the degree of disability. Current Norwegian law uses a tabular system as a basis. In many cases it is possible to determine the degree of disability by way of an authorized Disability Table. The system presupposes that tabular disability is an appropriate general gauge of the reduction of the capacity to exploit life's possibilities, to "enjoy life." This corresponds roughly to what were called leisure time activities under Sect. 2.3.

The table used for assessment of disability in cases of industrial injury is somewhat different from the tables applied by private insurance companies. When a doctor, for instance, says that the tabular disability of a particular injury is 40%, one has to know which table he is referring to in order to know what this statement implies.

Many countries have tables containing several thousand descriptions of injuries with appurtenant percentages. The Norwegian industrial injury table contains about 200 injury descriptions. It is rather detailed when it comes to finger injuries, the reason being that such injuries are very frequent.

The more comprehensive the table, the rarer will be the cases that fall outside the table descriptions. Where a definite injury is not specified in the table, it will be necessary to interpolate in order to determine the disability degree. Thus the table constitutes a collection of examples from which it is possible to analogize concerning the determination of the disability degree in connection with other injuries.

Special questions arise in cases of multiple injuries. These may be simultaneous or successive, where one of them only or several can be traced to the industrial accident.

The degree of disability is to be determined following an objective assessment of the injury per se, regardless of who the injured person is. This may be said to be in accord with the ideal of the law saying that all injuries should be treated equally. A definite injury should result in the same compensation, regardless of who has been injured. Such a principle does offer administrative advantages. However, there is some room for taking into account the extent to which the injury represents a drawback to the person in question (see Sect. 4.2).

As a rule, doctors play a central part in the appraisal of the disability degree. The primary task of the medical experts is to describe the injury itself. But also when stipulating the degree of disability, medical expertise is usually more important than legal knowledge. This is particularly so concerning injuries not listed in the table.

Where English law is concerned, Ogus and Barendt [13] have maintained that determination of the disability degree in such cases "is a question of fact, and the decision of the medical authorities will generally be regarded as conclusive." They refer to a case where "the claimant suffering from a condition of the finger which was more severe than on prescribed finger condition but less severe than another prescribed finger condition sought to argue that as a matter of *law* medical authorities were bound to assess at a finger between the two prescribed degrees of disablement. The argument was rejected. The discretion of the medical authorities was not to be fettered by thus enlarging the Schedule." According to the Norwegian conception it would be natural for the appeal instance (Commission) to review the decision of the medical authorities in a case such as this.

4 Grading of Medical Disability

4.1 Explanation of the Concepts

Medical assessment of disability is based on the disability tables. However, in addition to the objectively ostensible clinical symptoms, subjective symptoms such as sex, age, mental health, social position, capacity of adjustment, and similar individual properties are also taken into account.

Harlem and Lindén say that often the individual's occupation is also considered [7, 14, 15]. Dr. Strøm does not mention occupation as one of the factors taken into account in the determination of medical disability. In my opinion this factor should not be included in the medical concept of disability, as this might easily result in a mix-up with the occupational disability concept (see Sect. 5.1).

As a rule no distinction is made between the terms tabular and medical disability. They are normally taken to have the same connotations in prelegislative works, in legal literature, within the medical profession and other groups. As Dr. Strøm says, it is usage not only in Norway, but internationally as well, that medical disability equals tabular disability [8]. Dr. Harlem deserves credit for having made a distinction between tabular and medical disability.

Taking into account mental and social circumstances in addition to the physical injury and disease per se is in accord with modern medicine [4, p 97 ff.]. When determining the degree of medical disability it is not only the specialist on the disease in question who is "entitled to an opinion." Views from doctors with a special interest in social medicine, general practitioners, and psychiatrists are necessary or desirable. Members of other professions as well – particularly psychologists and social workers – may contribute significantly to the determination of medical disability.

In one respect, however, there is no difference between medical and tabular assessment of disability. Functional handicaps are not related to definite tasks which the individual should carry out (see, however, what has been said about occupation). This is incorporated in the table.

In short, one may say that assessment of medical disability is specific (individual) in one respect and general (abstract) in another respect: Consideration is given to the person's faculties (physical, mental, and social conditions), whereas consideration is not given to the areas in which he does not function.

4.2 *Industrial Injury Benefit*

Stipulation of the industrial injury benefit is not done only on the basis of a tabular determination of disability. It is possible to adjust the degree of disability if "age, sex, weight or other individual circumstances warrant the presumption that the injury causes particular inconvenience to the person concerned."

Adjustments can only be made in favor of the insured person, and to a limited extent. In practice the National Insurance Institution has been restrictive concerning such adjustments.

All things considered, one may say that the industrial injury benefit is determined on the basis of a combined tabular medical assessment of the disability, where the emphasis is on the tabular.

4.3 *Compensation for Noneconomic Loss*

By an act of May 25, 1973, a new form of compensation was introduced into the conventional Norwegian tort law, i.e., the compensation for noneconomic loss (the Act on Torts Sect. 3–2). This innovation in tort law was modeled on the industrial injury benefit.

In the prelegislative works the question of why this new form of compensation should be introduced was only scantily discussed. The Tort Law Commission mentions that the granting of compensation for noneconomic loss "must be presumed to be of considerable emotional significance to the injured person" [16]. The proposition says that "compensation in the form of money for the hardship which the injury in itself represents to the person concerned, can never "make up for" the disability. But the compensation is considered as a means for the injured person of alleviating the hardships caused by the disability" [17].

It is probable that the underlying reasons for introducing this form of compensation in 1973 on the whole were very similar to the arguments brought forward when the industrial injury benefit was introduced several years earlier (see Sect. 3.3). Social developments had given people more leisure time and longer vacations, and tort law had achieved its goal, which was to cover the entire economic loss. Therefore, it was only natural that in order to keep up with the development in society (including that of the economy) the tort law should take on new tasks. Contrary to the case with industrial injuries, no compensation had previously been given for the noneconomic loss in cases where compensation was otherwise awarded, although some form of "hidden" compensation for noneconomic loss probably existed [18]. But the Tort Law Commission stated that "it is quite evident that today legal practice bases the computation of compensation on the economic disability" [16, pp 12–13, 30]. Thus, it was not a question of carrying on a tradition, as with the industrial injury benefit, but of introducing a new form of compensation.

It will be seen from the Recommendation by the Tort Law Commission that the purpose of the compensation for noneconomic loss is to provide economic compensation for "limitations of the personal way of living and enjoyment of life which money cannot compensate." As examples are mentioned restricted opportunities to take part in outdoor life and leisure activities (e.g., not being able to go skiing or skating due to an injured foot), embarrassing face scars, a defective sense of smell or taste, and impaired sight or hearing [16, pp 30, 57]. On the whole it must be presumed that the purpose of the compensation for noneconomic loss coincides with the purpose of the industrial injury benefit.

According to the Act on Torts § 3–2, compensation for noneconomic loss is awarded to a person who "has sustained lasting and substantial injury of a medical nature." This formulation is almost identical with the formulation stating the terms for the right to receive industrial injury benefit. For a person to be entitled to an industrial injury benefit, an industrial injury must have occured. To establish a right to compensation for noneconomic loss, the injury must be due to an event warranting compensation – it must be a case of neglect or strict liability (including motor vehicle liability).

Compensation for nonecomonic loss is defined as "giving due account to the medical nature and extent of the loss and its implications for the personal enjoyment of life." The prelegislative works to the Act contain no explicit discussion of which category of disability assessment is to be applied in computing the compensation for noneconomic loss. The Ministry presumed basically that one should apply "the norms being in force at any time under Sect. 11–8 of the National Insurance Act." Possibly, the proposition of the Ministry [17] should be taken to mean that a tabular assessment of the disability, modeled on the industrial injury benefit, ought to be made. There are several indications of the proposition having been thus conceived during the debate in the Parliament (Stortinget). The Minister of Justice said:

> The proposition aimed at a system under which the compensation for noneconomic loss should be linked to the national insurance benefits. In the opinion of the committee this was rather too undifferentiated. Although it is a fact that a firm rule – so much for an eye, so much for a finger, as in the law of Hammurabi – might avoid conflict where otherwise agreement prevailed as to the compensation for economic injury, life is too manifold. The same injury or the same defect might have widely varying consequences for different persons regarding the opportunities for enjoying life, so that in the opinion of the committee each single case must be assessed individually. Here, as in so many other relations, it is up to legal practice to define a norm [19].

Against this background it would be correct to say that the courts, when stipulating the compensation for noneconomic loss, have far greater liberty to take into account a person's individual capacities and total life situation than the National Insurance Institution and the Social Insurance Tribunal have when determining the industrial injury benefit. It would probably be right to say that the compensation for noneconomic loss should be determined on the basis of a medical assessment of the disability. Special consideration should be given to the individual's possibilities for taking part in leisure activities.

So far only six court decisions concerning compensation for noneconomic loss are available in print [12 pp 312 ff.] On the basis of these decisions (only two of which are by the Supreme Court, Rt. 1977, p 782 and Rt. 1981 p 138) one should be a bit cautious in making general statements on the courts' attitude towards the assessment of disability when determining the amount of compensation for noneconomic loss. It is important to emphasize that the courts do not have to decide upon the degree of disability when determining the compensation, as they must when assessing the industrial injury benefit. It also seems as if comparatively little weight is attached to the percentages mentioned in the grounds for the court decisions. The description of the injury and its consequences to the injured person are considered most important. And on this basis a discretionary stipulation of the compensation for noneconomic loss is made.

It is not easy to determine how much weight the courts attach to individual circumstances. Computation of the compensation is based on a number of factors – the nature and extent of the injury, individual circumstances, the basic amount at the time of the court decision, the level of compensation for noneconomic loss as compared with the level of industrial injury benefits, etc. [20]. Somewhat varying significance appears to be ascribed to the different factors in different court cases. It seems, however, as if individual circumstances are considered as being of greater significance in the decisions on compensation for noneconomic loss than in computing the industrial injury benefit.

The assessments undertaken by the courts of the injury and the individual circumstances are very similar to the assessments undertaken when determining the degree of medical disability. This is in accord with what must be presumed to follow from the prelegislative works mentioned earlier.

5 Grading of Occupational Disability

5.1 Explanation of the Concept

The degree of occupational disability is determined following an assessment of the consequences of the injury or disease regarding the individual's capacity to continue in an occupation – usually the work which the person in question was engaged in at the time of the injury [21–23]. If the person concerned is unable to carry out any of his previous work at all, the degree of disability is said to be 100%. If he is able to do 50% of the work, the degree of disability is 50%. It is of no consequence whether he or she is able to carry out other kinds of work, personal tasks, and/or leisure time occupations.

Dr. Lindén says that tabular, medical, and occupational disability all neglect "the person behind the injury or disease" [14, p 201]. In my opinion this is not so where medical or occupational disability is concerned. When assessing occupational disability all the individual's resources – physical, mental and social – should be taken into consideration.

To be qualified to assess occupational disability a person must not only be a specialist on the disease in question. It is also necessary to be acquainted with the person's place of work. The assessment by the industrial medical officer is important when judging the occupational disability of an employee. When assessing a housewife's capacity to work in the home, the views of her general practitioner and of social workers may be significant.

Dr. Harlem believes that the concept of occupational disability ought to be done away with. His objection to the term is that it refers to whether the injured person actually has income from work, and not to her or his capacity to work. In Dr. Harlem's opinion, use of the term will result in those who do not exploit their capabilities (for instance because they are lazy) receiving too much compensation, with those who show initiative and make an effort to manage as well as they can getting a smaller compensation [7].

I believe that the distinction between the ability to do work and the will to carry out work (or to function in other respects) should not be applied when defining occupational disability. This is a general problem connected with all disability concepts which are not of a purely tabular character. In any case, the problem is an essential one in connection with the concepts of medical disability and economic disability. Dr. Harlem is a strong supporter of both [9, pp 206, 207].

Dr. Hanoa states that the terms tabular, medical, and economic disability are applicable when the disability is of a lasting (permanent) nature, whereas the term occupational disability usually applies to temporary disability. If his aim is to describe current Norwegian legislation, there is not much to be said against that. On the other hand however, I object, if the intention is to use the distinction between permanent and temporary disability as a criterion for differentiation between the term occupational disability per se and other terms of disability. The question of the duration of the disability is a general problem cutting right across the differentiation between the various concepts. There is, for instance, nothing to prevent the determination of the degree of tabular and medical disability at any stage during the development of a disease.

To summarize, it may be said that the determination of occupational disability is special (individual) in two respects. The assessment is to be made of the individual's resources, and the ability to function should be related to definite tasks – the individual's ability to carry out his occupation.

5.2 Sickness Benefit

Sickness benefit is to compensate the lapse of income during the first year after the disease occurs. Under Sect. 3-2 of the National Insurance Act the right to sickness benefit depends mainly on whether a person is unable to work because of sickness. Ohldieck, Litleré and Rygh say about this provision:

> If the insured person is to be considered unable to work only in respect of the work he had at the time when the disability occurred, but otherwise is capable of doing other work, sickness benefit should presumably not be paid, as sickness benefit pursuant to the National Insurance Act is not meant to be a benefit granted because of occupational disability. However, this provision ought to be applied with leniency, as the significance of the person being able to do other work must be judged on the basis of the circumstances in each separate case [24].

The practical result of the latter assessment is usually that no obligation to take up work in another trade is imposed on the sick person. This is especially so where it is a question of illnesses of short duration. This again means that a sick certificate can nearly always be issued on the basis of an assessment of occupational disability.

Only where the sickness is expected to last for some time will an assessment of economic disability be made.

5.3 Service Pension Plans

Most public and private service pension plans grant benefits in case of disability. The disability concepts applied vary somewhat under the different pension statutes and insurance conditions. I shall confine myself to the main principles of the Act of July 28, 1949 covering the Government Pension Fund.

According to Sect. 27, first paragraph, a member of the Government Pension Fund is entitled to "disability pension when he retires from his position because of sickness or injury and therefore is considered by the Pension Fund Board to be unfit for carrying out his duties in the service." Thus the Act aims at an assessment of occupational disability, but this is modified towards an assessment of the person's economic ability in Sect. 28, third paragraph: "The disability pension may be reduced or may lapse entirely even if the member is unfit for service in his position, if it is presumed that he may obtain other suitable occupation."

This implies that the Government Pension Fund refers to a combination of the two forms of assessment, that is, of the occupational disability and the economic disability.

5.4 Housewives' Disability Pension

The National Insurance disability pension is meant to compensate the lapse of income in case of permanent disability. When determining the degree of disability under Sect. 8-3 of the National Insurance Act, the basis as a rule is an assessment of the capacity to engage in other work (see Sect. 6.2).

Where housewives are concerned, the disability is graded on the basis of an occupational assessment. What is assessed is how much of the household tasks the housewife can manage with her handicap and how much she is unable to do [25-27]. If she only manages to carry out one-fourth of the household tasks the degree of disability will be 75%.

For nearly all women it is a disadvantage to be assessed in their capacity as housewives (if the intention is to obtain disability pension). Most women can do some work in the home. Therefore they often get a reduced pension or no pension at all (if the degree of disability is less than 50%). If a woman is being assessed in relation to the open labor market, it will often be impossible for her to find wage-earning work, and she will then be considered 100% disabled [28]. For categories other than housewives the occupational disability degree is normally above the level of the economic disability.

6 Grading of Economic Disability

6.1 Explanation of the Concept

Grading a person's economic disability means, just as in the case of occupational disability, assessment of the ability to work. However, consideration is given not only to whether he can reenter his previous occupation, but also to whether he will be able to carry out other kinds of work [29]. If a man used to earn 100000 kroner a year as a builder, and has to leave this work after an injury, but can then earn 40000 kroner a year as a caretaker, his degree of disability will be 60%.

Thus, when setting the degree of economic disability, one must determine how much the person concerned would have earned had the injury not occurred, and how much he can earn when the injury is a fact. The degree of disability is arrived at by calculating the percentage of the reduction in income due to the injury in relation to the income the person would be earning had the injury not occurred.

The characteristic feature of the assessment of the economic disability is that it is made on the assumption that the injured person is obliged to change occupations if there are other places of work which, after the injury, may provide him with an income or a better income than he would have received if he had continued in his previous occupation after having been injured. Usually, grants for education, reeducation, and other rehabilitation are introduced simultaneously with the introduction of the economic disability concept into a pension plan or a benefit plan. This began in the middle of the 1950s, when the industrial injury benefit plan moved from using a tabular/medical disability concept to the application of an economic disability concept (see Sect. 3.3). Along with the passing of Norway's first general act on the disability pension plan of 1960, an act was passed relating to rehabilitation grants. When it is required, by the manner in which the degree of disability is determined, that the injured person change occupations, the insurance plan must also cover the expenses incurred through such a change.

Normally, the person's incomes before and after the injury will be the safest guide for determining his economic disability. However, one must keep in mind that the amount of income does not always reflect the individual's ability to function. He may, for instance, receive help from colleagues, and it may also be that he does not utilize his possibilities completely [30, 31].

When determining the degree of economic disability, it is important to have the views and opinions of members of several professions. Doctors may throw light on the health condition, rehabilitation personnel may estimate the training and education potential, employment advisers may evaluate the possibilities of providing new jobs, and tax assessors may evaluate the income situation.

Dr. Harlem says economic disability should be interpreted as "the medical disability corrected by the effect of the patient's external surroundings, that is corrected by the possibility of obtaining the additional training or education that may furnish him with possibilities of employment, the external possibilities of moving to a place where he may get employment" [7].

Dr. Strøm states: "Economic disability is a medical disability where particular emphasis is laid on the patient's ability to earn an income, including the opportunity of receiving appropriate training and education and of obtaining employment" [8].

In my opinion one should not, when determining the economic disability, base this on the medical assessment of the disability. One should pass straight on to be person's general ability to earn an income by working. And in this assessment the health condition is only one of the factors to be taken into account [4, p 491]. Harlem's definition is probably connected with the fact that he includes occupational circumstances when assessing medical disability (see Sect. 4.1).

One may say, then, that the assessment of economic disability is special (individual) in one respect and semigeneral in another. When assessing a person's qualifications, his subjective properties are taken into consideration. The ability to function is not related to definite tasks, such as the person's previous occupation, but to a group of the tasks – working effort in some occupation or other – for which he can employ his resources.

6.2 Disability Pension Under the National Insurance Act

The right to disability pension under Sect. 8–3 of the National Insurance Act is conditional upon the reduction of economic ability by at least 50%. Under Sect. 8–5 the amount of the pension is graded according to the reduction in the insured person's ability to earn an income.

Sect. 8–3 contains certain guidelines regarding the principles for grading economic disability: "When assessing the degree to which a person's working capacity is deemed to be reduced, one shall take into account his actual possibilities of earning an income or of making an effort in a job which is suitable for him, compared to the corresponding possibilities before he became disabled ..."

What must be done, therefore, is to compare the income-earning capacity before and after the disability occurred. Determination of the degree of disability shall not depend on the actual earnings of the person concerned, but on his possibilities for obtaining such earnings. Capital income, pensions, and other forms of income not derived from work should not be taken into account.

These principles apply to everybody, but the practical problems arising in connection with determination of disability vary from one group to another. A division into four groups is practical: wage-earners, self-employed tradesmen, housewives, and children and young people who are not yet employed.

As for wage earners, the pay before and after the disability occured will nearly always be decisive when determining the degree of disability. Corrections must be made for pay changes, however. In addition, lost career opportunities and the loss of possibilities for making extra money (by overtime work) must be considered. Moreover, attention must be paid to whether the person concerned is very energetic or whether he does not do all he can to exploit his opportunities of earning something. It may be difficult, however, to prove that the disabled person could earn more than he actually does.

After the disability has occurred, a wage earner will as a rule either be able to continue in a full-time occupation or not be able to obtain any work. In the former case, the reduction of income will only exceptionally be so large that the insured person will be declared 50% disabled. If no work can be provided, the degree of disability will be fixed at 100%. Considering that the possibilities of finding part-time work are usually limited, employees will rarely get a graded disability pension.

Where self-employed tradesmen are concerned, it would also be natural to base the assessment on the income before and after the disability occurred. But in this case income will be a far less satisfactory indicator of the person's economic disability. Corrections must be made for a number of factors:

1. Fluctuations in the income of a self-employed person may often be attributed to a good year or a bad one, as for instance a bumper year for the farmer. Changes in income not connected with functional ability are not to be taken into account when determining the degree of economic disability.
2. As a rule, part of the income of a self-employed person is capital income [27]. Such income is not to be considered when determining the degree of disability. The same applies to consumption of capital, such as felling timber in the forest in excess of regeneration.
3. Part of the income of a self-employed person may frequently derive from the efforts of spouse, children and others [27]. The income of a farmer may for instance be the same before and after the disability occurred. Now, if he can manage only half of the work which he used to do, but the previous level of income is maintained by increased efforts on the part of others, he will be considered 50% disabled.
4. A self-employed person who previously did a lot of heavy manual work, may, after becoming disabled, often be able to carry out administrative work [27]. If his business is not too small, this effort might result in a satisfactory profit which ought to be taken into account when determining the degree of disability. A person should not be awarded a disability pension only because he cannot carry out the tasks he used to, and is "obliged" to change his "occupation".
5. Quite often the sensible thing is to change to another form of operation after the disability has occurred. The farmer may pass from the heavy and demanding work of growing root vegetables to the easier growing of grain. The resulting reduction in income is taken into consideration when determining the degree of the economic disability.
6. Changes in the income of a self-employed person may often be attributed to taxation issues, as for instance depreciation. Such changes are not due to alterations in working ability and are not to be taken into account when determining the disability.

Under Sect. 5.4 I have discussed how the degree of disability is determined for housewives. The decisive factor is the amount of the work in the home which the housewife can manage.

A woman who actually is a housewife is often assessed in relation to the open labor market ((a potential employee), for instance if the husband's income is too small for him to maintain her. According to the practice of the National Insurance Institution she is always considered as an employed person if the husband's income is less than twice the basic amount of the national insurance (at present 33 800 Norwegian kroner). She is also considered a (potential) wage earner if she is a widow, is separated or divorced, or if she has gone out to work before and has been staying at home temporarily only to look after small children [25, 27].

If a women is considered a (potential) wage earner, the amount of housework she is able to do is of no consequence. The determining factor as regards the grading of the economic disability is her possibility of obtaining income by working outside the home.

As regards children and young people who were not employed before becoming disabled, there is no previous income to which possible earnings after the disability occurred may be compared. In such cases one should probably compare these income-earning possibilities with the possibilities the person would have had, had the disability not occurred.

6.3 Compensation for Loss of Income

According to Sect. 3–1 of the Act on Torts, compensation for lost income and reduced future economic ability is to be determined by "considering the injured person's possibilities of earning an income by work such as may reasonably be expected of him, taking into account his faculties, education, practice, age and possibilities of rehabilitation".

The assessment to be undertaken here is thus an assessment of economic disability. Such assessment has also previously been used as a basis in court practice (see Sect. 4.3).

When deciding on compensation for loss of future income, the courts do not have to fix a definite degree of disability. The compensation may be determined directly, to equal the difference between the injured person's earning possibilities after occurence of the injury, and his earning possibilities had the injury not occurred. (Here I call attention to the fact that neither do the courts have to fix a definite degree of disability when determining the compensation for noneconomic loss [see Sect. 4.3].)

Assessment of economic disability is done along the sames lines in tort law as in National Insurance law. There is, however, one main difference: In tort law the income-earning possibilities after occurence of the injury are compared to what the income-earning possibilities would have been had the injury not occurred. In National Insurance law the income-earning possibilities after occurrence of the injury are compared to the income earned before the injury occurred. However, in practice the two different methods hardly ever lead to different results, because in social insurance law consideration is given to ordinary pay raises and also, to some extent, to promotion opportunities which no longer exist.

According to Sect. 3–1, second paragraph, last sentence, "the value of work in the home" is to be equated with income. The provision is particularly aimed at housewives, but has been given a general formulation. It should therefore be applicable to the efforts of any person in connection with personal tasks that may be classified as housework (see Sect. 2.3). It is not quite clear how compensation shall be stipulated when the injured person's possibility of carrying out housework has been limited. Two different principles are applicable:

1. To calculate the extra expenses incurred by the injured person's having to hire help, buy more expensive food, etc.; this is compensation for incurred and future expenses incurred because of the injury.
2. To presuppose an ordinary wage for housework, for instance by estimating the

housewife's work at what it would cost to hire a maid; if her functioning ability as a housewife is reduced by 60%, compensation should be 60% of a maid's income. This latter principle normally entails larger compensation than the former.

According to the wording of the act the latter principle should be the "correct" one. During the time preceding the passing of the Act on Torts, the former principle was the one usually adopted. It appears from the Recommendation of the Tort Law Commission that there has been no intention of amending previous law [16, p 55]. In my opinion, greater weight should be attached to the wording of the act than to the prelegislative works. Neither of these sources is very clear. I believe that real considerations speak in favor of the "housemaid principle," but I cannot go into detail about that here.

Since "the value of the work in the home" is to be compensated according to Sect. 3–1, the fact that the injury has entailed reduced possibilities of doing housework is not to be taken into account in the stipulation of compensation for noneconomic loss.

6.4 Disability Pension Under the Industrial Injury Insurance Act [32]

Sect. 3.3 deals with the assessment of disability in the accident insurance for industrial workers. In 1953 the following provision was incorporated into the relevant Act:

> When assessing the loss of economic ability, due consideration shall be given to the medical nature and the extent of the injury. Consideration should further be given to the injured person's occupation and his possibilities of earning an income before and after the injury.

Thus, a combined medical/tabular grading and grading of economic disability was introduced, but the chief consideration was to be "the medical nature and extent of the injury". In the new Act on Industrial Injury Insurance of December 12, 1958, the system of combined assessment was maintained, but the main weight was attached to economic factors:

> When assessing the loss of economic ability consideration shall be given to the injured person's possibilities of earning an income before and after the injury. Special consideration may also be given to the medical nature and extent of the injury.

This provision still applies to industrial injuries which occurred before January 1, 1971 (when the Industrial Injury Insurance was incorporated in the National Insurance Act).

6.5 Disability Pension Under the Acts on War Pensions

The war pension plans were forerunners of the industrial injury insurance regarding the transition from a tabular/medical assessment of disability to assessment of economic disability. The current provision in the war pension acts on assessment of disability conforms to the quoted provision in the act on industrial injury insurance. Consequently, a combined assessment of the disability is to be undertaken, and the chief weight attached to the economic situation.

In practice, determination of the degree of disability under both the acts on war pensions and the act on industrial injury insurance is done primarily on the basis of an estimate of economic disability. Then a supplement is granted for noneconomic loss. If the economic disability is 100%, there is no room for compensation for non-economic loss under this combined system. This is one of the reasons why a two-track system was adopted within the industrial injury benefit (see Sect. 3.3).

7 Assessment of Social Disability

7.1 Explanation of the Concept

Dr. Harlem defines social disability as a "disability which arises in relation to the contact with people both within and outside the family" [7].

The Director-General of Public Health states that social disability has been used "in connection with the disability which is due to the relationship between the patient, his next-of-kin and his environment in a wider sense. One may for instance talk of social disability where a person is being forced to leave work because he or she has to stay at home and take care of a chronically sick member of the family who is in need of nursing" [15].

Dr. Lindén says that an assessment of social disability means "an assessment of the individual's social adjustment ability" [14, p 201].

Judging from this, the definition of social disability is not very clear. It may probably be used to measure some of the functions which I have labeled leisure activities (Sect. 2.3). The example mentioned by the Director-General of Public Health points in another direction, primarily to the social causes of occupational disability.

When determining a person's degree of social disability, consideration must be given to physical, mental and social circumstances. The individual capabilities and life situation of a person may also be taken into account. In this respect the disability concept is individual/special.

However, in relation to the tasks/functions to which the concept refers, it must be said to be semigeneral. Social contact with other people covers a large and heterogeneous group of tasks, but does not encompass all the tasks which a human being is confronted with.

7.2 Section 5–8 of the National Insurance Act

Up to 1971, the concept of "social disability" had no place in Norwegian legislation. Generally, no economic compensation was awared for a reduced ability to maintain contact with other people.

However, an amendent of March 19, 1971 introduced a legal innovation into Sect. 5–8 of the National Insurance Act: "To a person whose capacity to function has been substantially reduced on account of sickness, injury or defect" may for instance be granted aid for buying a car, having a telephone installed, etc., to enable the person to escape an isolated existence.

When deciding cases under Sect. 5–8 there is no determination of the degree of social disability. But the decisions are based to a large extent on the same kinds of considerations as would apply in case of assessment of social disability.

8 Summary and Connections Between Assessments of Disability

8.1 Theory

Disability is a measure of how the individual manages or does not manage to cope with the tasks life presents. An individual's functional ability depends on a number of circumstances. I have distinguished between physical, mental, and social resources. And I have divided the tasks against which the ability to function is weighed in work, leisure activities, and personal matters.

Various concepts of disability are applied – tabular, medical, occupational, economic, and social disability. These terms may be defined as relationships between one or more of the individual's resources and one or more of the individual's tasks.

Tabular disability is used to measure the physical resources needed for undertaking an unspecified register of tasks. Medical disability is a measure of the aggregate resources (physical, mental, and social) needed for undertaking an unspecified register of tasks. Occupational disability is a measure of the aggregate resources needed for a person to carry out his previous occupation. Economic disability is a measure of the aggregate resources needed for the individual to carry out some kind of work suited to him. Social disability is a measure of the aggregate resources needed for maintaining contact with other people (part of the group leisure activities). Across these dividing lines there is a distinction between temporary and durable (permanent) disability, and also between an individual's ability and will to carry out certain tasks (ability to function/will to function).

8.2 A Survey of the Legislation and the Insurance Conditions

Norwegian legislation makes use of all five of these disability concepts and combinations of them. There are certain marked tendencies in applying the various concepts:

The tabular and medical concepts of disability are used when compensation for noneconomic loss is to be granted. Insurance companies and administrative bodies, when stipulating the compensation amount for such losses, lay most of the emphasis on the tabular disability (accident insurance and industrial injury benefit). When the amount of compensation is stipulated by the courts, the main weight is attached to medical disability (compensation for noneconomic loss). The insurance companies and the administrative bodies have a system which is quite easy to operate, whereas the courts have a system leaving considerable room for the discretion of the assessors.

The occupational and economic disability concepts are used when granting compensation for the loss of income. If this loss is temporary and/or concerns definite groups of persons, the emphasis is laid on the occupational disability concept (sickness benefit, service pensions and housewives' disability pension). If the loss of income is going to last for some time it is a question of compensation from general benefit schemes, the economic disability concept is applied (disability pension under the National Insurance and compensation for loss of income under tort law).

If, under the same category of benefit, compensation is to be made for loss of income and noneconomic loss, a combination of tabular/medical and of economic disability assessment is applied. If the benefit is primarily to compensate loss of income, the main consideration should be the assessment of economic disability (the war pension acts and the old Industrial Injury Insurance Act).

So far, the concept of social disability has not found a place in Norwegian legislation. However, decisions as to whether benefits shall be granted under Sect. 5–8 should be made on the basis of assessments which for the greater part correspond to the assessment of social disability.

Compensation for expenses after an injury is not determined on the basis of an assessment of the disability. In tort law it is the amount of the expenses involved which decide the amount of compensation. In social insurance law there are definite and detailed rules on which kinds of expenses are to be covered by the social insurance.

8.3 The Connection Between Grading of Tabular/Medical Disability and of Economic Disability

The definitions of the different disability concepts vary substantially. It is not surprising, therefore, that the degree of disability of an injured person may vary according to the definition on which the assessment has been based. I shall quote and briefly comment on some figures concerning decisions made in industrial injury benefit cases. Table 1 is contained in the report in health injuries subsequent to industrial accidents and the national insurance [33].

A total of 533 people were awarded industrial injury benefit and 174 people were awarded disability pension. Of these 121 received both benefits. This means that more than three-fourths of those who were considered 15% or more tabularly/medically disabled were not considered as much as 15% economically disabled. This is not very surprising. Most people who are disabled according to a tabular or medical assessment are not less able to earn an income.

What is more surprising is that nearly one-third of those entitled to disability pension did not have a tabular/medical degree of disability reaching 15%.

Table 1. The overlapping of tabular disability with economic disability

Tabular disability (%)	Degree of economic disability (%)								Total
	100	80	70	60	50	40	30	15–25	
15– 24	27	1	1		3		1	2	35
25– 34	18	2		1	1	2		3	27
35– 44	10		2		1		1	1	15
45– 54	16								16
55– 64	4			2	1	1		1	9
65– 74	9		1	1					11
75– 84	6								6
85–100	2								2
Sum	92	3	4	4	6	3	2	7	121

The majority of those entitled to both industrial injury benefit and disability pension have a low degree of disability according to a tabular/medical assessment. And a large majority of these have been regarded as 100% economically disabled. This goes to show that a low degree of tabular/medical disability often may lead to a high economic disability. As mentioned under Sect. 6.2, employees who have been injured either are often able to go on working full time or disappear entirely from the labor market.

References

1. Sundby NK (1974) Om normer. Universitetsforlaget, Oslo, pp 77 ff
2. Eckhoff T, Sundby NK (1976) Rettsystemer. Tammi, Oslo, pp 84 ff
3. Strøm A (1973) Lærebok i sosialmedisin. Fabritius, Oslo, p 38
4. Norges offentlige utredninger (1977) The disability concept under the National Insurance. NOU 14: 81–82
5. Harlem G (1976) Studies on the relation between impairment, disability and dependency. Kurer-Sats, Oslo, pp 7–8
6. Harlem G (1976) Uførebegrepet i teori og praksis. Sosial Trygd 1976: 171–172
7. Harlem G (1959) Invaliditetsvurdering. Tidssk Nor Lægeforen 1959: 380
8. Strøm A (1959) Invaliditetsvurdering. Tidssk Nor Lægeforen 1959: 690
9. Hanoa R (1975) Uførevurdering i praktisk medisin. Sosial Trygd 1975: 206
10. Nordic Commission (1963) Recommendation on assessment of disability, stipulation of compensation, tabular systems, etc. in the industrial injury benefit schemes in the Nordic countries. Oslo, pp 15–19
11. Selmer K (1982) Forsikringsrett. Universitetsforlaget, Oslo, pp 269–270
12. Kjønstad A (1979) Yrkesskadetrygden. Universitetsforlaget, Oslo, pp 185 ff.
13. Ogus AI, Barendt EM (1978) The law of social security. Butterworth, London, p 311
14. Lindén V (1973) Invaliditetsbegrepet. Ugeskrift for Læger 1973: 201
15. Director General of Public Health (1959) Ot. prp. No. 22, p 13
16. Tort Law Commission (1972) Recommendation, 1971
17. Director General of Public Health (1973) Ot. prp. No. 4 (1972–1973) p 21
18. Kjønstad A (1977) Trygd og erstatning ved personskade – utviklingslinjer, utbredelse og ulikheter. (see esp. Note 37) Universitetsforlaget, Oslo, p 30
19. Minister of Justice (ed) (1973) Odelsting debates, 1972–1973, p 257
20. Lødrup P (1980) Erstatningsberegning ved personskader. C. Lødrup, Oslo, pp 78–100
21. Strøm A (1958) Bedømmelse av invaliditet. Tidsskr Nor Lægeforen 1959: 76

22. Heiberg A (1968) Invaliditetsvurdering og erstatningsutmåling. Norsk Forsikringsjuridisk Forenings Publikasjoner No. 53, p 27
23. Selmer KS, Lundevall (1973) Rettsmedisian. Universitetsforlaget, Oslo, p 194
24. Ohldieck FW, Litleré J, Rygh H (1973) Lov om folketrygd. Sem og Stenersen, Oslo, pp 268–269
25. National Insurance Institute (1970) Circular of September 19 (08–02), pp 1, 4–5
26. Kjønstad A (1975) Sosialretten. In: Knoph (ed) Oversikt over Norges Rett. Universitetsforlaget, Oslo, p 699
27. Kjønstad A (1977) Et forsøk med bruk av EDB i rettsvitenskapen. Institutt for offentlig rett, Oslo. Stensilserie No. 16, pp 50–57
28. Norges offentlige utredninger (1977) Ytelser til hjemmearbeidende ektefeller ved uførhet. NOU 25: 24–25
29. Nord (1971) Medicinsk och ekonomisk invaliditet, Uppsatser i Försäkrings – och skadeståndsrätt, vol 2. Juridiska Föreningen vid Stockholms Universitet, Stockholm, pp 133 ff.
30. Gulbrandsen H (1960) Forskjellige faktorers betydning ved invaliditetsfastsettelsen. Det femte nordiske socialforsikringsmøde. Oslo, pp 12 ff.
31. Gulbrandsen H (1968) Invaliditetsvurdering og erstatningsutmåling. Norsk Forsikringsjuridisk Forenings Publikasjoner No. 53, pp 4–9
32. See Act of December 13, 1946, No. 21, on war pensions for military personnel, Sect. 3, paragraph 4, and No. 22, on war pensions for home guard personnel and civilians, Sect. 8, paragraph 3
33. Norges offentlige utredninger (1976) Yrkesbetingede helseskader og folketrygden. NOU 16: 38

Chronic Pain in the Medicolegal Aspects of Workers' Compensation Cases

D. W. Florence

1 Statement of the Problem

One of the more realistic nightmares of American industry today is the escalating cost of workers' compensation premiums. What was a very tolerable situation 10 years ago is a catastrophic disaster today. What are the reasons?

The benefits are more realistic than they were formerly, but the liberal scope of the courts has had the most devastating effect. The prevailing thought is, "Someone should pay – let's make it the employer – he has all the money."

Perhaps there was a day when that was true, but inflation and competition have totally rearranged the sites and scope of American industry. Very few companies enjoy a cushion of profits any more; austerity is the word.

To blame the problem totally on the legal system is completely unrealistic. There must be a vehicle to convey the individual or patient through the legal system, and that vehicle is the medical system.

The number of cases of work-related injuries has skyrocketed in recent years. Therefore, authorities have concentrated efforts on prevention of accidents and injuries, and without a doubt such efforts have been of some help. But one must realize that the greatest percentage of loss in workers' compensation cases is made up not of severe on-the-job injuries, but rather of minor accidents or incidents, following which the patient does not respond to standard medical care and does not return to his or her original employment.

What are some of the reasons for this lack of success? Certain types of patients tend to have these minor accidents or incidents, and then not respond to treatment. Such types are usually dependent and often inadequate personalities who do not really suffer serious physical injury but instead go through a psychosocial situation, after which predictable defense mechanisms come into play. The most striking example I call the "inadequacy syndrome." This affects a male with a very minimal level of education, who has done heavy labor most of his life, suffers a minor incident or accident, after which he is literally incapacitated. No form of standard medical care really relieves his pain. The average patient in this category has gone through every conceivable type of regular medical care (pills, prolonged rest, physical therapy, and often multiple surgery) before he is seen by the physician specializing in chronic pain.

The patient sits on the edge of the chair with his arms bracing his body as he holds frantically onto any adjacent piece of furniture. Ordinarily, any thinking physician, especially an orthopedist or neurosurgeon familiar with such musculoskeletal problems, knows that perhaps only two types of real lesions will produce such behavior, either an acute disc or a disc-space infection. Both of these entities are easy to diagnose by a complete physical examination and X-rays. Why, then, are physicians blind to the true answer, after doing such complete workups, plus possible myelography and EMG studies, and even a CT scan? The problem lies in the glaring fact that most American physicians do not take enough time to listen to the patient and to do a complete examination, which would demonstrate quite readily that the problem is really not primarily at the physical level. The greatest singular error in the fields of orthopedic and neurosurgery is the inability to recognize the difference between physical and psychological illness and to treat each accordingly.

Surgeons have not yet learned that emotional illness cannot be treated with a scalpel. Rather the opposite is true; psychological illness is enabled and perpetuated by surgery, as both the physician and patient then become convinced that actual pathology must exist or "why else would the surgery have been done?" In other words, the parties have conned each other, and frequently the cycle repeats and perpetuates itself, so that by the time the physician for chronic pain first sees the patient, three to six surgical procedures have been performed, and usually the patient is no better than he was before the first. Likewise, four to eight Pantopaque myelograms are the rule, and if there was no reason for the back pain before, there is now. So in essence, if a disability didn't really exist before, the surgeon has very neatly produced and perpetuated the problem, automatically rendering the patient legally disabled, even if the physician naively feels that the patient should be well. In other words, in the eyes of the physician, there is no reason for the patient to be regarded as having a disability.

At this point the principal enabling factor, the surgeon, has fed the patient into the legal disability system, in that a disability does exist after the back surgery, no matter how successful the surgeon thinks he has been, and the patient envisions himself as impaired. It is very interesting to read follow-up notes after surgery by physicians who state, "What a marvelous result the patient has had from the surgery." More often than not, the patient's perception of the end result is quite different. Both parties tend to be unrealistic. Physicians tend to tell patients what they think the patients want to hear (whether they realize it or not) while patients tend to tell physicians what the physicians want to hear, even though 10 minutes later the patient will convey a different message to another interrogator.

This is especially true with chronic pain, which is a behavior disorder and a perception illness. This may appear a dogmatic statement, but my years of experience with chronic pain in workers' compensation cases have left me with the unequivocal opinion that the patient with work-related chronic pain suffers primarily from a psychological and not a physical condition, no matter how serious it may be. There are very painfully crippled people who will repeatedly reply "just fine" to any greeting of "how are you?" There are also very healthly specimens who reply to "how are you?" with a 20-minute list of physical maladies.

This is particularly true of the workers' compensation-chronic pain patient, whose observed behavior can assume several different patterns in the course of just a few hours. For example, I recall a very fine patient, who had been out of work for 3 years after suffering two very insubstantial work-related injuries. As I walked with her to the exercise room one morning, she limped noticeably, even with the assistance of a cane. Twenty minutes later (when she did not know that I was observing) the patient walked without a cane and without a limp as she went to the water fountain. Five minutes later she asked for help to lift her leg onto an exercise table. Ten minutes later she was riding an exercise bike as if she were practicing for the Olympics. The first thought was "the patient is a fake." My definite conclusion (after spending three weeks with her on a daily basis) was that the patient was not fabricating. She actually thought she had the problem that she now manifested as a physical condition. Therefore, one was dealing with a behavior disorder, which is the primary diagnosis in workers' compensation chronic pain. It was no wonder that pills, rest, and physical therapy had not resolved the problem.

Let's return to the concept of psychosocial problems as the primary cause of work-related disabilities. No prevention program can affect this category of patient. To speak again of the inadequacy syndrome, the male patient with minimal education frequently has great difficulty with reading and writing, and is usually married to a more educated woman with a more skilled occupation. In all probability, the woman married the man to assume the roles of both wife and mother. After a number of years, when intellectual stagnation sets in and there is no common meeting ground, the situation can take one of two paths. Either the affection of the wife is such that it transcends all barriers or sheer frustration results. In the latter case, the macho male, who also frequently feels incapable of competing in the job market because of his limited skills, usually assumes the only socially acceptable role or attention-getting device available in our system, and that is "disability", usually work-related, following a minor accident or incident.

It is clear that rest, pills, physical therapy, and particularly surgery will not solve this type of problem, which is a psychosocial situation manifesting as a behavioral disorder. I could give endless examples of such syndromes. Physicians and attorneys must be made aware that such problems cannot be handled by a fragmented medical system; they must be treated in centers where a complete psychosocial work up, which should always precede any elective surgical procedure on a work-related injury, can be accomplished. I say elective, not emergency, as it has been my experience that the number of indications for emergency surgery (where open wounds do not exist) in a work-related situation are very few. This philosophy is not reflected in procedural practice in the United States.

Then how does the legal system handle such patients both during the prolonged treatment phase and after cessation of treatment. Unfortunately, the system is sorely wanting. Insurance companies will frequently deny benefits to the authentic case, while rewarding the fabricator. Frequently this is the fault of both the health care and legal systems, in that the medical team does not take time or is not capable of sorting out the problem, and the legal system overreacts to the folly of all parties involved, namely, the patient, insurance company, treating physician, and lawyer. The more liberal the state court system in workers' compensation cases, the less effort expended by defense attorneys to alter the decisions, since their efforts are simply not rewarded. The success of the plaintiffs in such litigation tends to perpetuate the process, by making people aware of the benefit structure, and of how to obtain disability benefits.

As long as patients with minimal injuries are rewarded to be ill, they will be. If patients can obtain workers' compensation payments along with Social Security disability, their tax-free incomes are often higher than their taxable incomes would be if they were working. More than one patient has frankly asked me whether I would do any differently.

The entire system has been developed to exchange finances and reward the disabled, while punishing the individual who returns to work, unless his motivation is so strong that money is not an issue. Unfortunately, few patients fall within that category.

Let's examine some of the avenues to disability stemming from a nonserious work-related injury. To begin with, the average physician will not seriously question the mechanism of injury in the history of a workrelated accident. The doctor will also rarely integrate the mechanism of injury with the subjective complaints or physical findings. I frequently see patients who have had an original minor injury to one part of the body, but who receive multiple surgery from head to toe, such as a patient with a minor injury to the midthoracic area who had surgery to the neck and lower back, plus an ulnar nerve transplant. True, the patient had developed symptoms in those areas and some of the workups were equivocal, but would not an examiner with a more probing eye and mind have proceeded with more caution? In the area of unnecessary surgery in workers' compensation cases, four categories seem most prevalent, in the following order of frequency: lower back (multiple), cervical, carpal tunnel, and ulnar nerve transplants. I guarantee that if a permanent disability did not exist before the surgery, it usually does after, and in the eyes of the law, all such procedures are compensable if a work-related status can be declared; it usually is.

Althoug most physicians in America function with honesty and integrity, the system is such that fraud has definite rewards. I have frankly been told by one successful surgeon, "If I don't operate on the patient, someone else will." That may be very true, but it reflects a defect in the system, namely, that patients with work-related chronic injuries should not be shuffled from physician to physician, but rather should be sent to centers where multidisciplinary teams of physicians and paramedicals are available to properly diagnose and treat such problems.

The State of Minnesota has a law that forbids elective surgery in workers' compensation cases without a second opinion. This is truly a step in the right direction. The same state now has an early mandatory rehabilitation law for injured workers, whereby a definite plan for treatment and rehabilitation must be registered with the state within 90 days. This is another positive step, and it appears to be more rigidly enforced than the second opinion rule.

But let's return again to my premise that most long-term workers' compensation incidents and accidents are of a psychosocial nature. If this is true, then it logically follows that a test similar to the MMPI could be developed, and one could accurately determine not only the likelihood of a particular individual being injured at some time during his or her employment, but also at what age such an incident might occur, and the type of injury or incident that could be expected. In fact, the pattern is so sterotyped that I can listen to a chronic-pain patient's story for the first 15 minutes and accurately predict what he or she will say in the next 30 minutes. Since none of these patients know each other, it would seem that the human brain tends to react in a similar fashion to a certain set of circumstances. Oddly enough, the same type of treatment approach in the chronic-pain patient is equally effective. In other words, no matter what the etiology of the chronic-pain patient's problem (be it physical, mental, or both) all patients respond to almost identical treatment systems.

Perhaps the most exciting avenues opening today in medicine are the neurosciences, and most specifically the behavior disorders, in that specialists from many fields are changing their approaches to these problems. Leaders in the field of chronic pain management include specialists in anesthesia, neurosurgery, orthopedics, psychiatry, and psychology. But we are gradually all acquiring a new point of view.

How does the legal system view this psychosocial approach? Attorneys and workers' compensation judges were well ahead of medicine on recognizing the psychological components of work-related injuries. The term "traumatic neurosis" has so long been accepted in legal circles that it is being replaced with more sophisticated terms such as sociobiologic, or occupational. In general, these are compensable conditions even if an indirect cause-and-effect relationship can be shown in a work-related event, or series of events. We now have the work-related heart attack in the white collar worker. The law (as well as medicine) has finally come to realize the importance of stress-related illnesses. The only question is: Who should pay the bill, the employer, the patient, or society? In our system the employer is losing, since the courts are applying socialist principles in a democratic society – probably a formula for disaster.

Most state workers' compensation courts differentiate sharply between psychological overlay at the conscious and subconscious levels, with the former being noncompensable and the latter compensable. Here again, the ability of the attorney and the individual fancy of the judge are major determining factors. Both can be very costly to the employer, and eventually to the consumer.

There is a tremendous difference in long-term treatment of workers' compensation patients, whether the problem is at the conscious or subconscious level. All potential patients should be screened by trained professionals, because consciously fabricated symptoms cannot be "cured" and frequently disrupt the treatment of the other pain patients. It is not always possible to identify malingerers on one office visit, and in-patient chronic pain observation may therefore be necessary. If the initial suspicion of fabrication is confirmed through observation and testing, the individual in question should be discharged from the program unless a face-saving plan can be agreed upon by all parties, given the issues enter the gray zone at times and due consideration should be given. On the other hand, for symptoms at the subconscious level, standard chronic-pain treatment is satisfactory no matter what the origin of the pain may be.

Medically, chronic pain is really a manifestation of stress-related situations, which one finds at the root of headaches, high blood pressure, ulcers, colitis, and other physical conditions. Other categories of illness, such as arthritis, collagen diseases, and even cancer have now extended into this area, and chronic pain should not be a surprise as a logical addition to the stress list.

2 Solutions Proposed

How does one prevent the subject of a workers' compensation case from becoming a chronic-pain patient? Medically, physicians should be educated to the signs and mechanisms of chronic pain, as some patients can be recognized as chronic pain individuals from the very onset of the problem, namely, shortly after the accident or incident occurs. The medical approach should be reasonable, utilizing the conservative approach, and recognizing that an urgent situation rarely exists, especially if the precipitating cause was of minimal significance. Structured goals must be set and rigidly adhered to as far as the recovery process is concerned. This is quite important in the early phases of treatment. If a more elaborate workup is required, newer and safer methods that have a lesser incidence of side effects should be employed, such as water-soluble myelography instead of Pantopaque. CT scans are totally noninvasive, and newer machines will, in all probability, soon replace invasive procedures.

If surgery is considered, a second opinion is a must, as personal prejudices can frequently cloud good judgment. This will be a difficult concept to apply in the United States but is absolutely essential.

In any case, early commencement of rehabilitation at a proper center is necessary to avoid time loss and mental fixation of pain. Chronic-pain treatment centers should take patients before workers' compensation litigation is settled, as delays tend to perpetuate rather than resolve the problem. In my experience, when third-party litigation for negligence is involved, any and all forms of treatment have a poor prognosis, as any recovery would tend to "destroy the case." For cases within the realm of workers' compensation settlements I have not found this to be true, although exceptions do exist.

Likewise, physicians must realize the psychosocial aspects of the workers' compensation case, from etiology to aftereffects, and treat them appropriately. Probably the most effective screening occurs before employment and job placement, but few organizations have reached that degree of sophistication.

Legally, the psychosocial aspects must be viewed as to their true etiology, that being life style, not work situation, and judicial decisions based in accordance. No employer has control over the employee's daily living patterns. Both the court system and physicians must become educated in chronic pain patterns and how these affect human performance and behavior.

Financial awards should be based on documented physical disabilities, with set periods of time established for expected recovery, depending upon the infirmity. The vast majority of disabled are capable of some form of sustained employment, unless the system perpetuates such disability with sustained rewards. If payments are contingent upon recovery and return to work, marked changes in patient behavior will be seen, and the total cost to the employer, taxpayer, and consumer will be dramatically reduced. In the long run, the patient and his or her family will be much happier and chronic pain significantly reduced.

The workers' compensation court system must also be more realistic in its decision-making process. Awards of large amounts should be made by two or three judges, which in the long run would probably be less expensive to the system, in that spurious or prejudicial opinions would be minimized. The legal system must realize the total economic effect upon society of all decisions made. Hopefully the day will come when panels of dedicated physicians and judges, working together for the good of the patient, will be able to make decisions based upon the concepts here stated, centered upon total rehabilitation of the injured worker. Only then will the system truly work and the cost of the workers" compensation system revert to a reasonable level.

III. Disability and Medicine

Psychosocial Aspects of Disability

M. Neumann

1 Introduction

When we speak of disability, we usually mean the result of an illness or injury to the body with a degree of irreversibility of the pathological process, or damage to the body or a bodily function.

The theme of this article is the psychosocial response to physical illness and disability, such responses being an integral part of any disease or disability.

2 Psychological Reactions to Disease and Disability

2.1 Intrapersonal Factors

Past experience with illness in himself and others may influence the opinion and attitude of the patient toward his particular illness or disability and its consequences. The psychological impact of any illness, injury, or disability differs according to when it appears in a person's life cycle. The experience of being sick and disabled and the capacity to cope are different in a case of congenital malformation, in a child, an adolescent, an adult, or an old person. Injury or disability incurred at any age may offer the potential of growth and adaptation, or lead to crippling maladjustment.

In addition to the age variable, the sex of the patient influences his or her reaction to an illness or an injury, especially one which impairs physical features or functions significant to the sexual role. In either sex, disease or injury affecting function or attractiveness may undermine the sexual role or sexual identity, and cause or intensify conscious and unconscious conflicts.

The personality of the patient has a great influence on the meaning and experience of illness and disability. Conscious and unconscious conflicts, ego strength, characteristic ego defenses and styles of coping, as well as intelligence, values and knowledge, body image, self-concept and self-esteem, all play a major part in determining the total psychic response to disease and disability.

2.2 *Interpersonal Factors*

The quality of people's interpersonal relationships before and after the onset of illness or injury exerts a profound effect on their experience and capacity to cope. If at the same time the patient is in a state of mourning over some significant loss, resistance to the traumatic effect of injury and disability may be diminished, and the reaction to it might be one of helplessness and hopelessness.

Family relationships are of crucial importance in influencing the course and outcome of illness. The same is true about the relationships with the health service professionale with whom the patient comes in contact.

2.3 *Natural Factors and Characteristics of the Disease or Injury*

Specific characteristics of the disease or injury also influence the patient's response to a large degree. Specific body parts, organs and bodily functions have different psychological meaning and symbolic value for each person, related to his or her unique life experience, body image, and personality.

2.4 *Sociocultural and Economic Factors*

Values, beliefs, and attitude related to matters of health, disease, and disability are generally shared by members of a given social class, or ethnic or religious group. These factors have a significant effect on every patient's emotional response and behavior toward illness, apart from the aforementioned intrapersonal characteristics.

Trust in scientific medicine varies with socioeconomic grouping. Sometimes it is too low and sometimes too high, with hopes for magical healing and recovery.

In a social welfare state such as Israel, the economic aspect of disease and disability has special significance. Hopes for financial compensation and indemnity payments can result in fixation of symptoms and disturbance of the adaptation and rehabilitation process. Sometimes the patient and his or her family feel entitled to special treatment and develop an unrealistic and demanding attitude, hoping that the misfortune of disease or injury and disability will be transformed into long-hoped-for good fortune. Such an attitude may spoil the efforts and good intentions of health service professionals and should be recognized and dealt with at an early stage. The interests of the legal agencies, who represent the patient and try to exaggerate the damage caused by the disease, injury (accident), and disability for the benefit of their client, often contrast with those of the medical professionals, who try to minimize the damage in order to reconcile the patient to the new situation. Sometimes rage and a desire for revenge aggravate the situation and make any therapeutic effort useless.

2.5 Physical Environment Factors

The physical environment of the sick or disabled person – be it home, neighborhood, hospital, or institution – has a significant psychological effect on him. Various nonhuman features of environment influence the patient, such as the aesthetic quality of the surroundings, noise, a pleasant or unpleasant atmosphere. The patient's well-being and mood may be very dependent on such conditions.

3 Psychosocial Response to Disease and Disability

3.1 Intrapsychic Aspects

There are several common trends in perceptual, cognitive, and emotional reactions to the experience of disease and injury. Egocentricity, a narrowing of interests, increased attention and responsiveness to bodily perceptions and functions, increased sensitivity, irritability, and a greater sense of insecurity are frequent. Suspicion anxiety, and regressive phenomena accompanied by longing for human support and closeness are commonly described.

3.1.1 Perceptual, Cognitive, and Emotional Patterns of Response

There are different patterns of perceptual style. There are people who are especially perceptive and tend to be more keenly aware of somatic sensations such as pain; they are more likely to interpret any bodily sensation as a threat or harm and to react with worry and anxiety. This type might be called augmenters. On the other side are the reducers, who tend to ignore and deny the significance of their symptoms. Their responses to various somatic stimuli are slow, and low. Such a perceptual style may help sometimes, but it may also be the cause of medical error and improper treatment.

The cognitive aspect of the psychological response is the reflection of the individual's cognitive reaction pattern or cognitive style. There are two extremes pertaining to the experience of illness. On one side is the worrier type, whose attention is constantly turned toward the body and its functions. The worrier needs to focus on the illness and to explain every illness-related perception or event, feeling that this vigilance is vital to his or her survival. On the other side are those with a tendency to play down, reduce, or minimize the significance of any perceived bodily changes.

An almost universal cognitive response to illness or injury is the need to explain the origin and mechanism of the disease. One common explanation is to blame oneself. The illness may thus be interpreted consciously or unconsciously as just punishment for repudiated wishes or actions, which have aroused guilt feelings. The other tendency is to blame others, or nonhuman agents such as bad luck, fate, etc. for the misfortune, with feelings of anger and revenge. The illness will be interpreted as something unjust, unfair, and terribly evil. This approach often enhances expectations and demands for excessive compensation.

Emotional aspects and responses to illness are, of course, interdependent on perceptual and cognitive aspects. They reflect and influence the personal interpretation of illness, the nature and degree of symptoms, and the relationship between the patient and his or her environment. The quality and intensity of the emotional response and its duration vary, and can change in different phases of the illness within the same patient. The most common effects are anxiety, grief, shame, guilt, and anger. Less common are apathy and indifference, or elation and euphoria.

3.1.2 Personal Meaning of Illness, Injury, and Disability

In order to understand a given reaction to disability, it is necessary to gain insight into what the particular illness and disability mean to the patient. People who especially value their physical appearance may react fiercely to any mutilation or disfigurement. A man whose major source of pride and self-esteem is his sexual prowess and ability to procreate is likely to be more disturbed by impotence (due to spinal injury, diabetes, or prostatectomy) than a man whose source of pride and satisfaction is his intellectual capacity; mastectomy or total hysterectomy in a woman may have similar emotional effects. People who attach particular importance to personal cleanliness are liable to feel dirty and devaluated after colostomy or due to urinary and fecal incontinence, as is seen in paraplegic patients. For a photographer, impairment of vision is a terrible loss, as hearing impairment is for a musician. There is actually no bodily dysfunction, damage, or loss that does not disturb the individual's sense of security and self-esteem.

An important category of meaning is the feeling of loss. In this context, loss means not only actual damage to the person's bodily integrity, but also symbolic damage. Deprivation of gratification may also be a blow to a person's sense of well-being. Any illness may result in a partial or total loss of gratification derived from certain functions such as eating and drinking, from physical, sexual, or intellectual activities, and from aesthetic pleasures.

The common emotional response to real or anticipated loss, whether concrete or symbolic, is grief. Grief is considered a necessary step in the psychological process of mourning, which results in acceptance of and adjustment to an irreparable loss. Lack of grief in the face of loss is usually attributed to the denial mechanism, which is also invoked when a person shows no anxiety in response to threat. Absence of grief or anxiety, like denial or avoiding and ignoring behavior, postpones the necessary process of mourning and should arouse the attention of those providing treatment. The danger of such a psychic reaction is depression at a later stage, which is referred to as delayed mourning reaction.

Sometimes the personal interpretation of illness and disability, for the most part-unconscious, is a psychological, social, and economic advantage for the patient. Illness may provide a legitimate excuse for avoiding conflictual situations and actions. Sometimes the expectation of economic or financial benefit has a similar psychological effect. When such psychic factors are present the patient may have a vested interest in maintaining his illness and disability, and may behave in a manner adverse to his improvement. These cases are also often referred for psychiatric evaluation to determine the psychological obstacles to recovery, adaptation, and rehabilitation, and to what extent they are conditioned by hope of compensation, whether conscious or unconscious. Thus, the personal meaning of illness and disability is sometime one of gain and relief.

3.2 Behavioral Aspects

The actions and communications of the patient in relation to his illness and disability constitute the behavioral aspect of his total psychological response. The content of the patient's communication, when he communicates, to whom, and how, are important for the doctor–patient relationship. The manner and style of communication are dependent, to a large degree, on sociocultural factors. A patient's style of coping may be classified as an active or fighting attitude, a passive or capitulating attitude, and an ignoring, avoiding, or denying attitude.

3.2.1 Active Behavioral Style

A patient with an active behavioral style will demonstrate a tendency to fight illness at any cost, and will cooperate fully with health service professionals. Sometimes this activity may be exaggerated and patients may do harm to their health in their overenthusiasm to regain lost skills and capacities. Most patients with such a behavioral style demonstrate good adaptive capacity. Their activity is rationally modulated and aimed at compensation for residual disability, and they search for new means of gratification to replace those lost.

Examples of coping devices spring readily to mind; counterphobias are striking. The defensive measure by which passive trends are turned into active ones is also positive. The range of such measures is enormous, covering almost everything from wishful thinking to straightforward courage. No greater example of the latter could be found than that provided by the legless fighters of the Second World War.[1] In disabled persons with strong egos, the conviction that only the physical disability holds them back from attaining their goals may act as a powerful and energizing motivation. All their psychic forces unite to overcome the disability, to triumph in spite of it, so that we see remarkable personal and social, as well as artistic and scientific achievements in this type of disabled person.

3.2.2 Passive Behavioral Style

Patients with a passive style of coping habitually deal with threats and losses by either withdrawing from people or clinging dependently to them. Their inadequate cooperation or excessive demands for support, reassurance, and care create problems for physicians and rehabilitation workers.

---

1 There were three legless fighter pilots among the Allied forces during the Second World War; they became famous for their courage and their triumph over their physical disability. One of them was Douglas Bader, regarded as a "fighter ace" because of the large number of enemy planes he had shot down

3.2.3 Avoidance/Ignorance

Avoiding and ignoring are active attempts to get away from difficulties and challenges. Such coping behavior is habitually displayed by people who cannot accept their illness or disability, which signifies for them a severe threat to their very existence and to their self-concepts as indepedent, invulnerable beings. The fact of weakness alone is a severe blow to their self-esteem, and they refuse to face and accept it. Their mechanism of defense is denial of illness and disability and resistance to the efforts of health service professionals to help them. These patients are often referred for psychotherapeutic treatment.

In the course of psychotherapy many such patients hold strongly to the conviction, conscious or unconscious, that were it not for the physical handicap all would be well and every difficulty would melt away. Every handicap, every emotional problem, every personal or social anxiety is then directly attributed to the physical disability. The psychotherapeutic aim with such patients is to undermine those mechanism for coping which put the disability at the center of every difficulty. Sometimes therapy shows that the disability is the confirmation rather than the cause of previous feelings of guilt, shame, and inadequacy.

3.3 Social Aspects

When one becomes ill, injured, or disabled, one adopts a new role which supercedes all others; this is the sick role. Although the fact of being ill does not mean than one's customary roles of parent, spouse, professional person or provider are simply dropped and the sick role takes over, being ill and assuming the sick role implies, to some degree (a) exemption from the responsibilities and obligations of the premorbid social roles in relation to the nature and severity of the illness, injury, or disability; (b) obligation to seek help and comply with advice and instructions of physicians and other health service professionals; and (c) surrender of the sick role as soon as possible and reassumption of the premorbid roles which were superceded by the sick role.

There are several different courses of action and behavior with regard to acceptance of the sick role. Patients may accept it realistically as society expects them to, and surrender it upon recovery. They may attempt to reject or avoid it by means of the denial mechanism, even if this is harmful to their health. They may adopt the sick role too readly, cling to it, and refuse (unconsciously and consciously) to give it up, despite the opinion of experts that they are fit to do so. People who continue in the sick role even when it is no longer justified are often referred to psychiatrists, because they are not ready to reassume their premorbid social roles.

All these patterns of sick role behavior are determined by the interplay between the patient as a psychological unit, the disability in terms of its somatobiological aspects, and the social environment. The sick role behavior is also determined to a considerable degree by the interaction between the patient, family members, and health service professionals.

4 The Patient and His Family

The impact of illness and disability on the patient and on the family varies according to the patient's premorbid social role. Illness in a parent is disturbing because of his or her unifying and emotional supporting role within the family. Such disability may deprive spouse and children of customary support, while imposing additional stresses and demans on them. Illness and disability of the mother or father as the main provider and status bearer undermines the family's sense of security and its entire social and economic position. The sick parent diverts the spouse's concern from home and children and thus deprives them of his or her support. The psychological effects on physically normal children of the permanent physical handicap of one of their parents is often a threat to their own bodily integrity and identity and to their own security and self-esteem.

Disability of a child could increase marital strain, enhance mutual blame and sibling rivalry. Children with congenital handicaps sometimes arouse feelings of guilt in their parents. The fact of bearing a disabled child may also be a blow for the mother, who feels she has not been able to produce perfection. The mutual nurture of pride becomes very difficult, leading to the impoverishment of self-love and self-esteem.

Disability in the parent who is the main provider often causes significant shifts in the respective roles of other family members, whose own roles are undermined in the process. There is also evidence of increased marital friction and decline in the social and economic status of the family. The healthy spouse complains of new and increased symptoms such as irritability, nervousness, and fatigue. Interpersonal conflicts may be increased, and both spouses tend to be depressed and nervous. Chronic illness and disability may aggravate animosities and complaints hitherto dormant in both partners.

An interesting relationship has been observed in couples in which the wife was severely disabled. The physical condition of the disabled woman was not a reliable predictor of need and marital satisfaction in either partner. There was no simple relationship between the wife's level of functional mobility and the husband's sexual satisfaction. The disabled woman's sexual satisfaction was positively correlated with her satisfaction in marriage and a positive relationship with her husband. Experience shows that the physical conditions of disabled persons have little effect on marital sexual activities and satisfaction. Similar observations have been made with paraplegic and quadriplegic patients of both sexes.

In every case of a married disabled patient, it is essential to inquire into the effect of the disabling illness on the respective roles of the marriage partners, their sexual adjustment, and the related marital tensions. The sense of sexual identity and sexual role in either partner may be undermined as a result of disability and reactivate intrapsychic conflicts. This may occur if one spouse is forced to play a more active role both as breadwinner or housekeeper and sexual partner, as the wife, for example, when the husband is paraplegic. The reverse situation and role shift may occur if the husband of a disabled woman has to assume housekeeping and other functions which conflict with his self-concept and self-image as a man.

Sometimes the sick role of the disabled spouse and the new role imposed on the healthy one fulfills unconscious wishes in him or her. The healthy husband may derive a lot of gratification from playing a supporting, nurturing, feminine role. A healthy wife may derive satisfaction from assuming her new role as the active sexual partner and the family provider. Either may enjoy keeping the disabled partner in the sick role, interfere with treatment, and foster dependence.

Chronic illness and disability often tend to accentuate ambivalence in the relationship between the sick member and the ones most concerned with his or her care. A vicious circle of resentment, blame, and guilt, and attempts at compensating for these negative feelings, is commonly observed and increases psychological stress in both partners. Such intrafamily frictions, tensions, and conflicts must arouse the attention of the health service professionals, and the problems must be treated within a psychotherapeutic framework. Sometimes it is not enough to treat the family members separately, and family therapy will be the treatment of choise.

We have stressed here some problematic themes and the need for a psychological approach in order to discern possible sources of pain and suffering within families of disabled persons. On the other hand, it is also commonly observed that illness and disability do not have only a negative effect on the family; it is astonishing to see how often sickness and disability in one family member helps to unify the family by rallying the members together.

5 The Doctor–Patient Relationship

Szasz and Hollender [1] describe three types of doctor–Patient relationship: (a) activity/passivity, (b) guidance and cooperation, and (c) mutual participation.

5.1 Activity–Passivity

The patient feels and behaves in a helpless and passive manner; the physician behaves as if he were the parent and the patient a helpless infant. Such a relationship, which is harmful for the patient, can be ascribed not only to the patient's unconscious dependency, but also to unresolved psychic conflicts within the doctor's personality.

5.2 Guidance and Cooperation

The patient is capable of following directions and exercising judgment. He is, however, expected to comply with the physician as a competent, mature guide. This model has its prototype in the relationship of parent and child. The paternalistic attitude is the traditional model of the doctor–patient relationship. The physician has all the autority and knowledge and the patient must have respect and confidence in him or her, as was expected between parent and child. Many physicians expect their patients to relate to them in this manner and feel annoyed and hurt if their expectations are not met. Today, with the continuing relinquishment of authority within the family and society in general, this relationship is becoming rarer.

Patients in Isreal do not have this kind of automatic respect for their physicians.

They do not feel toward them as the child does toward the parent. Patients demand explanations, information, and respect, and will criticize a paternal, all-knowing attitude, and eventually leave such as physician.

5.3 Mutual Participation

The model most appropriate for the management of chronic illness and disability is that of mutual participation, in which the patient is largely responsible for his or her own care. The physician gives the patient all the information available and makes the patient a partner in the treatment. The patient is helped to help him- or herself. This is a relationship between two adults.

The doctor–patient relationship may develop inappropriately, however, with resulting harm to the course and outcome of the illness. Both doctor and patient may be influenced by unconscious motives related to dependent, sexual, and/or power needs. The degree to which such elements enter into the doctor–patient relationship influences its quality and therapeutic efficacy.

A very important factor in the relationship is the information given by the doctor to the patient and the family. The patient's compliance and cooperation with medical advice and treatment is closely related to the degree to which his or her need for adequate information and explanation is met. The patient of today, like every citizen in a modern, democratic, Western society, expects maximal information about his illness and its course and outcome. The degree of information transmitted by the physician to the patient and the family depends on personal, ethnic, and cultural characteristics of both the physician and the patient and on the situation in which the information is communicated.

6 Conclusion

Clinical observation tells us that the chronically ill and disabled often go through varied phases and stages of psychological response. The reaction patterns are in no way static. Patients may experience shock and denial, grief and anger, acceptance and apathy, depression and euphoria, anxiety and courage. They may display a wide spectrum of emotional reactions and defensive strategies before settling into one or another response pattern. On practice, the physician must observe and consider the changing dynamic aspects of every patient's illness behavior. The health service professionals have to study and take into consideration the personality assets which are present to some degree in every patient. These must be used to the best advantage for each patient's rehabilitation. Even small gains in functioning may have considerable influence on self-esteem and meaningful existence, and are a worthwhile goal of rehabilitation efforts. Identification of the specific affective response and personal defense mechanism of each individual patient may offer important clues for therapeutic intervention, be it a pharmacological, behavioral, physiotherapeutic, psychotherapeutic, or combined approach.

There is a need for repeated evaluation and assessment of each patient's psychological state as the basis for a correct and individually suited management approach. The task of health service personnel is to be ever sensitive to shifts in the psychological responses of patients, and to encourage the most adaptive ones.

Reference

Szasz TS, Hollender MH (1956) A contribution to the philosophy of medicine: the basic models of the doctor–patient relationship. Arch Intern Med 97: 585

Psychosocial Factors in Successful Rehabilitation

U. Lowental

An important aspect of the successful rehabilitation of various bodily defects – apart from the technical aspects – is the subjective-individual parameter linked with the psychosocial dimension of illness or disability. One factor is the active/passive behavior pattern: Does the individual, whatever his sickness, try to cope by any means, hating the idea that he may need professional therapy? Or is his personality the dependent type, so that we welcomes all guidance and begs for detailed instructions? For optimal results, our therapeutic attitude should take this parameter into consideration.

We have measured the effects of two types of rehabilitation: a prosthetic replacement for lost teeth (the most prevalent human incapacity) and the rarely encountered maxillofacial prosthetics, e. g., an artifical nose, ear, or eye.

1 Loss of Teeth

The loss of teeth is very common in the elderly. Anxiety is involved, as in all contact with a dentist, causing people to avoid paying attention to their dental health, neglecting dental hygiene and periodic checkups. Thus, paradoxically, tooth decay and loss increase, until it comes to artificial crowns, bridges, and complete dentures. This "dental anxiety" is an indication of the tremendous emotional involvement of people with their teeth, and later with their dentures. Another indicator is the all too common denture dissatisfaction, which means a therapeutic failure. It may be presented by the patient either as a functional complaint, "I cannot bite and chew," or as an aesthetic one, "I look strange, repulsive, impossible!"

1.1 Study A

The subjects were 62 complete-denture patients. Some ethnocultural variables were recorded, after which each subject was presented with the following five questions:

How do you regard your
1. General health: perfect/not so healthy/some pains/sick/invalid
2. Feelings in Israel: better than abroad/as they were abroad/worse than abroad
3. Familial satisfaction: happy/O. K./endurable/bad
4. Professional (work) situation: wonderful/good/average/poor/bad
5. Housing and economic condition: wonderful/average/must be improved/bad

The combined score was measured as the Index of Personal Satisfaction (IPS). Finally, we asked whether the patient wanted to be fitted with natural-looking teeth on his new denture, or with beautiful white ones.

The IPS proved to be quite discriminative; natural-looking dentures were preferred by those with a higher sense of well-being, while dissatisfied individuale chose shining white teeth (perhaps as compensation?). Even more decisive, however, was the individual's ethnocultural background: Ashkenazi Jews chose the natural look, while Oriental Jews asked for beautiful white teeth. Apart from the socioeconomic correlations of ethnicity in Israel, less obvious at our low-cost University Clinic, the choice reflected the cultural norm in the diaspora, where Oriental people display their gold proudly on their neck, their arms, or in their teeth.

1.2 Study B

We examined 77 patients for the effect on them of bereavement after the death of a spouse or other close family member during the previous year. It is well known that such an event taxes a person's health, both physical and mental. We rated the IPS and found that older people require some encouragement in order to express their feelings. The state of bereavement did not cause great changes in, or extreme reactions in denture preference; rather it accentuated the ethnocultural difference, so that the complaints of the Ashkenazim diminished even more, while those of the Orientals increased.

The very frequent dental disability is as emotionally delicate as any other, and a successful rehabilitation depends on simultaneous consideration of all ethno- and sociocultural parameters. The diagnosis must reach far beyond the obvious anatomic-biologic aspect, and even beyond the functional aspects usually taken into account.

2 Maxillofacial Prosthetics

These stand at the other end of the rehabilitative "continuum". They are only rarely applied, have little functional value (no glass eye provides binocular vision), and are not connected with repressed anxiety as are dentures. The anatomical defect brings about instead reactions of incapacitating shame, inferiority, and a pessimistic hopelessness. A natural-looking prosthesis can restore a person's psychic equilibrium, his self-image and his social relationships, and can, figuratively, bring him back to life. Studies C and D covered the psychosocial factors that determine rehabilitative success.

2.1 Study C

We examined 39 patients by means of a self-image questionnaire, once before, and again 4 months after they had been fitted with a prosthesis. The overall improvement rate was significant ($P < 0.01$). Here, the ethnocultural background made no difference at all; the only variable which influenced the rate of success was the etiology of the defect.

The highest average response was measured where the cause of defect had been a traumatic injury (most often an auto accident), and the lowest was measured in the group of cancer patients, where surgery had removed neoplastic tissue (a considerable amount of time previously, resulting in a cure).

2.2 *Study D*

After the second group – 52 maxillofacial-defect patients – had responded to the questionnaire, a clinical assessment of the defect and the improvement was made by the prosthodontist-therapist himself, by an uninvolved physician – a stranger – and by a professional artist – a sculptor. The latter two saw only color slides of each patient, pre- and postrestoration, never the patients themselves, and they had no anamnestic data at their disposal.

The overall improvement was noticeable. Our (modified) questionnaire revealed less improvement than in study C, however. Both medical professionals proved to be very critical, and they noted an even lower improvement than was shown by the questionnaire results; the artist, whom we regarded as representing the "public's eye and opinion," rated the outcome much higher. Any effects of patients' gender or age on restorative success, subjective or objective, were negligible; once again, the original cause of the defect seemed most decisive. Even the double-blind evaluators who did not know the causes at all recognized the results: their improvement ratings were much higher for the injury patients than for the cancer group; the rates for subjects with congenital defects were intermediate.

The psychological dimension of illness and disability is demonstrated by the different rates of improvement with prosthetic rehabilitation in cancer patients as compared with injury patients. The disease or injury itself had been cured or healed in both groups; however, despite complete excision and healing, cancer patients often continue to perceive themselves as doomed. Their inner desperation persits and is observable, even when the original diagnosis is unknown to the observer. They therefore need much more than a technically perfect prosthesis for a complete and optimal rehabilitation.

Liability for Medical Malpractice in German Law

H. Stoll

The problems related to medical liability have recently become an issue of public debate in Germany. Legal literature on the topic is vast [1]; the number of court decisions involving medical liability have increased considerably [2], since claims for damages against medical practitioners and medical institutions are asserted more frequently nowadays than they were in the past. This development is reflected by the fact that the official Chambers of Medical Practitioners in almost all States of the Federal Republic of Germany have set up arbitration boards and committees of consultants [3]. There is, however, no compulsion to present a case to these conciliatory authorities. They also have no deciding power.

The debate on medical liability reached a climax during the 52nd Meeting of the German Lawyers' Association held in Wiesbaden in 1978. One section dealt with the question of whether it is recommendable and in the interest of both patient and medical practitioner to enact specific rules regarding medical contract law as well as medical malpractice. Various aspects of this issue pointed out by the more recent legal literature and court decisions make it difficult to choose those topics which could prove to have special significance for the foreign jurist. I have chosen such problems as have a bearing on general questions of contractual and delictual liability and which should therefore be of fundamental significance beyond the special field of medical malpractice.

1 General Outline of Medical Liability

Before dealing with particular questions, I would like to give a general outline of German law concerning medical liability. According to Sect. 823, paragraph 1, of the German Civil Code, the physician or surgeon is liable for bodily injury or wrongful death, should failure to use proper care in treatment prove detrimental to the patient's health or worse, fatal. As a result of this liability the medical practitioner must compensate all pecuniary losses caused by the impairment of health, as well as indemnify nonpecuniary harm caused by bodily injury (so-called *Schmerzensgeld,* S. 847 CC). Aside from this delictual liability, the medical practitioner's reponsibility can be based in a contract for professional services, if the physician or surgeon concerned has promised medical treatment contractually. He must, however, have acted with fault. In court practice as well as in the legal literature it is established that the medical practitioner, even within the framework of a contract of services, is only obligated to perform standard professional treatment and not to cure the patient [4]. As to the consequences, contractual liability does not extend as far as delictual liability. On the basis of a contractual claim for indemnification the patient is only entitled to damage for pecuniary loss, whereas any compensation for nonpecuniary harm is excluded, even in cases of bodily injury. This restriction of contractual liability is a peculiarity of German law, and, as Philipp Heck pointed out, no justification thereof is conceivable [5]. A further peculiarity of contractual liability under German law is the fact that in the most extrem case of breach of contract, i.e., when the medical practitioner culpably causes the patient's death, contractual remedies are not granted. The dependents of a deceased individual can claim compensation for the loss of maintenance suffered only on the basis of tort law, not on the basis of contract law [6]. The dependents do not participate in the physician-patient contract relationship and therefore do not enjoy the protection of contract law. This can be a disadvantage for the dependents as far as a limitation of claims is concerned. The statute of limitations on claims under the law of torts is 3 years after the victim has gained knowledge of the damage and identified the person liable for compensation (S. 852 CC), whereas that for claims based on breach of contract for professional services is 30 years.

These principles are also basically applicable in cases in which a so-called *Kassenpatient* (National Health Service patient) undergoes medical treatment. The health of a *Kassenpatient* is insured according to the rational insurance regulations. I cannot completely neglect this point, as the majority of the German people enjoy the protection of national health insurance. According so S. 368 d, § 4, Code of Social Security *(Reichsversicherungsordnung)* the *Kassenarzt* (i.e., a medical doctor admitted to the *Kassenärztliche Vereinigung,* a corporation comprising all doctors in a given district practicing with the authority of the national insurance agencies) who undertakes the medical treatment of a *Kassenpatient* is bound to provide the same standard of care as required by civil contract law. The same pertains to medically supervised institutions which share the medical treatment of National Health Service patients (S. 368 d § 5, Code of Social Security). The doctor or responsible institution is liable according to the principles of contract civil law, although the *Kassenpatient* is treated on the basis of a public law relationship between patient and medical practitioner or institution. Besides this contract-like liability under public law, the physician is also liable under the law of torts, if the deterioration of the patient's health or his death is due to the fault of the physician or surgeon.

According to the prevailing opinion in German legal literature. fault should continue to be a requirement for medical liability in the future. Strict liability of the medical practitioner is mostly rejected [7]. On the basis of such a liability, the physician or surgeon would have to ensure that medical treatment by no means impairs the patient's condition. A guarantee of this kind is, however, contradictory to the fundamental insight that even the most conscientious and most skillful practitioner does not have complete control over the outcome of his efforts. On the contrary, unpredictable factors, for example the patient's particular condition, his surroundings, or his behavior during or after treatment, play their part in the results. Despite medical progress, illness and the course of disease are even today often a question of fate, and it is not the purpose of medical treatment to ensure the patient against fateful deprivation of his health. The fact that medical practitioners have often taken out liability insurance, or that such insurance can reasonably be expected of them, does not justify strict liability, which is inconsistent with the very nature of medical treatment. Furthermore, American experience has shown that the tightening of medical liability entails a economically unreasonable increase in professional indemnity insurance and thereby jeopardizes the medical profession [8].

The basic adherence to the principle of fault, however, does not bar the extension of medical liability under certain circumstances or in certain cases in response to the patient's particular need for protection. A considerable number of the present problems of medical liability appear to be caused by the fact that in practice and theory the attempt is occasionally made to extend medical liability beyond the outline described above. It remains questionable to what extent this is admissible, and where the limits lie. One technique of extending medical liability used by the courts is to stress evidentiary law, especially shifting the burden of proof onto the medical practitioner. A consistent implementation of the fault principle would actually require that the victim fully prove the fault on the part of the responsible person as well as the causal relation between the wrongdoing and the injury suffered. Shifting the evidentiary burden with the effect that the defending party must prove that he has not acted with fault, or that he must rebut the causal relation, objectifies the fault principle. As a result a form of liability is achieved which holds the mean between pure fault liability and liability on the grounds of detrimental outcome. Furthermore, the liability of the medical practitioner is considerably extended, in that the mere infringement on the right to self-determination is regarded to be bodily injury, especially in the case of medical treatment without the patient's consent or without informing the patient sufficiently beforehand. Thus, out of consideration for the patient's right to self-determination, the right to bodily integrity as protected by S. 823, § 1, CC is interpreted in a broad manner. I shall examine these problems more closely, first dealing with the somewhat concealed extension of liability by means of evidentiary law, especially by a shift in the burden of proof.

2 The Increase of Medical Liability by Evidentiary Devices

The patient who as the result of malpractice suffers injury to his health often has difficulties proving his case. In many cases the patient does not have the necessary knowledge and experience to recognize and properly assess incorrect treatment [9]. Only the physician or surgeon has an exact view of the conditions and the course of therapy. This accounts for the high percentage of undetected or unproven malpractice cases, not to mention the fact that in medical liability litigation, expert witnesses of the medical profession are generally reluctant to make clear statements concerning the mistake of a colleague [10]. However, even if malpractice is certain, in many cases it is not clear whether this was the cause of the injury to health, or whether the injury would have occured in the course of proper treatment as well.

2.1 Prima Facie Evidence

There is little inclination in German legal practice to alleviate the patient's burden of proof by applying the rules of prima facie evidence. According to these rules, fault or causality is considered to be established if typical circumstances are given from which, by common experience, the physician's fault or causality between fault and injury may be inferred. If, however, a serious possibility exists that an unusual course of events took place, the prima facie evidence of fault or causality is refuted and the regular evidentiary rules come back into effect [11]. In the case of illness or impairment of health the patient can seldom refer to typical circumstances of this kind permitting prima facie evidence. Hence court decisions emphasize the fact that the unusual progress of a disease does not necessarily establish malpractice or fault on the part of the physician or the surgeon. The courts have specifically rejected finding fault solely because an operation did not progress as expected and proved instead to be detrimental to the patient's health [12].

Prima facie evidence may be brought by the patient most readily in such cases where infection sets in after negligent exposure of the patient by the medical practitioner or the nursing staff. For example, the German Federal Court found the causal relation to be proven in a case in which a patient contracted syphilis after receiving a blood transfusion. This occurred because the blood used came from a donor suffering from tertiary syphilis [13]. The fact that the transfusion of blood from a person afflicted with syphilis in this late stage of the disease very seldom causes transfusional syphilis was considered irrelevant; there were no grounds for assuming that the infection had been brought about in another way. On the other hand, the German Federal Court considered the prima facie evidence inconclusive in a case in which a prisoner held on remand contracted tuberculosis after being injustifiably placed in the cell of another prisoner suffering from the disease [14]. Apparently, according to expert evidence, the illness was caused by the reactivation of an old tuberculosis focus. The Court found that the rules of prima facie evidence were not applicable, since two possible sources could have independently caused the disease under normal circumstances. This decision shows clearly how difficult it is to establish conclusive proof by means of prima facie evivence, even in the case of hospital infections.

2.2 *Culpable Obstruction of Evidence*

The courts have attempted to relieve the patient of his diffcult evidentiary situation in yet another manner, where the patient appears to be particularly in need of protection. They ease the patient's burden of evidence in those cases in which the defending practitioner or medical institution can be reproached for culpable obstruction of evidence [15], for example, when an anesthetist disposes of a presumably defective tube after the patient has suffered brain damage in the course of an incubational narcosis due to an interruption of the oxygen supply [16]. A relevant obstruction of evidence, however, can only be assumed if the fault of the medical practitioner – negligence is sufficient – concerns not only the destruction of the object as such, but also the suppression of its evidentiary quality [17]. Until recently it was very uncertain to what extent inadequate documentation – for example, the complete omission of records, or inadequate, perhaps even incorrect, case reports – could be taken into consideration to the patient's advantage [18]. The German Federal Court originally favored the opinion that medical records only served as a memory aid for the medical practitioner and that he was, therefore, under no obligation, to the patient to keep the record complete and accurate [19]. However, in two fairly recent decisions, the German Federal Court expressly acknowledged that keeping accurate medical records is a duty incumbent on the pracititioner [20]. This accountability is similar to that which is self-evident in the administration of third-party property. A breach of this duty has evidentiary consequences irrespective of whether the physician or surgeon expects to defend himself in legal proceedings or not. There are, however, no rigid rules stating that in the case of failure to maintain accurate records the burden of proof is to be shifted to the medical practitioner. Easing the patient's burden of proof is indicated only insofar as leaving him with the full onus appears to be inequitable in view of the fact that the practitioner is responsible for obstructing the elucidation of the case [21]. Thus, with the aid of this flexible formula of equity, the German Federal Court has relaxed the patient's general burden to give evidence, as far as inadequate medical records impede the presentation of evidence. On the other hand, the medical practitioner is not always exonerated, even when the records kept speak in this favor. The German Federal Court requires the defending medical practitioner or medical institution to reasonably expound and prove the circumstances which can establish the general trustworthiness of the records. The defendant must prove for example, that the presented protocol of an operation was drawn up in immediate connection with the operation, and not modified afterwards [22].

2.3 Proof of Causality

If the physician has committed a gross error of treatment which is apt to and does cause damage to the patient's health, the German courts shift the burden of proof regarding causality onto the medical practitioner. In this case, it is presumed that the injury was due to incorrect treatment. The defending practitioner seeking to escape liability must rebut the presumption by producing counterevidence. Two different groups of cases must be held apart in this contested question. In the first group are those cases in which medical treatment is an adequate cause for the impairment of health, though it remains doubtful whether the same result would not have occured in the course of proper treatment as well. These doubts apply to the so-called *Rechtswidrigkeitszusammenhang* between incorrect treatment and injury (i.e., the injury must have been produced by the *error* of treatment), and not to the causation of injury as such (i.e., the injury must have been *caused* by the treatment). The following may serve as an example: a patient received burns after being X-rayed; the safety measures were insufficient. It remained doubtful, though, whether the X-ray burns would not have occurred even if the safety measures had been followed [23]. In the second group of cases, the causal relation between medical treatment and injury remains unproved. For example, after an appendectomy performed *secundum artem* (i.e., in conformity with established rules of treatment) heavy internal bleeding set in, resulting in the patient's death. Gross negligence must be imputed to the doctor, insofar as he did not become aware of the bleeding and did nothing to stop it. It could not, however, be ruled out that the patient may have died even if immediate treatment had been undertaken [24]. In this case, the doctor cannot be accused of having caused the patient's death by failure to render aid, for he thereby frustrated an uncertain chance of recovery only. Contrary to the opinion of the courts, I believe that these two types of cases must be treated under different legal aspects.

2.4 Obligation of the Medical Practitioner

Reversing the evidentiary burden as to the causal connection between incorrect treatment and injury can be justified according to the importance and purpose of the duty neglected by the medical practitioner. Implied are elementary duties aiming at the prevention of a dangerous course of events, which can generally be controlled and avoided, as medical experience shows. However, if such a course of events nevertheless takes place, the medical practitioner must exculpate himself. We are dealing with expanded duties oriented toward the outcome [25]. An X-ray burn is, for example, an elementary situation which can basically be controlled and avoided by utilizing medical skill. If the practitioner cannot exonerate himself in such a case, he is liable. In a decision of the former German Imperial Court, the defendant radioligst was justly expected to prove that while taking an X-ray, the correct distance had been maintained, or that the injury would have occurred in the same manner and intensity despite maintenance of the prescribed distance [26]. In another case, a patient died after receiving two consecutive injections of a highly concentrated morphine preparation. He had suffered from emphysema, and therefore had an impaired respiratory system [27]. It is appropriate in such a case that the physician bear the burden of proof, for a course of events of this type can, as medical experience has shown, be avoided by a thorough preexamination of the patient.

Recently the German Federal Court placed the burden of proof on the anesthetist, in a case in which the unconscious patient suffered brain damage because the oxygen supplied by the anesthetic instrument used in the operation was insufficient [28]. The anesthetist was required to exonerate himself. I believe that this conclusion clearly states the decisive aspect: In a case of inadequate performance of completely controllable duties incumbent on the medical practitioner, particularly the duty to ensure adequate technical facilities for proper and safe treatment, the rule that the patient must prove the fault of the defendent should not be applied. The decision shows that the use of technical equipment in modern medicine broadens medical liability by imposing duties of care which are oriented toward the outcome. In this manner, medical liability becomes liability based on the outcome of the unlawful act, modified by the possibility of exculpation on the part of the defendant. Such a stringent liability is only justified however, insofar as the performance of elementary duties is concerned.

Furthermore, the courts shift the burden of proof to the surgeon or physician acting with gross negligence, even though it cannot be ruled out that the impairment of health is a fateful result of the illness. Logically speaking, the fact that the physician or surgeon has caused the injury has not been proven. Culpable frustration of more or less uncertain chances of recovery is all that is established. Here a solution in substantive law is recommended; the medical practitioner should be held liable to the extent of the obstructed chances of recuperation. This solution has been developed by the French courts. In 1956 an action for damages against a physician was presented to the French Court of Cassation. An elbow dislocation had falsely been treated as a humeral fracture. By the time this mistake was discovered the health of the patient had suffered irreversible damage. It could not be ruled out, though, that these damages might have occured in the course of proper treatment as well. The action was granted only in part. commensurate with the extent of the "chance de guerison" (chance of recuperation) frustrated by the improper treatment [29]. In the aforementioned German case in which severe internal bleeding of the patient during an appendectomy was not recognized, and therefore not treated [30], the same solution should be applied. The dependents of the deceased would then be granted compensation for maintenance lost proportional to the patient's initial chances of survival or recovery. In these cases, whether the medical practitioner was grossly negligent should not be a deciding factor. There is no reference to a differentiation of this kind in the decisions of the French courts.

The solution in substantive law as suggested here presupposes that the general protection of life and health under private law involves legal protection of mere chances of recovery or survival to some extent. I find this view acceptable and appropriate. In this connection, the basic rights to life and bodily integrity guaranteed by the German constitution should be remembered. If the German courts derive a legally independent protection of unborn life from a general delictual liability for harm to life or health of another person [31], it is not daring to deduce from this same general liability an independent protection of chances of recovery under private law. In the relevant cases indemnification should be assessed commensurate with the value of the frustrated chance.

The range of legal protection afforded a mere chance of recovery or survival should be within reason however, in order to avoid excessive medical liability. As far as I can see, in all cases decided by the French courts only the total obstruction of such chances has led to compensation, and not every individual impairment or diminution of these. Otherwise every failure to apply proper treatment would entail liability as long as the treatment was not successful, for improper treatment almost always impairs the patient's chances of recovery in one way or the other. A claim for compensation was presented to the German Federal Court in a case in which a child contracted a staphylococcal infection while in hospital shortly after birth [32]. The child survived; but suffered permanent injury to its health: a severe deformity of the left leg and a handicap to the right arm. Due to the poor hospital conditions – crowded rooms, insufficient equipment and lack of isolation from other, especially septic, patients – the danger of infection was palpably increased, therefore diminishing the chances of successful treatment and care of the newborn child. It could not, however, be proven that the poor hospital conditions caused the infection. In my opinion award of damages should have been declined. The German Federal Court, however, reproached gross negligence on the part of the nursing staff and therefore shifted the evidentiary burden to the hospital. Thus the plaintiff was awarded full compensation. This ruling extends the private law liability too far. It cannot be allowed that jeopardizing the health of a patient is sufficient basis for liability and that the person endangered is indemnified in every case, irrespective of whether it can be demonstrated that the health hazard negligently produced by the defendent materialized and caused the damage.

3 Patient's Consent to Treatment and Medical Practitioner's Duty to Inform

3.1 Patient's Physical Integrity

According to established practice of the German courts, therapeutic intervention in the patient's physical integrity, even if it is performed secundum artem, is equated with assault and battery whenever the intervention is undertaken without the patient's consent. This legal view is upheld even if operational intervention improves or certainly does not impair the patient's condition [33]. The medical practitioner has no professional privilege in the sense that he is by virtue of his profession authorized to treat and heal a patient without the latter's consent – for example, on the grounds of the overriding interest in national health or on the grounds of the patient's own well-understood interest [34]. Even in cases of life-endangering illness or injury, the patient's consent to treatment cannot be omitted as long as communication with the patient is possible [35].

3.2 Patient's Right to Self-determination

This rigid standpoint of the courts is meant to protect the patient's right to self-determination. It is a significant achievement of the German courts that even in the period after 1933 this protected interest was given precedence. The controversial court decisions on the practitioner's duty to inform or disclose facts must be evaluated from this viewpoint. The courts consider a patient's consent valid only if he has been informed about the character and the extent of medical treatment as well as the risks involved beforehand [36]. Liablity of the medical practitioner is ruled out only if the treatment is legalized by the patient's "informed" consent, which requires that the patient has been adequately informed before giving his consent. Only informed consent can be considered an act of free self-determination. It is not a matter of the medical practitioner's discretion to what extent information and disclosure seems to be medically advisable, or jeopardizes treatment and should therefore be omitted. Thus, in a case of cancer a physician is not freed from his duty to disclose the specific dangers of radiation treatment [37]. The German Federal Court has stated that a surgeon who in the course of an ear operation discovers by chance an anomalous plaque of connective tissue causing a hearing disability is not authorized to simply remove the plaque. Instead, he must interrupt the operation to inform the patient of the enhanced risk connected with the removal of the plaques. Only after the patient's informed consent to this additional operational measure may the operation be performed. The decision is of course predicated explicitly on the supposition that the operation could be interrupted without danger to the patient [38]. The surgeon cannot claim that a reasonable patient would have consented after full disclosure of the pertinent facts relating to the operation [39]. Rather, the physician or surgeon who neglects his duty to inform carries the full burden of proving the patient's hypothetical consent. Doubts in this matter weigh to his disadvantage [40]. The physician or surgeon is liable if he cannot prove that the patient would have consented at any rate. On the other hand, the German Federal Court has also counteracted possible exaggerations of the duty to inform. For example, the patient must not be informed of those operational risks which materialize so seldom that their occurence must not be reckoned with [41]. The only requirement is that the patient has a general knowledge of the subject matter to which he has consented [42].

3.3 Failure to Inform the Patient

It is inherent in the case law described that every infringement on the right to bodily self-determination is equivalent to bodily injury. This poses a problem in cases in which medical intervention does not impair the patient's health, or perhaps even improves it. In a case decided by the German Imperial Courth the plaintiff had consented to an operation only because the defending medical practitioner had assured her that she would remain capable of giving birth [43]. In reality, however, the loss of this ability was to be expected as a side effect. It was found that the defending practitioner was obligated to inform the patient thereof. The plaintiff sued for damages after the said side effect developed, although it was plain that the operation had been necessary to save the plaintiff's life. Nevertheless, the German Imperial Court admitted that the plaintiff may have suffered damage in consequence of the unlawful operation. Had the defendent acted correctly, the patient would, at the very least, have saved the costs of the operation [44]. An annotator to this decision rightly remonstrated against the one-sided approach to the calculation of damages as outraging the sense of justice [45]. The preservation of life and health of the patient is a benefit which must come into consideration when damages are assessed, most definitely in the case of nonpecuniary harm. This benefit outweighed the disadvantages suffered by the patient. On these grounds the German Imperial Court should have dismissed the action.

However, cases of this kind are rare. The patient who has been treated successfully generally will not claim compensation, even if the physician or surgeon has failed to fulfill his duty to inform before undertaking treatment. Applying the tort law rules on assault and battery in cases of failure to inform involves, however, still another, far more dangerous consequence for the medical practitioner. He then carries the full risk that medical treatment, however, regular, may prove to be deleterious or to have caused detrimental side effects. The physician or surgeon who fails to inform his patient sufficiently as to extent and hazards of the operation is liable for its harmful effects, even if the operation is performed *secundum artem*. Therefore, some authors correctly point out that failure to inform the patient has developed into a subsidiary basis of liability of general importance: when incorrect medical treatment cannot be proven, the medical practitioner remains liable nonetheless for all injurious results of the treatment, as long as he cannot prove that he informed the patient sufficiently about the treatment and the risks involved [46].

These types of court decisions may lead to exaggerated liability of the medical practitioner. One may question whether it is appropriate to subject every case of failure to inform to the tort law rules on assault and battery, with the result that the medical practitioner is burdened with the operational risk. I would prefer the following differentiation. In many cases medical treatment is performed *secundum artem* only if the patient has assumed the risks involved after being informed of them. To illustrate this, let us examine the case of the ear operation mentioned earlier [47].

After partial detachment of the eardrum the defending surgeon discovered a plaque of connective tissue and removed it immediately. In the course of this procedure he severed an anomalously placed branch fo the facial nerve. According to the facts established by the court of appeal, the surgeon should have recognized the plaque of connective tissue as part of a congenital middle ear deformity, and should therefore have seriously reckoned with the unusual course of the facial nerve. This occurs in approximately 10% of "minor deformities of the middle ear." Under these circumstances the rules of the medical profession require that the surgeon disclose the anomaly to the patient. Only after the latter has assumed the risk may the surgeon undertake the operation. As the surgeon had failed to do so, he was rightly considered liable on the grounds of bodily injury. He not only violated the patient's right to self-determination, but also acted contrary to professional requirements. There is no reason in this case to apply standards of liability different from those applied in other cases of incorrect medical treatment.

In a second type of case the operational risks are so remote, or judged by medical indication so insignificant, that a reasonable patient would consent after being informed of them. Respect for the patient's right to self-determination requires, however, that even in such cases the patient's individual opinion be obtained and heeded. If this is not done, the patient's right to self-determination has been offended. The failure cannot, however, be considered a breach of the rules of the medical profession. Assuming that the patient is suffering from tuberculosis of the seventh and eighth thoracic vertebrae and is therefore constantly subjected to the danger of paraplegia, a reasonable patient would certainly consent to the curatively promising operation despite the risk that the operation may fail and itself result in paraplegia [48]. Nonetheless, the physician or surgeon must point out this risk out of respect for the patient's right to self-determination. Contrary to the opinion of the German Federal Court [49], the medical practitioner fails to fulfill his duty to inform if, upon the patient's questioning, he answers that the operation is no more dangerous than an appendectomy. On the other hand, one cannot accuse the practitioner of violating professional rules by undertaking the operation. The medical practitioner is only liable on the grounds of infringing on the patient's general right to self-determination and not on the grounds of bodily injury. Consequently he does not carry the risk for an operational failure. The patient is only entitled to damages for nonpecuniary harm insofar as his general right to self-determination has been infringed upon seriously [50]. This survey shows that the extension of medical liability beyond the general rules of fault liability requires a meticulous weighing of the interests involved. This can be subjected to abstract rules only with great difficulty. More often the specific circumstances of the singular case must be considered. This does not exclude working out general aspects for particular types of cases. The development of the law of medical liability should therefore be left primarily to the courts. Statutory regulations do not appear necessary or adequate. The same basic opinion governs the resolutions of the 52nd meeting of the German Lawyers' Association in 1978 [51]. There were, at any rate, no suggestions to implement legislation in regard to the fundamental questions of medical liability. The recommendations touching upon singular aspects cannot be presented here [52]. The most important recommendation concerns statutory rules on the physician's or surgeon's duty to document medical cases [53]. But even with respect to this special question, the necessity of legislative measures must be doubted in view of the fact the German courts have in the meantime developed adequate solutions within legislative intervention.

References

1. See Laufs A (1978) Arztrecht, 2nd edn (Beck, Munich) with numerous references to legal literature; further Deutsch E, Geiger M (1981) Empfiehlt sich eine besondere Regelung der zivilrechtlichen Beziehung zwischen dem Patienten und dem Arzt im BGB? In: Gutachten und Vorschläge zur Überarbeitung des Schuldrechts. Federal Ministry of Justice (ed) Bundesanzeiger Verlags GmbH, Cologne) vol II, pp 1049–1113; Giesen D (1982) Arzthaftungsrecht im Umbruch, JZ: 345–356, 391–403, 448–458; Laufs A (1982) Die Entwicklung des Arztrechts 1981/82, NJW: 1319–1324; Weyers L (1978) Empfiehlt es sich im Interesse der Patienten und Ärzte, ergänzende Regelungen für das ärztliche Vertrags-(Standes-) und Haftungsrecht einzuführen? In: Proceedings of the 52nd meeting of the German lawyers' association (DJT), Wiesbaden 1978, Expert Report vol I, Part A, pp 7–124
2. See e.g., Bürgmann W (1977) Widerrechtlichkeit des ärztlichen Eingriffs und Aufklärungspflicht des Arztes, NJW: 1472, 1476 ff.; Weyers L, loc. cit. pp 37–47
3. Weyers L, loc. cit., pp 49–51; Laufs A (1982) Die Entwicklung des Arztrechts 1981/82, loc. cit. 1323
4. BGH 15.3. 1977, VersR 1977, 546; 11.10. 1977, NJW 1978, 584 = JZ 1978, 275 Annot. by Deutsch E, VersR 1978, 82
5. Heck P (1929) Grundriß des Schuldrechts. (Mohr, Tübingen, p 57
6. An exception is allowed only in Sect. 618, § 3 CC, for the special case of the death of the employee due to the fault of the employer
7. von Caemmerer E (1971) Reform der Gefährdungshaftung de Gruyter, Berlin, New York, p 21; Deutsch E (1978) Rechtswidrigkeitszusammenhang, Gefahrerhöhung und Sorgfaltsausgleichung bei der Arzthaftung. In: Festschrift für Ernst von Caemmerer. Mohr, Tübingen, pp 329–332. To the same effect: Weyers L, in his expert report (10 c. cit., p 91). A proposal during the meeting of the German lawyers' association in 1978 to alter the present system of medical liability based on fault was rejected by the majority of the delegates, see the report by von Falkenhausen A (1978) Die Verhandlungen der Abteilung "Arztrecht". JZ: 767–769. It is still a question whether the patient's legal situation should be improved by an obligatory patient's insurance against risks of medical treatment. This question was not ripe for decision during the course of the conference. It was resolved that the Federal Ministry of Justice should set up a mixed committee to investigate the actual prerequisites and presumable effects of an obligatory patient's insurance of this kind (see von Falkenhausen, ibid.). See now Dinslage K (1981) Patientenversicherung. Alternative zur Arzthaftpflicht. VersR: 303–313; Klingmüller E (1980) Zu den Plänen einer neuartigen Patientenversicherung nach schwedischem Muster in der Bundesrepublik Deutschland. VersR: 694–696
8. See Franzki H, Franzki D (1975) Waffengleichheit im Arzthaftungsprozeß. NJW: 2225 ff.; Gerdes V (1976) Arzthaftung in den USA: ein fast unversicherbares Risiko. VW: 62–67; Kötz H (1974) Zur Berufshaftung im anglo-amerikanischen Recht. VersR: 613, 614; Kötz H (1977) US-Haftpflichtversicherung in Not. ZfV 28: 547–549
9. Cf. Baumgärtel G, Wittmann A (1979) Die Beweislastverteilung im Arzthaftungsprozeß. JA: 113–119, 114. In a decision handed down on July 25, 1979, the German Consitutional Court was divided on the question of whether the constitutional precept of fair trial cells for an alteration of the general rules on the burden of proof im medical malpractice litigation, because of the typical difficulties for the patient in proving his case (BVerfG, July 25, 1979, NJW 1979, 1925). In a dissenting vote, Hirsch, Niebler, and Steinberger held the opinion that the civil courts must decide in each individual case wether the burden of proof under the concrete circumstances still lies with the patient
10. See German Federal Court (1975) Decision from April 22, 1975. NJW: 1463, 1464: "even today there are a number of medical expert witnesses who have difficulty in freeing themselves, while

performing their duty, of antiquated professional usages which are contradictory to the legal system. This is mainly true in lawsuits for medical malpractice." The 52nd meeting of the German lawyers' association passed a resolution in which the medical profession is urged to make it clear in their rules for practicing that a medical practitioner in every case in which he has to deal with results of medical treatment must place objectivity before the interests of colleagues

11. Compare Palandt, Heinrichs (1982) Bürgerliches Gesetzbuch, 41 edn, preliminary remarks to § 249 Annot. 8a Beck, Munich
12. Compare RG 13.12. 1940, RGZ 165, 336, 338f.
13. BGH Dec. 14 1953, BGHZ 11, 227 = VersR 1954, 116; cf. also RG Dec. 13, 1940 loc. cit.
14. BGH Nov. 26, 1964, VersR 1965, 91
15. Compare in general Blomeyer A (1959) Die Umkehr der Beweislast. AcP 158: 97–106; Gerhardt W (1969) Beweisvereitelung im Zivilprozeßrecht. AcP 169: 289–316; Musielak, HJ (1976) Die Grundlage der Beweislast im Zivilprozeß. De Gruyter, Berlin, New York, pp 133–141
16. BGH June 24, 1975, VersR 1975, 952
17. BGH ibid; compare also BGH Nov. 26, 1964 loc. cit., p 92
18. Compare Weyers, L. loc. cit., pp 33–36
19. BGH Nov. 6, 1962, VersR 1963, 65 = JZ 1963, 369 Annot. by Steindorff E, Dec. 4, 1962, VersR 1963, 168
20. BGH March 14, 1978, VersR 1978, 542 = NJW 1978, 1681; BGH June 27, 1978, BGHZ 72, 132 = NJW 1978, 2337 = VersR 1978, 1022; see also already BGH May 16, 1972, NJW 1972, 1520 = VersR 1972, 887; cf. Laufs A (1981) Die Entwicklung des Arztrechts 1980/81, NJW: 1289, 1292 with further reference; also Hohloch G (1982) Ärztliche Dokumentationspflicht und Patientenvertrauen. NJW: 2577, 2578
21. BGH June 27, 1978, VersR 1978, 1024
22. BGH March 14, 1978 loc. cit.
23. Cf. RG May 21, 1937, HRR 1937 no. 1301
24. BGH Nov. 6, 1968, LM § 286 (c) ZPO no. 56b = NJW 1968, 2291 Annot. by Hanau P = VersR 1968, 850 = ZZP 82 (1969) 463 Annot. by Prölss J
25. Cf. Laufs A, *Arztrecht* loc. cit., pp 102–106; Stoll H (1976) Haftungsverlagerung durch beweisrechtliche Mittel. AcP 176: 155–158
26. RG May 21, 1937 loc. cit.
27. BGH April 28, 1959, LM § 823 (Aa) BGB no. 15 = LM § 823 (J) BGB no. 13 = NJW 1959, 1583 = VersR 1959, 598
28. BGH Oct. 11, 1977, NJW 1978, 584 = JZ 1978, 275 Annot. by Deutsch E = VersR 1978, 82
29. Cass. civ. 1 ère Dec. 14, 1965, D. 1966. 453 = J. C. P. 1966 II 14753 Annot. by Savatier R; cf. also cass. civ. 1 ère March 27, 1973, D. 1973. 595 = Gaz. Pal. 1973 II 630 Annot. by Doll P-J = J. C. P. 1974 II 17643 Annot. by Sevatier R; May 9, 1973, D. 1973. Somm. 116 = Gaz. Pal. 1973 II 631Annot. by Doll, P-J = J. C. P. 1974 II 17643 Annot. by Savatier R; May 2, 1978, D. 1978. I. R. 408 = J. C. P. 1978 II 18966 Annot. by Savatier R; March 24, 1981, D. S. 1981. 546 Annot. by Penneau J
30. Cf. BGH June 11, 1968, loc. cit.
31. Cf. BGH Jan. 11, 1972, BGHZ 58, 48 = NJW 1972, 1126 = JZ 1970, 363, Annot. by Stoll H
32. BGH Nov. 10, 1970, NJW 1971, 241
33. CF. Laufs A, Arztrecht loc. cit., pp 29 ff. with references
34. RG June 19, 1936, RGZ 151, 359; March 8, 1940, RGZ 163, 129
35. RG May 27, 1908, RGZ 68, 431
36. Cf. Laufs A, Arztrecht, loc. cit., pp 35–46, with references; Weyers L, loc. cit. , pp 23–25
37. BGH Jan 16, 1959, BGHZ 29, 176 = NJW 1959, 814 = LM § 276 (Ca) BGB no. 9 Annot. by Hauß F
38. BGH Nov. 2, 1976, NJW 1977, 337
39. BGH July 5, 1973, BGHZ 61, 118; Nov. 4, 1975, NJW 1976, 363 = VersR 1976, 634
40. BGH Nov. 4, 1975 loc. cit.; OLG Celle Aug. 17, 1977, NJW 1978, 593
41. BGH May 18, 1965, NJW 1965, 2005
42. BGH Oct. 16, 1962, NJW 1963, 393
43. RG May 19, 1931, JW 1932, 3328
44. RG, ibid.
45. Philipsborn A, Annot. to RG May 19, 1931, JW 1932, 3330: "Sense of justice remonstrates

against a claim of this kind, also against the ethics of the patient, who dares demand this at all. Should not an analogy to the principle 'compensatio lucri cum damno' be appropriate in this case?"
46. Laufs A, Arztrecht, loc. cit., pp 34
47. BGH Nov. 2, 1976, loc. cit.
48. Compare the case of BGH Nov. 25, 1975, NJW 1976, 365
49. Compare BGH, ibid.
50. Compare BGH Jan. 26, 1971, NJW 1971, 698; Palandt Thomas (1982) Bürgerliches Gesetzbuch, 41 edn; Annot. 15 F to § 823 BGB, with references. Beck, Munich
51. Compare the report by von Falkenhausen, loc. cit.
52. See also the recent proposals – by Deutsch E, Geiger M (1981) Empfiehlt sich eine besondere Regelung der zivilrechtlichen Beziehung zwischen dem Patienten und dem Arzt im BGB? loc. cit. – to insert special provisions regulating the contract for medical treatment into the Civil Code. The suggested provisions involve only minor changes in the present state of law. Their main purpose is to consolidate the case law and to incorporate it in the Civil Code.
53. Following recommendations were resolved:
    1. As to the questions concerning medical documentation (in particular, the obligation to document and to store records and the obligation of the medical practitioner to make these accessible to the patient or a person of his confidence, to the courts as well as to medical expert witnesses and the arbitrary boards) statutory regulations should be met.
    2. Should the rgiht to peruse medical records be regulated by statute, it must be guaranteed that this right also pertains to the dependents of the deceased patient in order to manifest claims for damages on the ground of medical treatment
    3. Every statutory or professional regulation of the obligation to present the medical records must guarantee that the patient's personal rights remain warranted

The Family and the Invalid: Who Needs Whom?

A. F. Halmosh

Marriage is a basic institution existing in almost all cultures and societies, which through the formal and ritual union of a man and a woman forms the family. With the birth of the first child the family becomes a group; hence, the laws and processes governing group interaction also apply to family dynamcis [1]. Most meaningful happenings in the family are conditioned by unconscious motives and serve them, bringing about homeostasis.

The forces that balance the relation between the family and the individual can be described as a circular process, in which change in one member affects the functioning of the rest [2]. Apart from the obvious roles of father, mother, child, and sibling, in this unconscious process each member is assigned a role that determine his behavior within the group. The striving, the hope, the competition and failure of each parent may be projected onto the offspring, thus shaping his or her special behavior from an early age, through identification or scapegoating [3].

If disaster occurs in the family, be it the birth of an abnormal child, the appearance of a chronic disease, or a serious accident, the homeostasis of the group is disturbed. A new equilibrium must be found and a reassignment of roles undertaken. The future of the afflicted individual depends to a considerable extent on the interaction of the unconscious needs of the group with his own.

The obvious, rational goal of everyone confronted with such a situation should be to join forces and means to achieve maximal adaptation and rehabilitation. However, people working in the field of rehabilitation sometimes find themselves facing unsurmountable obstacles to the attainment of just that goal [41]. The psychology of an injured person, or of one suffering from a chronic disease, is well known. The tendency to develop regression and dependcy, and through them to achieve unconscious secondary gains, is well documented [5, 6, 7]. Growing insight into family dynamcis has made apparent the significance of the role played by the next of kin in the process of adapting to and coping with the situation created by injury or chronic illness.

To illustrate the fact that rehabilitation is not just a simple technique by which the incapacitated person is taught skills to overcome his handicap, but a rather complicated process governed by interpersonal and intrafamilial relations, three case histories describing different family constellations that could almost be called standard situations are presented here.

1 Case 1

A 46-year-old engineer who had always been in good health suffered a sudden heart attack. Though clinically his recovery was satisfactory, he had difficulty in readjusting to his work. His entire personality and attitude toward life had changed. He became anxious and indecisive, and complained often of chest pains and asked to be taken to the emergency room. On examination there were no changes in the ECG, and he was sent home with a tranquilizer. His performance at work deteriorated, and after a year of being patient and forbearing, the management had a serious talk with him, informing him that they had to nominate an assistant engineer. The patient was not surprised by these developments; he had seen them coming, but was unable to prevent them. For an entire year he had refused several suggestions by the family doctor to be referred to a psychiatrist, but now he accepted. In the course of some 6 months of psychotherapeutic treatment the following dynamic pattern was revealed.

He was the only remaining son of a lower-middle-class family that had survived the Holocaust. The family resettled in Israel, via the Cyprus Detention Camp, when he was 12 years old. The aging parents, very anxious to shield him from any hardships he might encounter, fostered in him a very obedient and dependent personality. When he was called up for regular military serivce he wanted to prove to his classmates that he was not the mama's boy they considered him, and he volunteered for the paratroops. However, as the only son he needed the signature of his parents, who refused. He was stationed near home in a service unit. During service he entertained plans to study engineering and was promised full support by his parents. However, on demobilization he decided not to be dependent on his parents any longer, and took a job as a bankclerk, despite his mother's protest.

At the age of 24 he met a woman during one of his stints of reserve duty, and 9 months later they were married. At the insistence of the wife they set up house in another town, near her parents. Within 1 year his wife had persuaded him to study civil engineering. He accepted that his wife, with the aid of her parents, be responsible for supporting them during his studies. He had the intellectual capacity and was an excellent student. He passed the examinations with high grades and easily found employment. During the first few years he changed firms several times, always improving his position and increasing his responsibilities. He finally settled in the place where he was at the time of the heart attack, and was instrumental in developing a small factory into a medium-sized enterprise.

He had change considerably since his marriage. He gained confidence and his whole attitude to life took a 180° turn. His good-boy manners had changed into a somewhat arrogant self-assurance. He was respected for his talents, but he was not considered an easy man to work with. He was a solo player, incapable of teamwork.

His wife was a clever woman who knew how to handle him. She did not involve him much in family affairs. She gave him the credit, and did what she thought right in the family. He was not an excellent sexual partner, but his wife adjusted to that. She stopped working after the second child, enjoying the social position of her husband and finding satisfaction in voluntary work. Neither partner admitted to extramarital affairs, and for all practical purposes this marriage was considered a good one.

The relationship with his parents was mended when he started to climb the ladder of promotions, and they were proud of his success. He became a good son again, phoning them every day and visiting them every time he was in Tel Aviv on business. His wife and children remained more distant. This background is necessary to an understanding of what happened to this patient after his heart attack.

The aging parents tried to keep their only remaining son for themselves. The dominating mother made all the decisions in the house and had raised her son in an overprotective atmosphere, making him a weak and dependent person. She thwarted his attempt "to become a man" when she refused to let him join the paratroopers. He took his first revenge by refusing to study and becoming "only" a bankclerk like his father. He exchanged his mother for a strong-willed girl and avenged himself again by leaving his hometown to go and live where his wife wanted him to. As success came, he compensated for his weakness and dependency with arrogance and sarcasm. Similarly, at home he was the big boss, somewhat, aloof; he loved his wife and children in his way by being generous financially, but was unable to show really spontaneous feelings, neither love and joy, nor anger. His heart attack came as a total surprise at a time when he felt that the sky was within reach. The experience of the precordial pain and the hospitalization in the Intensive Coronary Care Unit shattered his outer shell of self-assurance and security. He had always been ironical and condescending toward emotional persons, having completely repressed recollection of his own youth. In his fear for his life, his basic insecurity and passivity emerged from the unconscious. In his attempt to cope emotionally with the event he found this formula: He, who had never given a thought to his own well-being, who had relentlessly devoted himself to his work and his family, now had to pay for his recklessness. From now on he would wath himself, care for himself, because no one else cared for him. He was angry about his wife, because he felt that she had pushed him in a way, and that it was her ambition that made him work so hard. Now she would have to "pay" for this and take care of him.

So the circle was closed. Under this guise and pretext of his heart attack, the patient maneuvered himself back into his primary personality structure. He needed his wife to take over her basically dominant role openly and by satisfying his need for dependency he also could express – camouflaged by disease – his feeling of aggression.

Therapy went on for about half a year, some of the sessions together with his wife. Their relationship improved, became more open, and they became closer. At his job he was able to slow down and to work with his assistant. He became more human in his relationship with his colleagues. Three years after treatment he had no relapse. He is still preoccupied with his health and becomes anxious from time to time, but he is able to cope with the situation. He is under regular medical supervision and visits the psychiatric clinic occasionally.

2 Case 2

A young soldier in regular military service had a severe automobile accident. He lay in bed with arms and legs attached to cords and weights. His mother arrived and did not budge from his bed, nursing him with untiring devotion. During the first

3 weeks he really needed full nursing care and the mother was a great help to the overworked nurses. One by one, the cords and weights were removed and physiotherapy was begun. His hands became free and the young patient was encouraged to use them as much as possible. At the beginning, every movement was very painful, but motivation was strong. He wanted to drink and grasp the glass by himself; his mother sprang to her feet and brought it to his mouth. He wanted to comb his hair; his mother did it delightedly, telling him at the same time how he used never to stand still when he was small. She was smothering him with her continuous care. At the beginning the man really tried to resist his mother's devotion, but her determination to meet all his needs and more made him give up soon.

Purely from the nursing point of view, it was no longer necessary for the mother to stay so much at his bedside, but all the suggestions and demands of the doctors and the head nurse were of no avail. No one could teach her what the duty of a mother was. In the meantine, her husband and two rather young children had to get along without her, and life at home was quite disorganized.

The psychiatrist was called in when the patient was supposed to get out of bed and start very active physiotherapy. There was no doubt that he was in bad shape, and he realized that he would be handicapped in his moving around. However, his hands were fairly free and mentally he was unhurt, so his prospects for independent rehabilitation were excellent. Nevertheless, his attempts at the exercises were weak and listless; he gave up easily and needed constant prompting. He was depressed and saw his future in gloomy terms.

When the psychiatrist came to see the patient it was difficult to persuade the mother to leave him alone with her son. Behind his hopelessness and depression we found despair, the feeling that, in any case, any attempt at being independent would be useless; he was an invalid and would have to spend the rest of his life on crutches.

During the talk the therapist had with the mother he realized that without working intensively with her, this boy would have no chance. It became evident that this was a very frustrated woman. She tended to be slightly overweight; she had pretty features, but now looked rather unattractive. Her husband was an easygoing, charming man, some 12 years older. She had felt very proud at the time that among all the other women who pursued him, she had succeeded in marrying him. He was the kind of eligible bachelor who was never able to form deep and strong relationships. In the first years of marriage, it seems, he continued to be that jovial kind of man, and the woman suffered much anxiety, especially as she interpreted his weak sexual drive, so typical for Don Juans, as being the result of her failure as a woman. They drifted apart; the quarrels ceased over the years and no real emotional ties existed between them. She bore the children to prove her womanhood and heaped upon them all her energy and love, but here she failed as well. The merry, outgoing way of their father, who never made problems out of anything, caused the children to be more attached to him than to the mother. She felt lonely and not really part of the family; for example, when they went to the beach on weekends, the mother remained at home nursing her headache.

In a way, her son's accident came to the mother as a godsend and gave her something to live for again. This time she would not give him up so easily to a physiotherapist or a rehabilitation worker to make him independent of her.

Surprisingly, this woman accepted therapy eagerly. At first she found relief in just being able to share her feelings with the psychiatrist, especially since he was not aggressive and rejective with her, as the nurses and the doctors on the ward had become. Only after a few sessions, once the relationship with the therapist was firmly established, did he begin to suggest that it was in the interest of her son for her to ease her grip on him. She was able to do that because of her therapy. The patient then needed only encouragement and hope to mobilize his own forces, and progressed satisfactorily toward maximum rehabilitation.

This case illustrates how much this mother needed her son and his dependence on her to compensate for her frustration and to give her life a purpose.

3 Case 3

Another constellation is usually found in families with an abnormal child or with a mental patient. Case 3 is hypothetical. He becomes the scapegoat of the family, or this lightning rod, needed to defuse the tensions that arise among the other members of the family. Such a case is almost always understood by the family to the the result of heredity and the child or patient is seen as the offspring of only one of the parents, the other parent and his family declaring solemnly that "on their side there was never such a case!"

These views are sometimes hinted at when the parents are interviewed together. The way these hints are expressed is very revealing of the relationship between the parents, as well as of their attitude toward the patient. The hints become recriminations, and sometimes is open accusations, when one speaks with each parent alone or with close relations, such as the grandparents.

The father is often able to avoid coping with the problem of the chronic patient under the pretext of working hard and earning overtime to provide for the family. So the main burden, the care of the patient, rests on the mother.

As years go by, the family organizes itself around the patient and many things that the family as a group, or every member individually, does or refrains from doing are explained by the exigencies of the patient. So much has this constellation taken root in the family that we are often witness to processes that unconsciously withhold, frustrate, or even sabotage attempts at rehabilitation.

4 Conclusion

This paper was intended to show that unsuccessful rehabilitation of the invalid is not only a case of the person concerned failing to cope with his deficiency. The patient's potential must be evaluated within the constellation of the family; unconscious forces interacting within it condition the behavior of the invalid. Uncovering these forces and treating the sources, which are often outside the patient, can bring about meaningful changes toward maximum rehabilitation and a better quality of life for all concerned.

References

1. Lidz T (1974) The family, the developmental setting. In: Arieti (ed in chief) The American handbook of psychiatry, 2nd edn, vol 1. Basic, New York pp 252–263
2. Ackerman NW (1972) Prejudice and scapegoating in the family. In: Zuk GH, Boszormenyi-Nagy I (eds) Family therapy and disturbed families. Science and Behavior Books, Palo Alto, pp 48–57
3. Deutsch H (1954) The psychology of women, vol 2. Grune and Stratton, New York, pp 294–331
4. Halmosh AF, Israel R (1983) Family interaction as modulator in the post-traumatic process. Int J Med Law
5. Titchener JL, Ross WD (1974) Acute and chronic stress as determinants of behavior, character and neurosis. In: Arieti (ed in chief) The American handbook of psychiatry 2nd edn. vol 3. Basic, New York, pp 39–60
6. Brüll F (1969) The trauma – theoretical considerations. Isr Ann Psychiatry 7: 96–108
7. Winnik HZ (1969) Second thoughts about psychic trauma. Isr Ann Psychiatry 7: 82–95

Self-concept of Rheumatoid Arthritis Patients

S. Navon, B. Fishel, and M. Yaron

1 Introduction

The idea that psychological factors play a role in the etiology and management of rheumatoid arthritis (RA) has been suggested by different studies, summarized by Pirkko Kiviniemi [1].

Most of the methods used in these studies were projective test techniques, e.g., Draw-a-Person-Test [2–4], Holtzman Inkblot Test [5], Rorschach Test [2, 4, 6–9], Sentence Completion Test [2, 10], and Thematic Apperception Test [3, 8]. Some of the studies reported used standardized psychological questionnaires, e.g., Cattell's Sixteen Personality Factor Questionnaire [11, 12], Minnesota Multiphasic Personality Inventory [6, 13–19], and Buss-Durkee Inventory [20, 21]. However, none of the studies mentioned utilized self-concept measures with RA patients.

The individual's concept of himself has been demonstrated to be highly influential in much of his behavior and also directly related to his general personality and state of mental health [22]. The individual's self-concept reflects the influence of phenomenological psychology, which focuses on how events are perceived by the individual [23, 24]. The individual's self-description thus becomes of primary importance in its own right, rather than being regarded as a second-best substitute for other behavioral observations [25].

People who regard themselves as undesirable, worthless, or "bad" tend to act accordingly. Those who have a highly unrealistic concept of self tend to approach life and other people in unrealistic ways. Those who have very deviant self-concepts tend to behave in deviant ways [22]. Interest also centers on the extent of self-acceptance shown by the individual. Thus, knowledge of how an individual perceives himself is useful in attempting to help that individual. This notion is very relevant to the medical and psychological treatment and rehabilitation of RA patients.

The present study examines and describes the self-concept of RA patients as compared with the self-concept of diabetes mellitus (DM) patients and healthy subjects (HS) – both as control groups.

2 Methods

2.1 Subjects

Sixty patients attending the outpatient clinic of the Department of Rheumatology and Physical Medicine with the diagnosis of definite or classical rheumatoid arthritis [26], were the subjects for this study. The sample had been selected consecutively from patient files by random selection and consisted of 50 women and ten men. Descriptive data are shown in Table 1.

Table 1. Characteristics of sample

Age group		*n*	%
20–29		12	20.0
30–44		12	20.0
45–60		25	41.7
61–70		11	18.3
	Total	60	100.0
M = 48.81			
Marital status		*n*	%
Married		45	75.0
Unmarried		7	11.6
Divorced		4	6.7
Widowed		4	6.7
	Total	60	100.0
Educational level		*n*	%
0–8 years of schooling		20	33.3
9–12 years of schooling		29	48.3
12+ years of schooling		11	18.4
	Total	60	100.0
Occupational distribution		*n*	%
Professionals and self-employed		7	11.7
Clerical and technical workers		29	48.3
Housewives, pensioners and others without occupation		24	40.0
	Total	60	100.0

2.2 Procedure

All 60 RA patients were classified into three functional stages of the progression of the disease [27] and into three time categories of disease duration. Descriptive data are given in Table 2.

Two control groups were matched with the RA patients for age, sex, marital status, educational level, and occupational distribution. The first control group consisted of 60 DM patients attending the diabetes outpatient clinic of the "Maccabi" sick-

Table 2. Stage and disease duration of sample (RA)

Stage		*n*	%
1 – early		12	20.0
2 – moderate		33	55.0
3 – severe		15	25.0
	Total	60	100.0
Disease duration		*n*	%
1–4 years		28	46.7
5–10 years		19	31.7
11+ years		13	21.6
	Total	60	100.0

fund organization, Ramat Gan. The second control group consisted of 60 healthy subjects.

The 60 DM patients were also matched with the RA patients for three progressive stage categories of disease severity (i.e., type of medical treatment required: first stage, diet therapy; second stage, oral tablets therapy; third stage, insulin injection therapy) and three time categories of disease duration. Descriptive data are shown in Table 3.

Table 3. Stage and disease duration of control group (DM)

Stage		*n*	%
1 – diet		12	20.0
2 – tablets		29	48.3
3 – insulin		19	31.7
	Total	60	100.0
Disease duration		*n*	%
1–4 years		19	31.7
5–10 years		20	33.3
11+ years		21	35.0
	Total	60	100.0

2.3 Self-concept Scale

The Tennessee Self-Concept Scale (TSCS) was chosen to be administered to all three groups [22]. It consists of 100 self-descriptive statements which the subject uses to portray his own picture of himself by checking each statement on a 5-point-scale level of agreement. The TSCS is self-administering for either individuals or groups and can be used with subjects 12 years of age or older and having at least a sixth-grade reading level. The TSCS has a Hebrew version [28] which produces 16 different scores of the TSCS per individual, by a computer scoring system.

2.4 *Analysis*

Four statistical methods were used:

1. The *t*-test for mean score differences between RA patients, DM patients, and HS on TSCS variables [29]
2. A two-way analysis of variance for stage factor and disease factor of RA patients and DM patients with TSCS variables, and for disease duration factor and disease factor of RA patients and DM patients with TSCS variables [29]
3. A chi square procedure for the three stage categories and the two types of disease, and for the three disease duration categories and the two types of disease [29]
4. A one-way analysis of variance for stage factor (independent variable) of RA and DM patients with TSCS variables (dependent variable) and for disease duration factor (independent variable) of RA and DM patients with TSCS variables (dependent variable) [29]

The null hypothesis was rejected when *P* values were less than 0.05. All statistical analysis was done on an IBM 370-168 computer, using the Statistical Package for Social Sciences (SPSS).

Table 4. Means, standard deviations, T values and two-tail probabilities of TSCS scores of RA group as compared with DM and HS groups

Variable	Group	Mean	SD	T value	Two-tail probability
Self-criticism score	RA	31.666	5.522		
	DM	29.516	6.049	2.03	0.044[a]
	HS	35.033	5.489	−3.35	0.001[b]
Total conflict score	RA	41.416	11.771		
	DM	37.283	13.564	1.78	0.077
	HS	28.516	9.051	6.73	0.000[b]
Total self-concept score	RA	339.716	29.446		
	DM	356.966	32.305	−3.06	0.003[b]
	HS	352.483	32.859	−2.24	0.027[a]
Identity	RA	115.766	10.304		
	DM	121.000	11.997	−2.56	0.012[a]
	HS	123.533	10.743	−4.04	0.000[b]
Self-acceptance	RA	111.666	12.039		
	DM	117.167	12.950	−2.41	0.018[a]
	HS	114.766	12.767	−1.37	0.174
Behavior	RA	112.283	12.328		
	DM	118.800	11.047	−3.05	0.003[b]
	HS	114.183	11.988	−0.86	0.394
Physical-self	RA	60.750	8.327		
	DM	66.238	9.136	−3.47	0.001[b]
	HS	69.283	7.647	−5.85	0.000[b]
Moral-ethical-self	RA	73.050	6.392		
	DM	76.800	8.207	−2.97	0.006[b]
	HS	73.150	7.499	−0.08	0.937

Table 4 (continued)

Variable	Group	Mean	SD	T value	Two-tail probability
Social-self	RA	69.183	8.699		
	DM	73.283	7.913	−2.70	0.008[b]
	HS	67.583	8.482	1.02	0.310
Total variability score	RA	51.800	10.086		
	DM	47.533	11.338	2.18	0.031[a]
	HS	39.400	11.576	6.26	0.000[b]
Defensive-positive scale	RA	63.483	11.112		
	DM	70.300	11.110	−3.36	0.001[b]
	HS	57.183	9.804	3.29	0.001[b]
General maladjustment scale	RA	91.733	9.648		
	DM	97.116	11.498	−2.78	0.006[b]
	HS	96.483	8.750	−2.82	0.006[b]
Personality disorder	RA	78.033	8.445		
	DM	82.550	11.554	−2.47	0.016[a]
	HS	76.283	8.918	1.10	0.272
Neurosis scale	RA	74.466	10.768		
	DM	80.200	11.647	−2.80	0.006[b]
	HS	82.750	10.369	−4.29	0.000[b]
General positive self-concept	RA	176.166	16.180		
	DM	186.150	17.349	−3.26	0.001[b]
	HS	174.033	16.943	0.71	0.482
General negative self-concept	RA	163.550	18.525		
	DM	170.816	20.564	−2.03	0.044[a]
	HS	178.450	17.130	−4.57	0.000[b]

$df = 118$
[a] $P \leq 0.05$
[b] $P \leq 0.01$

3 Results

Table 4 shows the mean, standard deviation, T values and two-tail probabilities of TSCS scores of RA vs. DM patients and RA patients vs. HS.

Generally, all HS scores were found to resemble the norm scores of the TSCS [22]; thus, any significant difference found between RA patients and HS should be regarded as such.

Of 32 scores on 16 variables measured by the TSCS, 25 scores (78.12%) were found to be significant – either $P \leq 0.05$ or $P \leq 0.01$. Compared with DM patients, RA patients were found to be significantly different on 15 of 16 TSCS variables (93.75%), and compared with HS, RA patients were found to be significantly different on 10 TSCS variables (62.50%).

Table 5 shows the F values for disease factor and stage factor. The results indicate that RA patients had significantly higher scores than DM patients in all three stages of disease severity on scales of Self-criticism and Total Variability Score, and lower scores in all three stages of disease severity on scales of Total Self-concept, Identity, Self-acceptance, Behavior, Physical Self, Moral-Ethical Self, Social Self, Defensive-

Positive, General Maladjustment (an inverse scale), Personality Disorder (an inverse scale), Neurosis (an inverse scale), General Positive Self-concept, and General Negative Self-concept.

The variance for stage factor was found to be significant on TSCS scales of Identity, Physical Self, and Neurosis. The disease × stage interactions were not significant for any of the TSCS variables. A 3 × 2 chi square procedure for the three stage categories and the two types of disease (RA and DM) revealed no significant

Table 5. F values of the analysis of variance of TSCS variables for disease factor and stage factor

Variable	Source of variations		
	Disease	Stage	Disease × stage
Self-criticism score	4.558[a]	0.834	1.684
Total conflict score	3.121	0.293	0.288
Total self-concept score	10.285[b]	2.228	1.118
Identity	8.116[b]	5.799[b]	1.227
Self-acceptance	6.031[a]	0.742	0.436
Behavior	9.692[b]	0.633	1.131
Physical-self	15.499[b]	8.052[b]	1.136
Moral-ethical-self	7.595[b]	0.215	0.082
Social-self	7.467[b]	1.434	0.441
Total variability score	5.296[a]	1.288	1.029
Defensive-positive scale	12.512[b]	2.303	0.465
General maladjustment scale	8.392[b]	2.173	1.208
Personality disorder	5.886[a]	0.049	0.477
Neurosis scale	10.028[b]	6.041[b]	1.804
General positive self-concept	11.362[b]	1.522	0.967
General negative self-concept	4.566[a]	1.648	0.673

Significance of F: [a] $P \leqslant 0.05$; [b] $P \leqslant 0.01$

Table 6. F ratios and F probabilities of TSCS variables for stage[a] of disease severity

Variable	F ratio	F probability
Self-criticism score	0.614	0.542
Total conflict score	0.282	0.755
Total self-concept score	1.725	0.182
Identity	4.983	0.008[b]
Self-acceptance	0.570	0.567
Behavior	0.388	0.679
Physical-self	6.256	0.002[b]
Moral-ethical-self	0.196	0.822
Social-self	1.281	0.281
Total variability score	0.988	0.375
Defensive-positive scale	1.622	0.202
General maladjustment scale	1.806	0.168
Personality disorder	0.018	0.982
Neurosis scale	4.890	0.009[b]
General positive self-concept	1.101	0.335
General negative self-concept	1.410	0.248

[a] Stage 1 – $n=24$; stage 2 – $n=62$; Stage 3 – $n=34$
[b] $P \leqslant 0.01$

differences for $P \leqslant 0.05$ ($\chi^2 = 0.694$; $2df$), thus allowing the RA and DM group combination.

In order to determine the impact of the stage of disease severity on the various TSCS variables, the one-way analysis of variance was carried out. Table 6 shows the F ratios and F probabilities of TSCS variables of RA and DM patients for stage of disease severity. The results indicate that both RA and DM patients had a descending order of scores across the three stages in ascending order of of disease severity: the lower the score achieved, the higher the stage of disease severity. This pattern is true for the TSCS scales of Identity, Physical Self, and Neurosis (an inverse scale). These results support the two-way analysis of variance.

Table 7. F values of the analysis of variance of TSCS variables for disease factor and duration factor

Variable	Source of variations		
	Disease	Duration	Disease × duration
Self-criticism	4.049[a]	0.053	0.335
Total conflict score	4.883[a]	3.085[a]	0.402
Total self-concept score	11.924[b]	3.206[a]	0.812
Identity	9.058[b]	4.751[b]	0.708
Self-acceptance	8.135[b]	3.367[a]	0.052
Behavior	10.139[b]	0.999	1.863
Physical self	13.841[b]	2.621	0.208
Moral-ethical self	7.677[b]	0.110	1.390
Social self	10.929[b]	4.892[b]	2.283
Total variability score	6.810[b]	3.118[a]	1.588
Defensive-positive scale	12.425[b]	1.134	0.392
General maladjustment scale	10.719[b]	4.712[b]	1.586
Personality disorder	6.913[b]	0.966	0.302
Neurosis scale	9.960[b]	2.782	0.123
General positive self-concept	12.301[b]	1.648	1.300
General negative self-concept	5.777[a]	2.921	0.245

Significance of F: [a] $P \leqslant 0.05$; [b] $P \leqslant 0.01$

Table 7 shows the F values of the two-way analysis of variance of TSCS variables for disease factor and disease duration factor. The results indicate that RA patients had significantly higher scores than DM patients in all three time categories of disease duration on scales of Self-Criticism, Total Conflict Score, and Total Variability Score.

RA patients had significantly lower scores than DM patients in all three time categories of disease duration on scales of Total Self-Concept, Identity, Self-acceptance, Behavior, Physical Self, Moral-Ethical Self, Social Self, Defensive-Positive, General Maladjustment (an inverse scale), Personality Disorder (an inverse scale), Neurosis (an inverse scale), General Positive Self-concept, and General Negative Self-concept. The variance for duration factor was found to be significant on TSCS scales of Total Conflict, Total Self-concept, Identity, Self-acceptance, Social Self, Total Variability, and General Maladjustment.

The disease × duration interactions were not significant for any TSCS variable.

A 3 × 2 chi square procedure for the three disease-duration categories and the two types of disease (RA and DM) revealed no significant differences for $P \leqslant 0.05$, ($\chi^2 = 0.162$; 2*df*), thus allowing the RA and DM group combination.

Table 8. F ratios and F probabilities of TSCS variables for duration[a] of disease

Variable	F ratio	F probability
Self-criticism score	0.039	0.962
Total conflict score	2.222	0.112
Total self-concept score	1.905	0.153
Identity	3.477	0.034[b]
Self-acceptance	2.175	0.118
Behavior	0.593	0.554
Physical-self	1.639	0.198
Moral-ethical-self	0.129	0.878
Social-self	3.067	0.050[b]
Total variability score	2.069	0.130
Defensive-positive scale	0.480	0.619
General maladjustment scale	3.196	0.044[b]
Personality disorder	0.444	0.642
Neurosis scale	1.679	0.191
General positive self-concept	0.813	0.445
General negative self-concept	2.083	0.129

[a] 1– 4 years – $n = 47$
5 – 10 years – $n = 39$
11+ years – $n = 34$
Significance of F: [b] $P \leqslant 0.05$

In order to determine the impact of the duration of the disease on the various TSCS variables, the one-way analysis of variance was performed. Table 8 shows the F ratios and F probabilities of TSCS variables of RA and DM patients for duration of the disease. The results indicate that both RA and DM patients had a descending order of scores across the three time categories of disease duration: the lower the score achieved, the longer the time of disease duration. This pattern is true for the TSCS scale of Social Self. On scales of Identity and General Maladjustment, there is a sharp decline in the score level from the first time category of disease duration to the second time category, after which the score level rises somewhat from the second time category of disease duration to the third.

These results partly support the two-way analysis of variance: only TSCS scales which were significant at the $P \leqslant 0.01$ level for Duration factor on the 2-way analysis of variance were found to be significant at the $P \leqslant 0.05$ level on the one-way analysis of variance.

5 Discussion

The results of this study seem to indicate that RA patients generally have a lower self-concept than either a control group of chronically ill patients (DM) or a control group of healthy subjects (HS).

As compared with the other chronically ill patients, RA patients seem to be less defensive and to have a greater capacity for self-criticism (Self-criticism subscale). They are less capable than DM patients of describing themselves and their basic identity (Identity sub-scale). They have a lower opinion of themselves than DM patients and thus put more limitations on how pleased they are with the way they see themselves (Self-acceptance subscale).

Rheumatoid arthritis patients are less pleased with the way they act or function (Behavior subscale). Their views of their body, state of health, physical appearance, skills, and sexuality trouble them (Physical-Self subscale). RA patients seem to undervalue their moral worth and to be dissatisfied with their religion or lack of it (Moral-Ethical Self subscale). They feel that they are less adequate and worthy than other people in their social interactions in general (Social Self subscale), and they exhibit greater inconsistency from one area of self-perception to another (Total Variability subscale). RA patients lack the usual defenses for maintaining self-esteem (Defensive-Positive subscale). They feel that they are generally less well adjusted (General Maladjustment subscale), have more personality weaknesses (Personality Disorder subscale), and bear greater resemblance to neurotic patients (Neurosis subscale).

Finally, RA patients, as compared with DM patients, have more difficulty in seeking and referring to positive elements in their self-concept (General Positive Self-concept subscale), but they "refuse" to accept more negative elements in themselves as well (General Negative Self-concept subscale).

The following points are unique to the comparison of RA patients with the second control group (HS): RA patients appear to be more defensive than HS (Self-criticism subscale), have more conflicts, and exhibit more contradictions in the area of self-perception (Total Conflict subscales).

Finally, in contrast to the comparison with DM patients, RA patients have more defenses than HS do for maintaining their self-esteem (Defensive-Positive subscale), which correlates with their defensive trend on the Self-criticism subscale mentioned earlier.

5.1 Stage Factor

It seems that the stage factor of disease severity is deterimental for the chronically ill patients (both RA and DM) especially in the areas of the patient's identity, physical self, and his or her neurotic reactions to the severity of the disease. The mean scores on each of these variables across the three stages of disease severity indicate that during the first stage of disease severity both RA and DM patients ($n=24$) keep up with the normal value scores of the TSCS; however, those patients classified in the second ($n=62$) and third stages ($n=34$) become worse with regard to their identity, physical self, and mental health self-perception.

5.2 Duration Factor

Like the stage factor, the duration factor has a similar pattern in two areas of the self-concept of the patient, identity and general maladjustment. Those patients ($n=47$) in the first time-category of disease duration (1–4 years) resemble healthy subjects. However, as their disease becomes chronic by its duration, those patients ($n=39$) included in the second time-category (5–10 years) become worse with regard to identity and general maladjustment. This pattern of a descending order of scores changes for patients ($n=34$) who are sick for more than 11 years (third time-category of disease duration): these patients do not do worse than patients included in the 2nd time-category of disease duration in regard to these two self-concept variables, and they even slightly improve; however, not to the degree of 1st time-category patients. It seems, therefore, that patients who have suffered from their chronic disease more than eleven years become somewhat "adjusted" to their poor condition and become "compliant" with their sick role, lacking the mental energy to cope successfully with their disease (30).

5.3 Mental Variables

In addition, the preoccupation of patients categorized according to the duration of their disease with "mental" variables, such as Identity, Social Self, and General Maladjustment, perhaps suggests that they lack the Physical Self variable. This is in contrast with the presence of this variable for patients categorized according to the stage of their disease severity mentioned before. It seems, therefore, that the duration of the disease itself impairs the psychological balance of the patient more than his or her physical balance does.

A summary of the results obtained with characterological questionnaires shows depression as the feature that emerged most clearly (1). It is probably the depressive reaction of RA patients to their disease which brings about impairment in the various areas of their self-concept. According to some authors, such as Rimon [20], the depressive reaction of RA patients did not differ appreciably from that of control subjects. But Rimon's control group consisted of patients with other diseases; hence his results suggest that depression is a common psychic component of disease in general, especially of chronic disease. Our study confirms the notion that both severity and duration of the disease might affect the patient's self-concept whether he has RA or DM. However, an RA patient generally feels worse about himself than a DM patient.

The results of the present study suggest a focus on some specific areas of the RA patient's self-concept for formulating psychological therapeutic goals in helping him to deal with problems and frustrations resulting from the disease. Further investigations using larger samples and additional phenomenological measurement techniques are needed to assess the individual's view of himself.

6 Summary

The study indicates (a) that RA patients are more impaired in various areas of their self-concept than the control group of DM patients, and even more so as compared with HS; (b) that the stage factor of disease severity for both RA and DM patients has a pattern of descending order of negative impact across the three stages of disease severity on their Identity, Physical Self, and Neurosis; (c) that the duration factor for both RA and DM patients also has a pattern of a descending order of negative impact across the three time-categories of disease duration on their Social Self; and (d) that patients classified in the third time-category (11 years and longer) improve slightly with regard to their Identity and General Maladjustment, but not to the degree of patients classified in the first time-category of disease duration (1–4 years), who resemble more healthy subjects.

References

1. Kiviniemi P (1977) Emotions and personality in rheumatoid arthritis. Scand J Rheumatol 6, Suppl 18: 1–132
2. Cleveland SE, Reitman E, Brewer EJ Jr (1965) Psychological factors in rheumatoid arthritis. Arthritis Rheum 8: 1152–1158
3. Mueller AD, Lefkovitz AM, Bryant JE, Marshall ML (1961) Some psychosocial factors in patients with rheumatoid arthritis. Arthritis Rheum 4: 275–282
4. Rekola J (1973) Rheumatoid arthritis and the family. Scand J Rheumatol 2, Suppl 3: 1–117
5. Cleveland SE, Fisher S (1960) A comparison of psychological characteristics and physiological reactivity in ulcer and rheumatoid arthritis groups. I. Psychological measures. II. Differences in physiological reactivity. Psychosom Med 22: 282–289
6. Geist H (1966) The psychosocial aspects of rheumatoid arthritis. Thomas, Springfield
7. Prick JJG; Van de Loo KJM (1964) The psychosomatic approach to primary rheumatoid arthritis. Davis, Philadelphia
8. Shochet BR, Lisansky ET, Shubart AF, Fionco V, Kurkland S, Pope M (1969) A medical-psychiatric study of patients with reumatoid arthritis. Psychosomatics 10: 271–279
9. Williams RL, Krasnoff AG (1964) Body image and physiological patterns in patients with peptic ulcer and rheumatoid arthritis. Psychosom Med 26: 701–709
10. Nurimen E (1975) Parent-child relationship in rheumatoid arthritis and bronchial asthma. Scand J Rheumatol 4, Suppl 8: Abstract S01–12
11. Moldofsky H, Rothman AI (1970) Personality, disease parameters and medication in rheumatoid arthritis. Arthritis Rheum 13: 338–339
12. Robinson H, Kirk RF Jr, Frye RL (1971) A psychological study of rheumatoid arthritis and selected controls. J Chronic Dis 23: 791–801
13. Bauer B, Leistner K, Tanner E, Kunath H, Schwartz R (1973) Vorkommen von klinischen, sozialen und Persönlichkeitsmerkmalen bei Patienten mit progressiv chronischer Polyarthritis. Beitr Rheumatol 20: 173–189
14. Bourestom NC, Howard MT (1965) Personality characteristics of three disability groups. Arch Phys Med Rehabil 46: 626–632
15. Moos RH, Solomon GF (1964) Minnesota multiphasic personality inventory response patterns in patients with rheumatoid arthritis. J Psychosom Res 8: 17–28
16. Moos RH, Solomon GF (1965) Psychologic comparisons between women with rheumatoid arthritis and their nonarthritic sisters. I. Personality test and interview rating data. II. Content analysis of interviews. Psychosom Med 27: 150–164
17. Nalven FB, O'Brien JF (1964) Personality patterns of rheumatoid arthritic patients. Arthritis Rheum 7: 18–28
18. Polley HF, Swenson WM, Steinhilber RM (1970) Personality characteristics of patients with rheumatoid arthritis. Psychosomatics 11: 45–49

19. Woff BB, Farr RS (1964) Personality characteristics in rheumatoid arthritis. Arthritis Rheum 7: 354
20. Rimon R (1969) A psychosomatic approach to rheumatoid arthritis. Acta Rheum Scand Suppl 13: 1–154
21. Rimon R (1973) Rheumatoid factor and aggression dynamics in female patients with rheumatoid arthritis. Scand J Rheumatol 2: 119–122
22. Fitts WH (1965) A manual for the tennessee self-concept scale. Department of Mental Health, Nashville, pp 1–31
23. Kelley GA (1968) The psychology of personal constructs, vol. 1. A theory of personality. In Anastasi A (ed) Psychological testing. Macmillan, New York, pp 531–532
24. Snygg D, Combs AW (1968) Individual behavior: a perceptual approach to behavior. In: Anastasi A (ed) Psychological testing. Macmillan, New York, pp 531–532
25. Anastasi A (ed) (1968) Psychological testing. Macmillan, New York
26. Hollander JL, McCarthy DJ Jr (1976) Arthritis and allied conditions. Lea and Febiger, Philadelphia pp 403–404
27. Steinbrocker O, Traeger CH, Batterman RC (1949) Therapeutic criteria in rheumatoid arthritis. JAMA 140: 659
28. Fitts WH (1974) Tennessee self-concept scale (Hebrew version by Franckle JJ). Bar-Ilan University Press, Ramat-Gan, Israel,
29. Fergusen GA (1966) Statistical analysis in psychology and education. McGraw-Hill, London, pp 125–126, 227–241, 242–263, 157–178
30. Kiviniemi P (1976) Psychological problems in rheumatoid disease. In: Answell B (ed) Rheumatism and the psyche. Huber, Bern, pp 29–32

Definitions of Rehabilitation in Legislation

P. J. Blommestijn

This article concerns ways in which definitions, terminology and nomenclature in law, legislation, and other statutory documents can be used, and why they should be used, to promote more effective, relevant, and just responses to the needs and the rights of disabled and handicapped persons. Generally received definitions will be reviewed, and attempts will be made to formulate alternatives to them. This paper is not primarily concerned with problems of a handicapped person in court or in the penal system (as offender, defendant, criminal or prisoner), although the situation of a handicapped plaintiff or rightful claimant in civil law and administrative law may be dealt with. It discusses general conditions for entitlement to the provisions of the various welfare sectors (health, labour, education, social work, housing, social security, recreation, sports, culture, etc.), and how to improve their availability. It is the result of experience in the sectors of legislation, administration, policymaking, and social security, especially regarding rehabilitation of the mentally, physically, sensorially, and socially handicapped.

1 The Why and Wherefore in General

Many definitions are of minimal value; they have a symbolic significance only, or satisfy the personal scientific needs of an outsider. Many definitions incorrectly describe rehabilitation as essentially a medical problem; others see the objectives of rehabilitation above all as enabling a disabled person to work or to earn an income. Definitions of a handicapped person often describe the individual as a (medical) patient instead of as a consumer or client with many needs, desires, and potentials. Recent definitions, too, do not sufficiently emphasize that the handicapped person – "a person with a handicap" would be a more preferable term – does not want to undergo rehabilitation passively, but rather to decide for himself, in all phases, content and range of his rehabilitation. Although it is everywhere acknowledged that a handicap has especially social consequences i.e. that a person experiences his handicap mostly through (a lack of) social relations and through his environment, definitions too often deal only with the individual without appreciating that in most cases it is above all the environment (social as well as technical and physical), the milieu, the next-of-kin or society at large that are the determining factors.

Many definitions are inspiring, but offer no real starting points for the formulation of policy or the designing of a structure or type of organization. Definitions can also stigmatize and segregate people; in fact, the purpose of a definition is to label. But labeling does not have to diminish the dignity of a person. In some cases it is even essential, since some help can be given only when the person in question is labeled handicapped. But definitions and terms not only define and mark; they also limit and restrict. Some persons and facilities fall outside the realm of laws and regulations; definitions can give rights but can just as easily deprive a person of such; e.g., one who is not designated as handicapped may still need help and care; a definition can block access as much as it can further it. Definitions, therefore, must be not only clear, specific, and complete; they must be just socially flexible as well.

It follows that definitions and terms have important juridical and social meaning: they label, codify, limit, give or withold rights, and can also be a social yardstick.

The WHO Expert Committee on Mental Health reported in 1955: "Most of the existing mental health legislation is unsatisfactory, although in some countries laws based on outmoded concepts of mental abnormality, when interpreted liberally, can be made to work fairly well in practice . . .". [1]

This statement also seems to have value in defining rehabilitation and handicapped persons. A striking example is the definition (see Sect. 4.1) formulated at the conference in Vienna in 1955 on rehabilitation and "care of the disabled" [2]. Although it must now, 25 years later, be considered outmoded, many countries appear to live well with it, the practice in these countries often being more advanced and more progressive than that which has been codified in law, or other regulations elsewhere.

The importance of definitions should not be overestimated. However, it would be unwise avoid defining things, or to be content with outmoded formulations for the simple reason that one can live with them in practice. The effect would be legal insecurity, hindering certain developments in rehabilitation, while stressing others too strongly.

The Vienna definition has also operated as an inspiring and orientating instrument, has opened up new concepts of rehabilitation, has introduced especially the multidisciplinary and multifunctional character of rehabilitation, raising it above the status of a predominantly medical activity with additional vocational aims.

Even if most definitions "only" reflect the development of general social awareness, and are in that sense a form of codification, they are at the same time an expression of the political intent to allow social awareness to be effective.

There is yet another aspect: Where a country has no generally accepted definition of, e.g., rehabilitation of the handicapped, or where a country rejects the Vienna definition as outmoded, it will very often be evident that specific legislation exists there for limited aims, such as insurance against employment disability, provision of jobs by government, admission to day-centers or hostels, admission to special education facilities, provision of aid, all precisely and clearly laid down and effectuated. However, the effect of such separate positive legislation, with good definitions, is not the same as that of a total model.

Naturally, it cannot be assumed that a country with the best definition will be a model in rehabilitation, nor should we consider a country lacking generally accepted definitions of rehabilitation underdeveloped in this field. However, the possession of good, generally and officially accepted definitions of disability and rehabilitation can be, for any particular country, a measure of the level and the range of rehabilitation and care of handicapped persons. By a "good" definition we mean not only a technically and conceptually good one, but also one corresponding to ethical standards of humanity and dignity. Only then will it be a social yardstick. If the democratic quality and the greatness of a country and its inhabitants are determined by the degree to which the weakest citizens in that society are cared for – and the handicapped form a part of this group – this should be reflected in the terminology, too. By this is meant changes in the use of words with the passage of time, e.g., misshapen, deformed, crippled, destitute, imperfect, defective, invalid, disabled, and now handicapped.

Terms reflect the views of a society and a people. They are, on the one hand, the effect and the concrete shape of concepts and ideas, but on the other hand they can change existing views. A persistent problem is that new terms and names are introduced merely because the existing ones are considered wounding, outmoded, or simply no longer relevant, and then soon suffer the same fate themselves.

However, in our society the formulation of definitions and please for better terms often encounter opposition, too. There is a current prejudice that definitions and the making of them are the territory of perfectionists, extremists, bureaucrats, or technocrats, who have no appreciation of the human being behind the definition. But there is much ambivalence here: those who reject definitions must often admit the need of them, just as many people who say they hate politics state their opinions on political events, daily, and complain that no person with authority ever listens to them.

Definitions order social traffic, just as traffic rules and definitions are needed on public roads. But there is resistance here, too: the government of any country realizes that pronouncing upon social policy, in the form of official acknowledgement of a general, normative definition, can have radical consequences for the budget, for training capacity, for building capacity, and social security at large. And civil servants realize that definitions can affect their autonomy as well.

The danger of overestimating the importance and the effectiveness of general definitions has been pointed out. But we should not underestimate their value either. On the contrary, in a certain sense, the examples of resistance and opposition are arguments for their significance.

It was striking that at the 14th World Congress of Rehabilitation International, in 1980 in Winnipeg, Canada, almost without exception Swedish amendments to draft definitions were welcomed (see [3]). These amendments were progressive, but it was the new nations and so-called developing countries present who greeted the proposals for far-reaching adaptation of the tabled definitions of rehabilitation, etc. as especially positive. Their representatives said that they felt a strong need for progressive definitions from which they could derive a stimulus and a world-wide recognition of the importance of rehabilitation and care of the handicapped, and which could help them to persuade their Governments of the value of paying more attention to minority groups in their societies.

Another important point is that a high level of economic and social development can act as a brake on countries. History shows that especially countries which we now call developing or underdeveloped can catch up on progress and knowledge very quickly. They do not need to go through all the stages of development, but can – stimulated by the urgency of their backward state – take over the newest concepts, developments, and ideas at once, according to the local situation and the possibilities. They can benefit from what we call "the law of leap-frogging" or "the law of stimulating arrears." Naturally, there are limits to what general, norm-setting definitions can attain. Neither definitions nor laws can change moral norms or guarantee progress and happiness; "Law cannot make mores," as U.S. Senator Charles Sumner (1811–1874) said in a speech on the right s of man. But laws and a standard-setting nomenclature can create conditions for greater well-being.

Definitions based on political decisions reveal that a certain development is necessary, that society feels a responsibility for the realization of that development, and that it is obliged to find the means for its realization. In this respect, definitions also play an important part in the catalyzing and educational functions.

I will now indicate more systematically why, and in which situations definitions are necessary, and with which requirements and qualification definitions, terms, and nomenclature must comply. Problems in this connection will also be outlined.

2 Arguments, Conditions, and Problems

2.1 Differences of Purpose

There is a sharp distinction to be made between general definitions of rehabilitation (handicap, being handicapped) and definitions for a specific purpose or group, e.g., in special legislation.

2.1.1 General Definitions

General definitions serve as points of orientation, frames of reference and as norms or criteria for further use in more specific regulations. General definitions set standards, or at least are supposed to serve as standards. A general, universal nomenclature for the areas of disability and rehabilitation is lacking, especially in legislation, administration, and scientific literature. The reason is that the effects of a handicap are different for different people, depending on age, on social and cultural aspects and on the type of handicap or group of handicapped persons. The administration and the legislative machinery follow a mostly step-by-step policy, if any. Persons in need of help are defined under a given regulation, according to the aims or purposes of a benefit or service system. The initiative in legislation and planning bodies is primarily group-oriented. There are various motivating or inhibiting factors: social policy arguments such as the state's philosophy, the political tide, the diversity of political forces, government action as the last resort, the laissez-faire theory, "every man for himself," or public responsibility in a welfare state for all deprived minorities or deprived persons; economical and budgetary considerations; the influence of pressure groups; or simply the lack of awareness, neglect or even denial of needs, depending on sociohistorical developments in a given country or culture. It is impossible to formulate one general, universal definition suitable for use in every sector, every area of care, help, and service. It is equally wrong to act in particular sectors while lacking general, norm-setting definitions, as a frame of reference.

2.1.2 Specific Situations

For special situations there are in fact as many definitions as there are values in use: conditions governing the access of handicapped people to medical treatment, to employment, to special education, to day-care centers or hostels, and conditions on entitlement to social benefits or facilities, to parking facilities for a handicapped driver, or to a driving license. In the sphere of taxation there is a need for specific assessment rules. Specific definitions are also necessary for civil law, penal law and medical registration (for matters of prevention, early detection, etc.).

In most of these cases definitions may decide on access, which in some situations really means on an existence worthy of human beings. General definitions, then, are valuable as points of departure, as the highest norms fostering the ideal objectives.

We have observed that in those countries where rehabilitation and care of the handicapped began with specific regulations for specific groups or needs, without having or using general orientating definitions, such regulations are experienced as arbitrary, as unjust and discriminatory towards other, comparable groups, and as a barrier in the way to broadening and extending care.

At the beginning, a step-by-step development is the only possibility; however, the next aims must be broader and more differentiated.

2.2 Definitions for Governmental Purposes

Definitions are needed for the relation between the three branches of government. We make use of the generally accepted terms "executive" and "legislative" power, which, together with the judicial power, form the "trias politica." The actual forms taken by these powers differ from country to country, but they are generally recognizable and the terms are internationally useful. The government of a country cannot give an optimal account of its actions to parliament without a clear and mutually accepted terminology. And a people's representation cannot optimally call to account or stimulate a government when both parties use different terms and languages. Is a mentally handicapped child included in the term "handicapped person"? Is a blind or deaf person also included in the concept "disabled person"? Does rehabilitation comprise more than medical treatment? One cannot discuss and decide on planning, organization, the burden of taxation and social premium, on extension of social security and training of personnel, on the relation between (expensive) intramural care and (mostly cheaper) ambulant care, or on the juridical position of fellow citizens, when a terminology, a "language," common to all is lacking. This is also true for the relations within the executive branch of government, e.g., between ministers or secretaries and departments and for the relations between the executive and legislative branches and organizations of consumers and providers of services. That which applies to the Executive as a body applies also to the traffic between parts of this power. Ministers and ministries have to know which mutual competences and duties they have, on which points they must cooperate and what support they can give each other. In some countries, ministers and ministries dealing intensively with matters of rehabilitation and care of the handicapped – the so-called *keyministers* of rehabilitation – cooperate closely under the charge of a co-ordinating rehabilitation minister. The advisory body of officials is then an interministry steering committee on rehabilitation policy, a board of high civil servants drawn from the ministries concerned.

There are several variations on this operating system:

1. The rehabilitation ministers and the interministry steering committee can maintain official, systematic, and periodic contacts with the national organizations (professionals, lay persons, parents, consumers, etc.) for rehabilitation and care of the handicapped.
2. A national advisory body on rehabilitation, consisting of representatives of national organizations of and for the handicapped and of the lower government (provincial, local) advises the government in all important matters of rehabilitation, projected legislation included. A council on a legal basis is preferable, with clear guidelines on themes, competences, and the obligation of the ministers concerned to ask advice.
3. An interministry steering committee of high officials is complemented by representatives of national organizations as full members.

We prefer variant 1 with a fundamental widening as shown in Fig. 1.

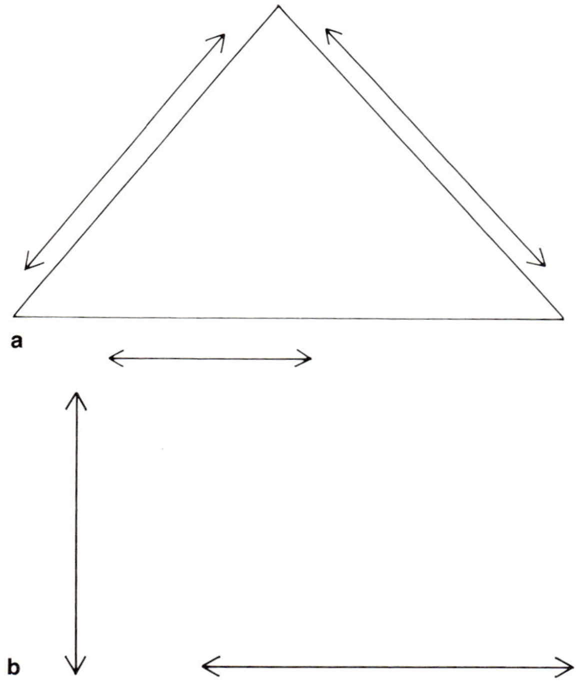

Fig. 1a, b. A comparison of systems for dealing with rehabilitation at the governmental, policymaking level. **a** illustrates the triangular network of reciprocating circulation, and **b** diagrams the classic linear system with lateral openings

Curran and Harding [4] describe variant 3 for the evaluation, review, and improvement of mental health legislation. Although several constitutional, administrative, and structural objections could be raised to this model, their arguments, based as they are on the interpretation of the legislative and constitutional situation in so many countries, are so relevant that they will here be elucidated in detail.

Curran and Harding[1] give as reasons and considerations for their choice:
1. public attention and prestige;
2. time and resources for a careful review process, including longitudinal assessments;
3. involvement of a range of professional groups with relevant expertise;
4. availability of information and ability to plan necessary information collection;
5. lay participation;
6. involvement in programme planning and execution;
7. international links (governmental and non-governmental organizations, academic links, etc.);
8. research capability [4, p. 793].

The combination of these characteristics – some may be incompatible, as the authors themselves say – leads to the formulation of the following mechanism:

> ... An interministerial standing advisory committee (ISAC) could provide such a model. Its chairman and members would be jointly appointed by those ministers with responsibility for health care social and welfare services, ... The secretariat would be drawn from the health ministry .... The committee would be informed directly of the national mental health policy and programme, would have access to the national health information system, and would be able to request the collection of additional data. The committee members would include: one or more members of the legislature; senior civil servants from the ministries involved; senior mental health professionals (including those representing professional associations); representatives of lay mental health associations; an academic; and one or more additional members. Total membership would not be more than 20. Such a committee need not meet as a total group more than once or twice annually. The aim would not be simply to provide a forum for discussion and exchange of views but to initiate and maintain a cycle in which mental health programme objectives were reviewed, the potential contribution (or negative effect) of existing legislation identified, and a series of detailed objectives for such legislation agreed upon ...
> Recommendations would be made directly to the government in a report which could receive wide publicity.
> The suggested model is a hybrid; it might suffer from bureaucratic inertia, and in many countries modifications would obviously be necessary. Some mechanism of this kind may, however, be the only way to ensure prestige, wide representation, relevant information input, necessary expertise, an adequate secretariat, and independent opinions. Obviously, if such a committee was set up it

1 I am indebted to Curran and Harding; many ideas in the article derive from their study.

could address the wider problems of coordination of mental health programmes at the national level [4, p. 794].

The authors offer their model with realistic restrictions and reservations. The fundamental advantages are the high administrative level, the direct link between the government and the welfare system, and the concentration of all relevant sectors; the model produces full representation. But too many different sectors and individuals seem to be lumped together, within a model that would be critized by the official democratic system: in most countries the parliament is the official (part of the) legislative body, also controlling the government; the necessary cooperation between parliament and government may find in this model an overprivileged competitor, when even lay associations and professional groups may deliberate and negotiate with the government on equal speaking terms. Such associations and groups are interest groups, it lies in their nature to underestimate the role of other groups and to be preoccupied with the needs, the interests, the role, and the contribution of their own group. They do not form an objective, independent counterbalance. We should remain aware of the fact, however, that specialized civil servants from the ministries may have their own subjective, narrow-minded aspirations!

The crucial question, raised by this concept, is whether nongovernmental groups or individuals can participate equally in a governmental setting or not. If in a given country they can, all conceivable advantages are present; if they cannot, the disadvantages are clear: no direct influence, longer lines of communication and information. In that case, an official advisory council to the government, with civil servants or other government representatives as advisory members only, would not form a sufficiently comparable alternative. In many countries, too, legislators, policymakers, and governmental and parliamentary circles are against the establishment of more categorial group councils concerning problems of youth, the handicapped, the elderly, and other minorities; they prefer functional or general advisory councils on the broader issues of health care, education, labor, welfare, housing, etc. So, in my view, an official, separate "noninterministerial" advisory council will form neither an easy alternative nor a fully satisfactory one.

Nevertheless, even when the given model is not adoptable in some countries, the construction or conception is likely to give incentives for other solutions. The government and nongovernmental organizations are not the only ones interested in evaluation and improvement of legislation; the parliament is, too! A good representation of the people will appreciate having regular, periodic contacts with national organizations as well as systematic relations with the government (i.e., the ministers), in matters of a specialized and quantitatively important character (in terms of numbers of people and amounts of money involved), such as rehabilitation, mental health, care of the elderly, etc. One instrument for this in many countries is formed by a standing parliamentary committee for rehabilitation, which by its existence and status alone can act as a group of experts, and as a counterbalance, controlled by the parliament that represents all the people's interests.

It is for these reasons that we advocate an open triangular network between the government (key ministers for rehabilitation and their interministry steering committee), the parliament (its standing committee), and the national professional and lay organizations in the field of rehabilitation (as they cooperate with the government according to alternative A, Fig. 1). Within this network all parties concerned can cooperate and communicate; it gives a structure for consultation, negotiation or just communication, by which structure alone the importance of rehabilitation and care of the handicapped will be perceived by the community in a very special, accessible form.

Such a triangle will naturally have its own stimulating, generating value; but the different, sometimes contrary, competences have to be indicated clearly. Definitions, if accepted among the members, may contribute to clarity here.

The effectiveness of such a triangular cooperation will be broadened when all parties concerned can restrict or limit their efforts and objectives to those which reflect the most pressing needs or gaps in the aid system; five-year plans may constitute an effective revolving system of survey, evaluation, and future-oriented planning.

In order to be able to contribute to this cooperation, the organizations of and for the handicapped should be encouraged, developed, and financially supported by the government.

2.3 Statistics and Comparability

Definitions and uniformity of terminology are needed for collecting statistical material, for (medical) registration, for applied science, for the translation of science into practical policy, and for international comparison. This argument is closely related to Sect. 2.2. Statistics are equally an instrument for policy and politics – e.g., censuses – and international comparison. Moreover, international comparison can be stimulating though at the same time discouraging. (Medical) registration has its importance in prevention, for population research, for diagnosis and treatment, and for evaluation of the effectiveness of the service system.

2.4 Social and Ethical Yardsticks

Definitions label, but can also stigmatize and restrict. Generally adopted definitions are not an absolute guarantee for a high level of rehabilitation and care of the handicapped, but by good definitions a community gives expression to its attitude toward its fellow citizens and the value that it sets on their welfare. But there is a discrepancy between norm and reality (the Universal Declaration on Human Rights!).

Yet without a norm there is no progress and no criterion for measuring progress. Moreover, there is a difference between verbal and intellectual acceptance, e.g., of equality of the handicapped with the nonhandicapped, and the actual experience and recognition of equality. For all these reasons, we postulate that definitions *can* be social yardsticks.

2.5 *Protection of Human Dignity*

Definitions should respect and promote human dignity; they must at least serve to prevent social stigmas. It is important to prevent labeling that can lead to social discrimination and segregation, or to the creation of a subculture, instead of promoting integration and participation. This means that the words most suitable to a particular country or culture should be used with regard to the handicapped, thereby promoting better attitudes in the population at large. Although there are cleary important semantic reasons for distinguishing, for example according to the Anglo-Saxon concepts, between impaired, disabled, and handicapped, it is regrettable that the officials of the United Nations, knowing that a disability expresses itself primarily in social effects – a disability is a social phenomenon more than personal misfortune – have pressed to organize an International Year of the Disabled rather than of the the Handicapped. The latter term is internationally more useful and has, in our experience, a more positive emotional value.

We have distinguished (Sect. 2.1) between general and specific or subdefinitions. In this context we used the term "(intended) use value". Depending on the intended use, one might prefer a term that in another context could be experienced as discriminatory or unpleasant; it is acceptable and, in the light of growing international mobility, preferable to use the term "invalid" for the indication of parking places or on public transportation vehicles. The term "handicapped person" would have a socioliterary, emotional value, instead of a nonpersonal, useful value.

2.6 *Participation of Those Defined*

Definitions should be determined with the participation of the persons primarily concerned. This argument relates to that under Sect. 2.2. "Full participation and equality" – motto of the International Year – must apply particularly to the formulation of terms. Handicapped people have a right to a say in the formulation of regulations which concern them, a say in the implementation of these regulations, in the programming of their rehabilitation process, in the design of their own future. In practice this means participation in the management of rehabilitation services as well. Participation is nowadays acknowledged to be a basic social right, especially for those who are very dependent on services and institutions. "Having a say" means codetermination, taking part in the process of self-determination.

2.7 *Making Definitions Official*

General, norm-setting definitions should be laid down in official documents. The form of official embodiment will differ from country to country. In any case all should strive for embodiment in the most official, authoritative form. In one country, that may mean insertion in a general rehabilitation law; in another, insertion in the terms of reference and duties of a coordinating minister for rehabilitation (see Sect. 2.2); in a third country the government and the national organizations concerned could convene to draft a special document, separate from legislation.

Furthermore, a government may opt for declaring its adhesion to the formulation of definitions of organizations like the WHO, the ILO, the UN, Rehabilitation International or the International Conference of Social Welfare; such a declaration should, however, take the most official form possible.

We see here – depending on the political and administrative situation in a given country and the level of rehabilitation – an important task for political parties, trade-unions, organizations of the handicapped, churches, prominent industrial leaders, and the mass media.

2.8 Integration of all Aspects

General definitions must not exclude in advance any particular sector of life; therefore, they should also create the conditions for the extension of the service system and for full integration of the handicapped. A handicapped person is, like all of us, an individual to be treated as a whole, as a sociopsychosomatic entity. It is generally accepted that rehabilitation and care of the handicapped have a broad content and significance, reaching far beyond the original purposes of medical and vocational care, and that handicapped persons ought to be helped in all their human, social, and functional aspects, with no area excluded. That means also that the responsibility for rehabilitation and care of the handicapped ought to be anchored broadly in the cabinet's policy; mindful of the saying, "qui trop embrasse, mal étreint" (he who tries to achieve too much achieves nothing), we may distinguish between key ministers and ministers in the second line.

Full rehabilitation demands the covering of all social risks within the social security system (consequences of sickness, disease, social deprivation, disability irrespective of the cause, unemployment age, etc.) and not only the classic professional risks (primarily unemployment and disability). The newer dimensions of rehabilitation are accessibility, independent living, participation, road and traffic safety, and technology.

3 The Main Principles and Concepts of Rehabilitation

Difficulties arise not only from nomenclature, but also from confusion about underlying concepts and objectives.

3.1 Coordination

Rehabilitation is an interdisciplinary, multifunctional process for the planned, coordinated, combined, and comprehensive use of all relevant facilities – medical, social, educational, vocational, cultural, religious, legal, economical, psychological, sexual, and recreational – supported by legislation in the fields of housing, social security, and taxation, and by provisions on physical accessibility, transport, traffic security, technology, prevention of accidents at work, mass media, etc. In fact, no aspect of life should be excluded.

3.2 Preventive Measures

Rehabilitation also includes prevention and early detection or identification; it includes custodial care and long-term care needed by severely disabled persons in institutions, as well as persons being threatened by a disability or chronic illness. Although definitions neither represent absolute truths nor justify boundless claims on all aspects of being handicapped, as involved in the process of rehabilitation, we are against the idea of using the term "care of disabled" in place of "rehabilitation" if "such care is not intended to bring about a change in the condition." This statement is found in a WHO working document [5]. Is such care really "not intended" to bring about a change even if "the condition" is regarded only as a medical or biological one? And is the involvement of the family with a severely disabled child or adult really not a part of the rehabilitation objectives?

3.3 Equal Rights and Participation

People with handicaps have rights equal to those of all other people within their society; the handicapped have a fundamental right to determine their own way of life. In consequence, they have the right of participation in the law-making process and in deciding about rehabilitation policy at large which affects their position. They should take part in the planning, conducting and evaluation of their own rehabilitation program, and participate in the management of rehabilitation facilities and in the social security advisory bodies. This right implies, in turn, their duty to contribute to these processes and procedures to the maximum of their capabilities. This requires that organizations of the handicapped be acknowledged, encouraged, and financially supported.

3.4 Legally Based Participation

The right of participation, as discussed in Sect. 2.6, should be laid down in respective laws and regulations.

3.5 Social Integration

Integration and participation in the life of the community are the most important aspects of rehabilitation; only through integration and full participation as equals can handicapped persons achieve independence and self-determination. These norms and aims imply for example that intramural life or stay in residential institutions should be seen as transitional, preparatory, or temporarily replacing stages on the way to living in the community or society, instead of being permanent or long-term refuges for certain groups; the focus of rehabilitation efforts should constantly be on providing care in the community. The slogan, "Care in the community goes for intramural care" implies that a stay in intramural settings shall not be made financially more attractive than a stay in the community. The norms also mean that the provisions available to the population in general (medical, social, educational, vocational, etc.) should be open to the handicapped as well, as far as this is possible for and desired by the handicapped, themselves. This is preferable to establishing or maintaining specially categorized provisions and services, thereby segregating or isolating and labeling the handicapped.

It should be noted that to plead for the reduction of "categorial" provisions is not to say that we do not need a categorial or rehabilitation policy; on the contrary: each society needs a specialized, stimulating, evaluating focal point of knowledge, experience and means concerning the problems and needs of its handicapped fellow citizens.

3.6 Individual Effects

Disabilities and handicaps result from different problems with different effects and solutions. Handicapped people do not constitute a separate social, medical, mental, or economic group. Especially negative attitudes towards handicapped people, or stereotyped images of them in the light of existing social norms, produce the phenomenon of handicapped persons seen as forming a special group or social category.

Even existing legislation on rehabilitation has a discriminatory effect and keeps handicapped persons from collecting their due. Handicapped people should not be discriminated against in respect of benefits and pensions. There are no decisive arguments with respect to entitlement to social security schemes and rehabilitation programs to distinguish between being handicapped by birth, or by accident or sickness in later years, or between becoming handicapped during work or leisure activities. The effects and consequences of a handicap, rather than its cause, must be adopted as the yardstick of the need for rehabilitation. Distinctions in the field of social security based on the causes of an impairment, disability or handicap instead of the effects, may result in unjust financial arrears and – even more blameworthy – in the social phenomenon of privileged and underprivileged handicapped fellow citizens. Statistical data and scientific classifications are frequently cause oriented, not based on the principle of "finality."

3.7 Benefits

3.7.1 Social

The social benefits of providing rehabilitation are perceptible in the growing number of handicapped – or formerly handicapped – fellow citizens living a (fairly) normal, independent life, in a normal, sometimes adapted dwelling; going through the streets or being a driver or passenger in traffic (an unmistakable criterion for measuring the effects of rehabilitation and the level of integration); having enjoyed normal education and adapted vocational training; having a job or performing another activity; having enough income from work or social insurance; having a family of their own or living in a family, sometimes in a hostel or a group home which replaces the family; enjoying or living life in a physically accessible and safe environment in society at large; in short, feeling comfortable at their own level, sometimes with absolute limitations, the acceptance of which may depend on the extent to which society can accept them, mentally, intellectually, and in practice.

The foregoing does not include the many handicapped patients confined, more or less permanently, to a hospital or other "closed" institution, or those who are homebound for the rest of their lives. The aims of rehabilitation will remain the same for them; not all handicapped can reach the same stage of rehabilitation or social level, something many leaders of organizations of the handicapped sometimes seem to forget, preoccupied as they are with the interests of better educated, more informed, and more capable individuals.

3.7.2 Economic

The economic benefits of providing rehabilitation have been demonstrated in savings in the cost of health and other social services, in the reduction in the cost of public assistance and social security plans, by the reduction in intramural care in favor of more open care, which is cheaper, and in the gains to society from goods and services produced by handicapped workers, contributing in the process many tax and social service premiums. However, it should be noted that in times of economic stringency such as we are experiencing now, the employment chances of handicapped workers will be disproportionately endangerd.

Further arguments, formulations, and proposals can be found in the "Charter for the 80s", drafted at the International Conference of Rehabilitation International in 1980 at Winnipeg, Canada (see Sect. 4.1.6) [15]

3.8 Criteria of Effective Rehabilitation

The criteria for assessing the effectiveness of rehabilitation policy and provisions are [6]:

1. Demographic indices
2. Measures of the incidence of certain personal and social conditions which can be calculated on the basis of censuses, administrative records, or surveys
3. The existence and the range of certain services and benefits (measures of input)
4. Measures of uptake of certain services and benefits (measures of output)
5. The existence of certain laws, regulations, and administrative or management provisions
6. The existence of certain incentives

4 Definitions

> Everyone is handicapped, but some so evidently that they are labeled as blind, deaf, crippled, or spastic. (Dutch motto)

Definitions do not demonstrate absolute truths; they are based on official arrangements and have an inherently arbitrary character. These arrangements refer to content, meaning, range, and validity or legitimacy. So the persons and authorities concerned, having agreed, for example, that psychiatric patients should be included by analogy in the definitions of "rehabilitation" or "handicapped" – with regard to registration and certain benefits – may equally declare that this category is not included in the actual rehabilitation policy and service system. They may declare, too, that people popularly regarded as socially handicapped, such as drug abusers, shall not be defined as handicapped, but should be covered nevertheless by some part of the social security rehabilitation system originally reserved for handicapped people. These restrictions illustrate the fact that a definition is a simplification and a condensation with a certain goal. Definitions, like classifications, are subordinate to a purpose.

4.1 Rehabilitation

4.1.1 The Vienna Definition

"Rehabilitation is a complex of measures and provisions aiming at developing and/or maintaining the physical, mental, social, vocational and economic abilities of a disabled individual to the individually highest possible degree" [2]. In 1955 this definition represented a keystone and a new starting point, introducing rehabilitation as much more than a medical field and with broader aims than vocational progress only; today it is considered outdated. The definition takes for granted what a disabled person is. It deals with the individual only, and not in relation to his or her family or broader environment, not as he or she relates to nonhandicapped persons of the same peergroup. It starts with the person as he or she *is*, excluding measures for prevention; moreover, it does not comprise conditioning or taking measures to make public life more accessible to the handicapped. It formulates an offer to a person, as an object of care and help. Furthermore, it tends to overstress performance and competition. The definition sounds like a functional instrument, listing a series of potentialities.

To date the Vienna definition is the only one acknowledged worldwide in the field of rehabilitation; it is amazing that we can still live with it. Fundamental turning points – like this definition – have a persistent duration. It is as if we could live with love without defining it or having a need to redefine it.

4.1.2 *Definition of the WHO Expert Committee on Medical Rehabilitation (1969)*

"Rehabilitation is the combined and coordinated use of medical, social, educational and vocational measures for training or retraining the individual to the highest possible level of functional ability" [7]. Our problems with this formulation are approximately the same as those we enumerated against the Vienna text.

4.1.3 *Definition Adopted by the Council of Europe in 1976*

"Rehabilitation is the continuous process designed to maintain, increase or restore the disabled person's capacity to pursue a normal activity.

This process includes a variety of complementary measures, applied simultaneously, as the case may be:

A. medical rehabilitation and
A.[1] medical and educational processes;
B. psychological rehabilitation;
C. social rehabilitation;
D. industrial rehabilitation;
E. vocational rehabilitation . . ." [8]

This formulation expresses a terminological struggle for life. It shows little or no progress compared with the other definitions. In particular, the term "complementary measures" is surprising; the measures are essential and basic, and form the very nucleus of rehabilitation.

4.1.4 *German Definition*

"Rehabilitation is a total, comprehensive process, comprising the securing of measures for prevention, for the most durable integration, reintegration and safeguarding of the reintegration of disabled persons in labor, occupation/school, and/or society" [9, p. 55]. This formulation is more society-oriented than the others. It includes prevention, but takes for granted what a disabled person is and enumerates objectives, not means or instruments. The definition is not individualizing; it takes rehabilitation and integration as absolute objectives, not relating a rehabilitee to his or her peers or environment. If we take the sequence, disease – impairment – disability – handicap (see Sect. 4.2) and know that one can be impaired without being disabled and disabled without being handicapped, then we may question whether the definition stresses the social aspects too strong.

For the rest, this definition – taking for granted many of the terms in it – is a good one, precisely because of its simplicity.

4.1.5 Definition by the Bureau on Rehabilitation (Canadian Department of National Health and Welfare, 1980)

"Rehabilitation services are services which have as their objective the reduction or removal, to the fullest extent possible, of the effects of an impairment which substantially limits a disabled person's ability to obtain employment, to retain employment, or to undertake the activities of daily living in the community." This is a very useful formulation, though perhaps overstressing functional abilities while neglecting social aspects. The definition gives absolute objectives, and does not relate to the circumstances of other, nonhandicapped fellow citizens with regard to age, education, and cultural background, as independent living projects are frequently ghettos.

4.1.6 Draft Text of the "Charter for the 80s" [3]

"Rehabilitation is a process for the combined and coordinated use of medical, social, educational and vocational measures to assist the disabled individual to achieve his or her highest possible level of functioning and to integrate within society"

It is really remarkable to find such a formulation in 1980 under the auspices of Rehabilitation International. In fact, the definition is only a slight improvement over that from the WHO (see Sect. 4.1.2) and follows the disciplines approach of the Vienna definition from 1955 (Sect. 4.1.1) [2].

4.1.7 Swedish Amendments to the Draft Text of the "Charter for the 80s"

"Habilitation and/or rehabilitation is a process aimed at enabling a person to reach an optimum physical, mental, and/or social functioning level, thus providing him/her with the tools to change his/her own life. It may involve measures intended to compensate a loss of function or a functional limitation (for example by technical aids) as well as measures to facilitate social adjustment or readjustment" [3]. This definition is, by its intention, a sympathetic one and making valid comments is not an easy task. It contains objectives and instruments, and comprises individual functional aspects as well as the social aspects. It leaves it to the person (the handicapped one?) to play an active role. But it does not relate to the circumstances of nonhandicapped persons of the same peer group; it raises questions about what one's "optimum" level is or should be. Moreover, it leaves open the important question of whether rehabilitation is concerned or has to deal with the handicapped or disabled person only, or primarily as the central subject of rehabilitation measures. In our view, within a family both the relatives and the handicapped family member may encounter "problems," in some phases of rehabilitation the relatives more than the handicapped person. Or only the relatives may have problems, or measure "optimum" differently (e.g., the situation or condition of the handicapped person cannot be changed, temporarily or permanently; in terms of the definition, he or she has reached his or her optimum, which can really be a minimum as compared with the situation of his or her peers).

Finally, we are against the introduction of the word "habilitation" implying that some handicapped persons were not "habilis" or "valid" before. It is not the etymological origin that gives a word its meaning but the use of it and the emotional value that society at large or the language-making community attaches to it [10].

4.1.8 U.S.S.R. Definition

A noteworthy description of rehabilitation is also given by Zakharov and Tsivilyov [11]:

"Rehabilitation is a long, drawn-out process covering comprehensive convalescent treatment of the disabled person (medical rehabilitation), his being drawn out of a state of mental depression (psychological rehabilitation), restoration or development of his ability to do suitable work and the actual provision of such a job (vocational rehabilitation). All these stages are closely interlinked and intertwined, and are also supplemented by other measures."

4.2 Impairment, Disability, Handicap, and Disabled or Handicapped

The International Classification of Impairments, Disabilities, and Handicaps [12] brings brand-new, outstandingly elaborated attempts at defining basic terms and aspects of the field of rehabilitation and the care of disabled or handicapped people. The classification schemes in this manual are offered "as frameworks to facilitate policy development in response to the problems, clarifying the potential contributions of medical services, rehabilitation facilities, and social welfare respectively."

The manual [12] uses the sequence

→	disease or disorder	→	impairment	→	disability	→	handicap
	(intrinsic situation)		(exteriorized)		(objectified)		(socialized)

In this graphic representation a problem-solving sequence is portrayed, intervention at the level of one element having the potential to modify succeeding elements. The authors state clearly that their representation does not simply suggest a linear progression along the full sequence; the situation is in fact more complex: handicap may result from impairment without the mediation of a state of disability; one can be impaired without being disabled, and disabled without being handicapped. We may add: one cannot be handicapped without being (or having been) impaired or disabled or having (had) a disease or disorder,[1] so it is a very logical, unidirectional sequence.

---

1 The authors' example of someone who can be handicapped without being disabled is the individual who has recovered from an acute psychotic episode but who bears the stigma of being a "mental patient"; his impairment or disability does not exist at the time the handicap develops

The distinctions between impairment, disability, and handicap are not new in the English-speaking countries. We are not aware of any close synonyms in other languages.

The distinction between the medicodiagnostic (or physiological, biological) aspects (impairment) and the physical and social consequences or effects, or between the intrinsic situation and the exterior aspects seems especially attractive. For the purpose of medical classification and other scientific or research activities, the proposed international classification has the highest value. The authors say that "it is perhaps vain to hope that the tide of careless usage can be reversed, but at least in serious discourse the logic of terminology should be exploited to reinforce the conceptual framework." Nevertheless, words like "handicap" or "handicapped" do have a stronger emotional value, and their psychological meaning should not be underestimated. It is possible and desirable for policy makers, field workers and administrators to use the words handicap and handicapped, provided they keep themselves informed with more sophisticated, differentiated, scientific background knowledge, such as that presented in the manual. We prefer the public at large to use the more dignified terms "handicap" or "handicapped" as well, just as handicapped persons themselves prefer them. It is our experience that these terms (or their derivatives) are becoming adopted in many languages, all over the world.

One point made by the authors should be noted especially: to say that someone has a disability (a handicap) carries much less risk of being dismissive and attributing stigma, than to say someone is disabled (handicapped).

With these annotations and qualifications we quote the definitions of the WHO manual [12].

4.2.1 Impairment

> In the context of health experience an impairment is any loss or abnormality of psychological, physiological, or anatomical structure or function.

4.2.2 Disability

> In the context of health experience, a disability is any restriction or lack (resulting from an impairment) of ability to perform an activity in the manner or within the range considered normal for a human being.

4.2.3 Handicap

> In the context of health experience, a handicap is a disadvantage for a given individual, resulting from an impairment or a disability, that limits or prevents the fulfillment of a role that is normal (depending on age, sex, and social and cultural factors) for that individual.

We have some fundamental problems with these three distinctions. Some basic disabilities are role dysfunctions, therefore producing a handicap more as a disability only; some disabilities (e.g., speech impediments) may also be marked as impairments. Six "survival roles" in the classification of handicaps are given: orientation/ physical independence/mobility/occupation/social integration/economic self-sufficiency; this designation is very impressive, but the communication role, as described under communication *disabilities,* is missing.

For these and other reasons we would persist in using the overall terms "handicap" and "handicapped person" as being more adequate for general use, and because the social aspects and consequences of an impairment or disability are the most striking ones. "Handicap . . . represents socialization of an impairment or disability" [12].

4.3 Other Definitions

4.3.1 "Disabled Person"

"The term 'disabled person' means any person unable to ensure by himself or herself, wholly or partly, the necessities of a normal individual and/or social life, as a result of a deficiency, either congenital or not, in his or her physical or mental capabilities" [13].

This formulation alone, compared with the definition of "handicap" from the Manual, illustrates that the term "handicapped person" is preferable. In addition, the relation with age, sex, and social and cultural factors, as well as the relation with one's peers, is missing.

4.3.2 "Disabled Person" Equated with "Handicapped Person"

" [A] person who, on account of an injury, disease or congenital deformity has serious difficulties or is unable to undertake activities which a person in the same group would usually be able to undertake" [8]. This is a formulation with good elements, but it is too compact, there by suggesting rather than defining.

4.3.3 "Physically Handicapped"

> The physically handicapped are understood to be those persons who have one or more functional disorders to at least a certain degree. Functional disorders are disorders in function of the legs, arms/hands, sight, hearing, speech, endurance (mainly heart/lungs), micturition, defecation, balance (incl. epilepsy), or other functions [14].

This is a useful working definition, but the words "to at least a certain degree" leave much to interpretation. The degree of a functional disorder is not a matter of an individual functional scale only but depends more on environmental, social, or cultural factors.

4.4 *Alternative Definitions*

We conclude with alternative definitions that we have formulated for "handicap," "handicapped person," and "rehabilitation," based on our preceding comments, and on discussions with handicapped persons.

4.4.1 Handicap

A handicap is a disadvantage or affliction suffered by a given individual in a given society resulting from an existing or threatening disease, disorder, deficiency, impairment, or disability, or combinations thereof, that limits or prevents the fulfillment of functions and roles which are normal – depending on age, sex, education, skill, and social and cultural factors – for that individual, and that affects the personal environment of the individual in such a way that the persons in this milieu experience, wholly or partly, comparable disadvantage or affliction.

4.4.2 Handicapped Person

A handicapped person is an individual in a given society who experiences serious, and/or long-lasting or permanent limitations in the fulfillment and development of functions and roles in all sectors of life which are normal for his or her age, sex, education, skill, and social and cultural factors, which limitations result from an existing or threatening disease, disorder, deficiency, impairment, or disability, or combinations thereof.

4.4.3 Rehabilitation

Rehabilitation is the comprehensive and coordinated complex of actions – whenever possible with the participation of the handicapped persons concerned – existing in individual and societal, general and group-specific measures, facilities, and provisions, offered to handicapped persons and those in their personal environment, so that they can maintain and develop themselves and feel integrated in all sectors of life and in all kinds of environments, to the highest possible level according to their stage of life and their aspirations in relation to their social and cultural environment.

It would have been possible to link elements from one definition with elements in the others, e.g., to replace the full definition of "handicapped person" simply with "a handicapped person is a person with a handicap", but we felt the need of autonomously readable formulations of the main terms.

References

1. WHO Expert Committee on Mental Health (1955) Fourth report. Legislation affecting psychiatric treatment. WHO Technical Report Series No. 98, Geneva
2. WHO Specialists Seminar (1955) Vienna
3. Fourteenth World Congress of Rehabilitation International (1980) Charter for the 80s. Winnipeg
4. Curran WS, Harding TW (1978) The law and mental health: Harmonizing objectives, a comparative survey of existing legislation together with guidelines for its assessment and alternative approaches to its improvement. WHO, New York
5. WHO (1976) Working document A 29/Inf. Doc. I, p 13
6. United Nations (1980) Criteria for assessing the effectiveness of child welfare policies. European social development program report SOA/ESDP/1979/3. UN, New York
7. WHO Expert Committee on Medical Rehabilitation (1969) Technical Report Series, No. 419
8. Council of Europe (1976) Glossary and list of principal terms used in the rehabilitation of disabled persons (English, French, German, Italian, and Dutch). Council of Europe, Strasbourg
9. Government of Nordrhein-Westfalen (1978) Landesbehindertenplan.
10. Moulijn CD (1964) Rehabilitation – the way to self-reliance for the handicapped (in Dutch). De Toorts, Haarlem
11. Zakharov M, Tsivilyov R (1978) Social security in the USSR. Progress, Moscow
12. WHO (1980) International classification of impairments, disabilities, and handicaps – a manual of classification relating to disease. WHO, New York
13. United Nations (1975) Declaration on the rights of disabled persons. UN, New York
14. Netherlands Central Bureau of Statistics (1978) The physically handicapped in the Netherlands 1971–1972, Part 6 (English summary)

Medicolegal Considerations in the Care of Severely Disabled Newborn in Canada

J. E. Magnet

The newborn mortality due to low birth weight and congenital deformity in Canada used to be cataclysmically high. Not long ago, many Canadian doctors thought that this was in the nature of things. The low-birth-weight infant suffered from an immature respiratory system which made breathing problematic. High mortality in deformed populations was perceived to be nature's way of eliminating its mistakes. Only in very selective cases did doctors intervene with the medical techniques then available.

Quantum leaps in all areas of pediatric medicine radically changed the survival potential in cases of low birth weight and congenital deformity. With this progress, many practitioners modified their views about treating seriously ill children. In 1962, under pressure from medical staff, hospitals in Toronto and Montreal established experimental neonatal intensive care centers to combat high infant mortality and long-term disability. The neonatal intensive care center is a small, highly specialized, interdisciplinary facility within the hospital, charged with front-line responsibility for treatment of serious pediatric cases.

These first units were remarkably successful in reducing infant mortality and long-term disability; consequently, the neonatal intensive care concept has spread throughout Canada. Today, twenty-nine units are in place, and several more are under construction or in the planning stage.

Although neonatal units experience a diverse case load, the majority of cases referred are low-birth-weight babies suffering from respiratory distress. These cases pose a dilemma because techniques for estimating their progress are unreliable. In one third of extreme asphyxiation cases, newborns, unlike adults, recover completely, even if spontaneous respiration is absent for 30 min. Two thirds of such patients, however, suffer severe damage, which in many cases destroys all capacity for socialization and self-awareness. Many become ventilator-dependent vegetables. A similar problem arises with the smaller population admitted for anomalies distinct from immaturity.

The success of Canadian neonatal intensive care has thus been accompanied by spectacular failures, which present intractable ethical and legal dilemmas. Neonatal intensive care makes life possible where it would have been unimaginable just yesterday. It ranks among our foremost achievements that nature's rejects are brought into the human family. But neonatal intensive care also leaves grossly deformed survivors, many of whom require permanent institutional care and never achieve a cognitive existence. In consequence, many Canadian doctors think that some seriously ill children should not be treated. All of the neonatal units practice selective treatment. With children considered unsalvageable, beyond feeding and warmth, care is simply withheld. The child is allowed to die, in some cases assisted in dying.

I have no intention of debating whether passive euthanasia of defective newborns is ethical or legal. All Canadian units practice selective treatment. Although under the child protection statutes, in three cases, Canadian courts have compelled treatment, it is more to the point to notice that, in defense of standard medical practice, Canadian law tolerates passive euthanasia in most cases. In some provinces, deputy attorneys general have suppressed prosecutions commenced by junior staff. Similarly, on the ethical front, while some have spoken out against selective treatment – most notably the Canadian psychiatric association – there is a distinct absence of outrage or clamor for public attention on the part of most interested Canadians. Having made these prefatory observations, I now wish to probe the *process* of selection for treatment, covering the following questions: (a) Who is the proper decision maker; (b) what is the proper procedure of decision; (c) what paramedical data properly figures in the decisional formula; (d) what is the proper role of the parents; and (e) what is the proper interim care?

Through practice Canadian neonatologists have developed standards of acceptable medical conduct to cope with such dilemmas. The standards are articulated in medical *practice* only, but nowhere drafted in writing. These practices condition the behavior of staff, including new members, in the units. A neonatology resident, for example, will observe, absorb, and be instructed in approved routines. My thesis is that such routines – which of course can be documented empirically – constitute an ethic of medical practice, professionally established in the systems of institutional medical life. These routines are practical ethics in the sense that this is what doctors actually do and feel pressured to do, even if they are not certain that what they are doing is right.

Being a lawyer by profession, I felt that nothing worthwhile could be said about passive euthanasia until I knew precisely what I was talking about. With the help of several student research assistants I interviewed over 200 neonatologists, pediatric specialists, nurses, residents, and parents in all Canadian neonatal intensive care centers. What follows are certain observations and conclusions emanating from that research program.

The first important issue was to identify the proper authority – whether the parents, the court, variously constituted committees, or the doctors – to make the decision for passive euthanasia of a defective newborn. The research results leave no doubt whatever that in Canada, a professional medical consensus exists on this issue. Where doctors conclude that treatment is improper, they retain decisional authority. Even of parents specifically demand surgery, doctors may refuse. "The decision is ours," a chief neonatologist told me, "but we take the parents' wishes into every consideration." One neurosurgeon said with great emphasis:

> In don't let the parents make the decision. I don't think it's fair letting the parents make the decision. I think we are the responsible ones to make the decision ... anyway, they should not be able to make a decision. They can't make a decision. Therefore, we make the decision for them after discussion back and forth with them.

Although the parents' views about treatment are important to the medical team, and figure significantly in the decision-making formula, sharp parental disagreement about medical protocol results in assertion of medical authority. Three mechanisms are employed: first, doctors use their control over the flow of medical information to the parents to shape the parents' views; second, coordinated interchanges between neonatal staff and the parents influence the latter; third, doctors refuse outright to treat, and advise the parents to seek care elsewhere. If the problem occurs because the parents refuse to consent to treatment that is deemed medically necessary, medical authority is asserted by the same means. In addition, the hospital legally compels treatment by application under the child protection statues for court-ordered substituted consent to proceed.

The established consensus that doctors are the proper decision-makers results in certain disquieting phenomena encountered repeatedly throughout my research. The most obvious is a failure to inform parents, adequately and objectively, of available medical alternatives. Associated with this is a failure to inform parents of actual medical decisions which have been taken about their child, and which will result in death. Parents usually are not told, for example, that a decision was made not to ventilate their child, or that ventilation having been initiated, a subsequent decision was made to turn the ventilator off. Parents may not be told about available transplantation if the doctors opt for passive euthanasia. I found several instances where doctors bypassed established hospital channels – such as the transplant committee – after having made a decision not to treat a particular newborn. I also discovered numerous cases where doctors initiated treatment without parental, court, or committee consent.

Existing Canadian law on informed consent is inadequate to meet the challenge of these cases. The speed required for decisions in the intensive care nursery precludes long explanations and court or committee proceedings. Medical opinion in these cases, being interdisciplinary, frequently resists easy, nontechnical summation in the form of yes or no options. Parents are often overwrought emotionally when confronted with a severely damaged newborn. It is unrealistic in these circumstances to postulate a cold, rational risk-benefit analysis by the parents.

Legal control by the familiar adversary, process of civil and criminal litigation is inappropriate and unproductive in governing such abuses. One should consider whether a more appropriate assertion of legal authority would be accomplished through internal administrative control by the hospital's medical agencies. An internal unit could develop standards and guidelines, continually revised in light of mandatory research, for the contentious cases that repeatedly occur in the intensive care nursery. The process could be given teeth in the form of powers of internal discipline. The disciplinary machinery could be engaged by internal or external (parent-initiated) complaint. This form of control would improve the quality of medicine through a continuous program of review and research, and would generate standards having the sanction of those in a position to know. Of course, if the hospital were negligent in its review and supervision of the process, as by articulating indefensible standards, or failing to initiate continuing review and research, civil liability would follow in the ordinary way.

Existing ethical precepts require redefinition in light of these cases. The models of self-determination and privacy are grossly artificial when applied to the newborn. Even the language of "substituted consent" smacks of unreality. We need clear-headed, ethical analysis of the smaller issues involved – such as the proper decision-maker or decisional process.

A second dilemma relates to the procedure by which decisions to withhold treatment are made. Assuming that doctors are the decision-makers, which doctors should decide, and, if more than one, what procedures should govern the decision-making process? Established Canadian routines reveal a professional consensus on that issue. While the neonatologist retains formal responsibility for the decision, established procedure requires that his formal authority be tempered by the opinions of interdisciplinary specialists. Institutional practice requires the neonatologist to initiate appropriate consultation with pediatric colleagues in order to coordinate a decision under his leadership.

The interdisciplinary approach to serious neonatal cases is a key rationale for the neonatal unit. Meningomyelocele, for example, produces deficiencies in urological, neurological, and orthopedic functioning. A urologist would not be competent to treat meningomyelocele, but, as a member of the neonatal team, he could illuminate for other doctors whether the urological system was repairable, and describe the expected quality of the child's life from a urological point of view. Neurological and orthopedic data would be separately assessed by pediatric neurologists and orthopedists. The neonatologist collates, assembles, and discusses all the data with participating members. Decision-making follows a team approach.

The research revealed that the interdisciplinary approach is vulnerable. Where an anomaly of one system is pronounced, the specialist evaluating that system becomes the pivotal person. Not uncommonly, that doctor regards the patient as his or hers alone. This may affect the doctor's willingness to consult with or accept the advice of pediatric colleagues.

In neurosurgical cases, this problem is conspicuous. Neurosurgeons jealously guard their perceived prerogative of deciding whether to operate. Consultation withers; the interdisciplinary approach shatters. A one-man approach destroys the interdisciplinary raison d'être of neonatal intensive care and undercuts the demonstrated strength of its team approach to medicine. An ultrasophisticated facility metamorphoses into a neurosurgical satellite.

What has Canadian law contributed to resolving these difficulties? Some hospital regulatory statutes stipulate an obligation to consult in serious cases. However, enforcement is through the torts system, thus depending on parent-initiated complaint to the courts. This has never happened. The Canadian Medical Association's Code of Ethics requires consultation acceptable to the patient when diagnosis or treatment is difficult or obscure. Again, the problem is enforcement through the torts system, or by parent-initiated complaint to an external body, the College of Physicians and Surgeons. More successful is the requirement to consult imposed by the bylaws of many hospitals. The bylaws are enforceable by informal internal administrative discipline. One should consider whether, if refined, this might prove useful. Continuing review and research could enlighten decision-making procedures which could be adopted as standards by the hospital's medical agencies. The standards could be enforced by inspection. Disciplinary machinery capable of being set in motion by internal or external complaint would give the process clout. Ultimate court control would enter only if the hospital were negligent in establishing a research, review, and inspection program.

A third problem is the information which must be gathered prior to deciding to withhold treatment. Neonatologists generally agree that the anticipated quality of life must be determined by extensive medical assessments of the child's separate body systems. "Quality of life" refers to the child's potential for physical and mental development, and environmental factors which have a bearing on his potential for development. Where the anticipated quality of life does not decisively indicate whether treatment should be initiated, the parents' wishes are ascertained and figure as a separate factor in deciding whether to treat.

The use of socioeconomic and personal data in medical decision making is a special problem. Most Canadian neonatal centers take the initiative in collecting paramedical facts to weigh in the decision-making process.

Many units employ social workers as paramedical fact-gatherers. They are charged with responsibility for interviewing the family and preparing reports containing paramedical data. The reports are attached directly to the child's medical chart.

The following is a list of the paramedical data repeatedly emphasized as relevant during the course of our research:

1. The marital status of the baby's parents
2. The nature of the parents, including such things as intelligence and psychological adaptability
3. The effect which addition of a deformed child would have on the family
4. The economic position of the baby's family
5. The ability of the parents to have additional children
6. The presence of mental retardation

Such factors are considered important because, as a chief neonatologist told me:

> There is no use in sending a baby who required complicated management and care back to a mother who is unmarried, who has an I.Q. of 70 and is quite unable to deal with it. She may have part-time work or something like that, or six other kids in the family. We know it's not going to work . . .

A cardiologist said you *have* to consider:

> . . . if you are dealing with a [poor] psychological situation . . . if you fix this child surgically, is he going to make it in the post surgery? . . . It's a very big part of pediatrics.

Canadian law again has little to contribute to the debate about use of paramedical data in medical decision-making. The Medical Association's Code of Ethics, enforceable through the torts system, requires doctors to consider the patient's well-being first. One should consider whether appropriate legal intervention could come from an internal disciplinary body supported by continuous review, research, and standard-setting. If all units researched the use to paramedical data and methods of quality control, would not medical practice improve? Clearly, this has to be a major objective of legal control.

A final dilemma concerns the proper care to be provided to a child whom the doctors decide not to treat actively. There is general agreement that the child should be fed, kept warm, and have its fluids managed. The consensus is that nothing further should be done for it. No antibiotics should be administered, no minor surgery performed, and no resuscitation attempted.

If anything, Canadian law relevant to interim care has had a deleterious effect on medical practice. The nineteenth-century common law cases hold that any omission of life-saving essentials, including medical treatment, is sufficient to engage the manslaughter and murder sections of the *Criminal Code*, in a hospital context. As previously mentioned, prosecutions have been started on this basis, but subsequently discontinued. In addition, Sect. 199 of the *Criminal Code* imposes a special duty on physicians who commence treatment to continue if failure to treat could be dangerous to life. These provisions, general in their application, need rethinking as applied to the intensive care nursery. It would be most unfortunate if a widely publicized prosecution were commenced, for it would hinder the entire development of neonatal practice. Would not it be preferable to assert legal control through an internal administrative organ, based on a sound program of research and review? In this way, the twin goals of improving the quality of medicine and providing machinery to settle disputes swiftly, certainly, and with justice, could be harmonized.

Rehabilitation of Heroin Addicts with Methadone Maintenance: A Five-Year Clinical Experience

R. Stolberg-Acosta and L. Seda-Mendoza

Ever since Nyswander, Dole and other researchers [20] published their early works on the treatment of heroin addicts with methadone, a synthetic opiate derivate, this modality has evolved into one of the most widely used treatment alternatives [22, 35] for heroin addicts in the United States. At present, it is administered to nearly one-third (32%) of all U.S. heroin addicts under treatment [35].

Althougth methadone was initially successful and is still considered the most effective treatment for heroin addiction [22, 25, 37], concern has grown owing to the mounting number of objections and drawbacks associated with it that have been reported in the literature over the years [9, 16, 17, 19, 22, 26, 32]. Some of these are:

1. Methadone maintenance treatment programs have had relatively low success in producing significant rates of abstinence for extended periods of time once treatment is terminated. Accordingly, relapse to drug-taking behavior has been high [1, 4, 5, 6, 7, 8, 27, 30, 34, 35], which has led some researchers to urge that the methadone modality be seen as a strategy of indefinite duration, and that no pressures be applied to detoxify [7, 8, 34, 35]. This has brought the objection from critics that methadone treatment is merely the substitution of one addiction for another.
2. Methadone maintenance has been consistently associated in the literature with an increase in and/or a shift to the use of other nonopiate addictive substances, predominantly alcohol [2, 4, 10, 11, 15, 21, 23, 24, 29, 30, 33, 34, 35]. Estimates of concurrent alcohol abuse begin at 10% in a given population [35].
3. Reports on criminal activity, acknowledged as a difficult parameter to measure, have shown uncertain, or at best, mixed trends. In general, although the number of drug-related offenses has dramatically dropped, the same cannot be categorically stated for non-drug-related crimes [3, 18, 31].
4. Another series of associated problems reported in the literature with a certain consistency has been the creation of methadone "black markets" through illegal diversion of the substance with unauthorized self-medication and primary methadone addiction as sequelae [12, 13, 14, 28].

On the other hand, defense of methadone maintenance has been based on two points:

1. Evaluation of its overall effectiveness should take into consideration the fact that the population served is a high-risk, hard-core, socially deprived population and therefore, any measure of rehabilitative success is significant [25, 37].
2. Although methadone has its acknowledged drawbacks, no other treatment alter-

native has had a similar measure of success and patient acceptance within this group [25, 37].

Experience on the island of Puerto Rico, a Commonwealth of the United States, with methadone maintenance treatment programs has tended to mirror overall trends in the United States. Initially established in 1969 as an experimental project, by 1972–73 it had evolved into a fully established program, serving 900–1300 heroin addicts per year at seven different treatment centers. Follow-up of the treated population has been facilitated through the establishment of a computerized information bank system.

On the basis of a 5-year active clientele programm population (1973–1978, $n = 1847$) for which reliable data is available, the population served is a relatively homogeneous Hispanic, Spanish-speaking urban population with the following demographic characteristics: 92% are male, 8% are female; 78% are married or living in common-law relationships, 14% are divorced or separated, and 6% have never married; the median age upon admission was 26.2 years with the range 18–54. The median number of school years completed was 6, and the socioeconomic level was predominantly low (84%).

Median age of beginning heroin use was 17 years with 22% indicating onset of addiction between 12 and 14 years of age. At the time of admission there was some evidence of current multiple drug use and alcohol abuse among program participants. Approximately 12% reflected regular use of a nonopiate drug, predominantly minor tranquilizers, although 72% reported having experimented with other substances in the past. Of the 89% who reported using alcoholic beverages, 21% reflected definite problem drinking or alcoholism. Median length of stay in the programm is 3.8 years. Of the 46% who had been charged with two or more non-drug-related criminal offenses, 16% had been convicted. Of a total of 34% charged with drug-related offenses, 29% had been convicted. Approximately one-third (37%) were working at the time of admission.

Services rendered to clientele in the program consisted of methadone dispensa-

Table 1. Results of 2-year follow-up ($n = 1847$)

	Prevalence (%)		Net gain/loss
	At admission date	At 2-year follow-up	
Illicit nonopiate[a] substance abuse (2 months or more)	12	35	+23%
Alcohol abuse[a]/alcoholism (2 months or more)	21	54	+33%
Drug-related offenses (convictions)	16	3	−13%
Working (1 months or more)	37	44	+ 7%

[a] Approximately 17% of population fall into both categories.

Abstinence attempt	Drug-free-1 year later
17% ($n = 214$)	4.3% ($n = 80$)

tion on a day-to-day basis, weekly individual and/or group therapy sessions, occupational therapy, recreational activities, vocational rehabilitation counseling, and remedial teaching geared to basic writing and reading skills where applicable. Average daily maintenance dosis was in the range of 40–60 mg. Clientele was encouraged to gradually decrease methadone intake in an individualized manner.

The 2- and 3-year follow-ups of this population (see Table 1) offered the following findings. Of the total population, some 214 (17%) had attempted one or more program-sponsored detoxification and abstension periods after gradual dose decrease. Average time elapsed between admission and detoxification was 1.83 years. Of the 214, 80 (4.3%) were drug free 1 year later. Seen from another perspective, some 291 abstinence attempts were made, which indicates a successful attempt rate of 27%.

As Table 1 shows, there was a significant increase in the trend to simultaneous alcohol and/or multiple drug abuse in this population. Some researchers have proposed the explanation that with effective blockade of the pleasure-producing effect of opiates by methadone, clients tend to shift to other substances not affected by methadone in search of "high."

Occupational status reflected some percentage gains, while convictions on drug-related offenses showed the greatest improvements. These last two paramters reflect what some authors such as Goldstein [14] have referred to as the "life-style-stabilizing potentiality" of such a modality.

Judging from results, one may at first glance be tempted to conclude that cost- and effort-wise methadone maintenance modality has not achieved desirable standards. The crux of the issue lies, however, in the fact that although gains have been modest, methadone maintenance may very well be the only alternative readily available to address and provide solutions, however partial, to the needs of a segment of the addict population characterized by marginal social functioning and chronic pharmacological deterioration.

References

1. Anderson GS (1975) Clients and outcomes of a methadone treatment program. Int J Addict 10: 937–948
2. Bihari B (1974) Alcoholism and methadone maintenance. Am J Drug Alcohol Abuse 1: 79–87
3. Bowden CH (1978) Arrests before and during methadone maintenance. Int J Addict 13: 921–931
4. Cohen M, Stimmel B (1979) Chemotherapy: methadone in rehabilitation and treatment aspects of drug dependence. CRC, Boca Raton
5. Cushman PJr (1978) Methadone maintenance: long term follow-up of detoxified patients. Ann NY Acad Sci 311: 165–172
6. Cushman PJr (1977) Ten years of methadone maintenance treatment: some clinical observations. Am J Drug Alcohol Abuse 4: 543–553
7. Dole VP, Joseph H (1977) Methadone maintenance: outcome after termination. NY State J Med 77: 1409–1412
8. Dole VP, Joseph H (1978) Long-term outcome of patients treated with methadone maintenance. Ann NY Acad Sci 311: 181–189
9. Epstein EJ (1974) Methadone, the furlong hope. Public Interest 36: 3–24
10. Gearing FR (1971) Evaluation of methadone maintenance treatment programs. In: Einstein S (ed) Methadone maintenance. Dekker, New York, pp 171–197
11. Gearing FR (1977) Report on evaluation of methadone maintenance problems; alcoholism and drug abuse problems. Int J Addict 290: 769–774

12. Goldman FR, Thistel CI (1978) Division of methadone: illicit methadone use among applicants to two metropolitan drug abuse programs. Int J Addict 13: 855–862
13. Goldstein A (1976) Can the community be protected against the hazards of take home methadone? (Proceedings) Natl Inst Drug Abuse Res Monogr Ser 8: 62–63
14. Goldstein A (1975) On the role of chemotherapy in the treatment of heroin addiction. Am J Drug Alcohol Abuse 2 (3–4): 279–288
15. Gould LC (1974) Changing patterns of multiple drug use among applicants to a multi-modality drug treatment program. Arch Gen Psychiatry 31: 408–413
16. Gossop M (1978) A review of the evidence for methadone maintenance as a treatment for narcotic addiction. Lancet 1: 812–815
17. Greaves D (1972) Medicine, methadone, and morality. Int Pharmacopsychiatry 7: 71–77
18. Jacobs PE, Doft EB, Karras A, Koger J (1978) Methadone and criminality: a suburban perspective. Am J Drug Alcohol Abuse 5: 51–58
19. Jacobs PE, Doft EB, Karras A, Koger J (1979) Methadone evaluation: some additional thoughts. Int J Addict 14: 207–213
20. Jaffe J, Zaks M, Washington E (1969) Experience with the use of methadone in a multi-modality program for the treatment of narcotic users. Int J Addict 4: 481–490
21. Jain NC, Budd R, Olson B, Sneath T (1977) Patterns of drug use among methadone maintenance patients in Los Angeles county. Bull Narc 29 (2): 45–53
22. Kaim SC (1976) Evolution of the national academy of sciences study of naltrexone. Natl Inst Drug Abuse Monogr Ser 9
23. Liebson I, Bieglow G, Flamer R (1973) Alcoholism among methadone patients, a specific treatment method. Am J Psychiatry 130: 483–485
24. Maddux JF, Elliot B (1975) Problem drinkers among patients on methadone. Am J Drug Alcohol Abuse 2: 245–254
25. Newman RG (1976) Methadone maintenance treatment: will it survive? NY State J Med 76: 1536–1537
26. Peck DB, Cox TJ (1976) Methadone maintenance: a review and critique. Br J Addict 71: 369–376
27. Perkins ME, Bloch HI (1971) A study of some failures in methadone treatment. Am J Psychiatry 128: 47–51
28. Resnick RB (1977) Problems of methadone diversion and implications for control. Int J Addict 12: 803–806
29. Scott NR, Winslow WW, Gorman DG (1973) Epidemiology of alcoholism in a methadone maintenance programm. Proceedings of the fifth national conference on methadone treatment, New York, pp 284–287
30. Scott NR, Orzen W, Musillo C, Cole ET (1973) Methadone in the southwest; a three-year follow-up of chicano heroin addicts. Am J Orthopsychiatry 43: 355–361
31. Sechrest DK (1979) Methadone programs and crime reduction, a comparison of New York and California addicts. Int J Addict 14: 377–400
32. Senay EC (1972) Critique of theories of methadone use. Int Pharmacopsychiatry 71: 64–70
33. Siassi I, Alston DC (1976) Methadone maintenance and the problem with alcohol. Am J Drug Alcohol Abuse 3: 267–277
34. Stimmel B, Rabin J (1974) The ability to remain abstinent upon leaving methadone maintenance, a prospective study. Am J Drug Alcohol Abuse 1: 379–391
35. Stimmel B, Cohen M (1978) Alcoholism and polydrug abuse in persons on methadone maintenance. Ann NY Acad Sci 311: 99–109
36. Wallace DB, Keil TJ (1978) Illicit opiate use during methadone maintenance. Int J Addict 13: 241–247
37. Zinberg NE (1977) Sounding board. The crisis in methadone maintenance. N Engl J Med 296: 1000–1002

Rehabilitation of Traumatic Brain-injured Patients

A. Ohry and J. Rattok

1 Introduction

There is a rising number of brain-injured patients (BIP), due to road traffic accidents, work or sport injuries, and gunshot wounds. Rehabilitation centers are increasingly aware (unfortunately belatedly) of these patients' particular meeds, calling for special remedial programs. All the tremendous efforts directed toward the utmost rehabilitative results may be in vain if the intellectual, cognitive, neuropsychological, and psychosocial aspects are neglected during the rehabilitation process.

Unlike receptive or expressive defects, cognitive dysfunction is not necessarily associated with injury to a particular cortical area. Therefore, most of the "failures" in the rehabilitation of these patients are results of these cognitive-intellectual impairments and of the lack of a comprehensive approach. We will also "fail" if there is no receptive and understanding family or employer. Thus the rehabilitation efforts must also include the participation of "significant others."

A special new programm for BIPs has been established in Tel Aviv and New York. During the few years since the program was started, several ethical issues have been raised which we would like to share in this paper.

2 Definition of a BIP

A BIP is usually a young adult who, prior to injury, was a healthy and productive working person with no record of neurologic or psychiatric problems. Due to a usually external trauma the patient loses his or her consciousness for a relatively long period of time and suffers from various degrees of post-traumatic amnesia. Following resuscitation and neurosurgical treatment, the patient wakes up and is later transferred to a rehabilitation center. The severe BIP may suffer from locomotive, sensory, and autonomic problems, speech and communication disturbances, visual or auditory impairments, etc. Approximately one-third of BIPs will not be able to benefit fully from rehabilitation services because of cognitive, intellectual, behavioral, and psychosocial problems. Thus, all efforts must be made to treat these aspects of brain injury particularly.

3 Ethical and Medicolegal Considerations

Participation in a long-range rehabilitation program requires persistence, concentration, attention, and full cooperation on the patient's part. Some of these capabilities may be impaired, and will have to be worked on by the rehabilitation team. Consent to participate in such a program has to be given by the patient and his family. However, if the BIPs judgement is impaired, or if he does not exactly know which of his faculties are damaged, what is the value of his consent? The best results the rehabilitation programm can obtain depend on the patient's motivation. But many BIPs insist they are not impaired intellectually, which is part of the denial phenomenon typical in these injuries. In our view, after a period of assessment, the patient should be informed of his problem (in a tactful manner), and the improvements which may be expected as a result of the programm should be explained to him or her.

Another problem to be faced is the selection of patients from a vast number of candidates. We have developed several criteria for selection: IQ, age, time elapsed since injury, and lack of neurological and psychiatric troubles prior to injury. But how can we predict after selection who will benefit most from the programm? Our assessment system contains neuropsychological, behavioral, and social tests designed to help in this regard.

When is the optimal moment to start the BIP on our programm? Some say immediately upon his or her awakening from the prolonged coma, at which point orientation, attention, and concentration must be evaluated. However, we lack specialized people and sufficient funds to start treatment so early on so many patients. We therefore take the view that if severe cognitive defects are still present about 1 year after injury, the patient is "ripe" for our program.

Finally, we would like to point out that traditional neurological and psychological evaluation methods generally accepted by various public authorities do not accurately reflect the actual abilities and inabilities of BIPs. Our experience shows, for example, that high IQs achieved by BIPs do not automatically translate into everyday living skills. Thus, we must ask whether a BIP with a good IQ who has nevertheless lost his general integrative capacity should be permitted to drive a car. It is also necessary to decide the extent of such a person's legal responsibility as a witness in court or in other legal situations.

All these important questions await answers. We do, however, have a very affirmative answer based on our experience as to this program's value. We are convinced of its success in improving the quality of the BIPs personal, vocational, and social life.

Prostheses for Disabled Elderly Amputees

T. Mashiah and A. Mashiah

In aged patients who have advanced peripheral occlusive arterial diseases and diabetes mellitus, together with mental confusion, there are no premonitory symptoms to herald the onset of gangrene, and amputation of the limb becomes a life-saving procedure [1].

For the past few years the expenses for fitting a limb prosthesis have been paid from public funds. As a result the patient or his family very often demands a prosthesis, and the cardinal question is, "Does every elderly amputee need prosthetic rehabilitation?"

In Israel, especially in the Tel Aviv area, the geriatric percentage of the population is getting higher (Table 1), and ever more elderly amputees are in need of rehabilitation.

Table 1. Geriatric population (%) to date

	1961	1972	1976	1982
Tel Aviv	6.6%	12.8%	15.9%	17.3%
Israel	3.9%	7.7%	8.9%	

Harzfeld Hospital, a 304-bed geriatric rehabilitation center and hospital for chronic diseases, which is situated at Gedera, south of Tel-Aviv, admits patients who have undergone lower limb amputation and require rehabilitation. The following is a review of lower limb amputees hospitalized in Harzfeld over the 5-year period from 1975–1979.

1 Patients and Methods

The patients had their amputations in hospitals from the Gush Dan and the Shifela areas and were sent to Harzfeld hospital 7–10 days postoperatively. Those in good mental and physical state were fitted with a prosthesis while those in poorer condition were rehabilitated in a wheelchair. On becoming sufficiently independent they were sent home or to an old-age home.

In the years 1975–1979, 102 lower limb amputees were admitted, their age ranging from 57 to 91 years (mean 71.9); 63 were men and 39 were women. Of the patients, 43 had below-knee amputation, 56 above-knee. There were 24 bilateral amputations; eight of these were below-knee and six above-knee. Ten patients had combined levels of amputation.

The orientation of 61 of the patients on admission was good, while the remaining 41 were in different stages of mental confusion. There were 19 patients who had undergone reconstructive vascular surgery, including major operations of more than one procedure. Twelve patients had had surgical or phenol sympathectomy. These procedures postponed the need for amputation for 2 months to 3 years [2].

2 Results and Discussion

2.1 Rehabilitation

The 61 patients who were admitted in good mental and physical condition were able to be rehabilitate 25 with prosthesis, 36 in a wheelchair. Of the 41 patients who were not fit for rehabilitation, 32 died in the hospital, 1 week to 2 years after amputation (mean of 10 weeks).

Usually, 6 weeks enough for rehabilitation in a wheelchair, and most of the patients achieved a fully, active daily life. Once the decision for wheelchair rehabilitation had been made, the rehabilitation team [3] and the family prepared the patient to leave the hospital in 2 months' time. Of the 36 patients in this group, 26 went home on time. The time needed for fully prosthetic rehabilitation was 3–6 months with a mean of 4.5 months [4].

2.2 Use of Prosthesis at Home

Only 12 of 25 (48%) of those who went home with a prosthesis (8 of 16 men and 4 of 9 women) are still using it regularly, among them, a 90-year-old man and an 83-year-old woman. A 57-year-old man, a double amputee (one side above the knee), is using his prosthesis and is back to working full time on his farm.

Some of the rest use the prosthesis only in public, to maintain their physical self-image. It has been determined that 60%–70% of elderly amputees never use their prosthesis.

2.3 Survival

The length of survival of the 25 patients with prosthetic rehabilitation ranged from 5 months to 4 years, with a mean of 27 months.

3 Factors Preventing Rehabilitation

3.1 Concomitant Disease

Most of our patients, 69 of 102 (67.6%) had concomitant disorders such as myocardial insufficiency, hypertension, cerebrovascular insufficiency, and chronic lung disease.

3.2 Postoperative Complications

Pneumonia, sepsis, myocardial infarction and cerebrovascular accidents were the causes of death in 32 of our amputees.

3.3 Brain Insufficiency

Of 41 unrehabilitated lower limb amputees, 30 were in very poor mental condition.

3.4 Poor Musculoskeletal Condition

Eleven could not be rehabilitated due to muscle or joint disorders such as fixed flexion contractures and marked spasticity, motor paralysis after CVA and proximal muscle weakness.

3.5 Cardiopulmonary Insufficiency

A great amount of energy is needed to use crutches and above-knee limb prosthesis; below-knee limb prosthesis requires less.

Many older people with heart failure complain of extreme fatigue and inability to walk more than a few steps. Other elderly live for several years with such poor lung function, that even slight exertion causes severe breathlessness; such patients are unfit for prostetic rehabilitation. However, an aged amputee who can use crutches properly can be fitted with a limb prosthesis either above or below the knee.

3.6 Underlying Disease

Of our patients, 78 (76.4%) were diabetic, and of these 22 were also arteriosclerotic. In 24 patients, arteriosclerotic peripheral vascular disease was the primary cause of the amputation.

It is clear that both diabetes mellitus and arteriosclerosis are generalized diseases, affecting the arteries of both legs (Fig. 1). Very often the blood supply to the other leg of a single amputee is poor (Fig. 2), and the risk of becoming a double amputee is very high.

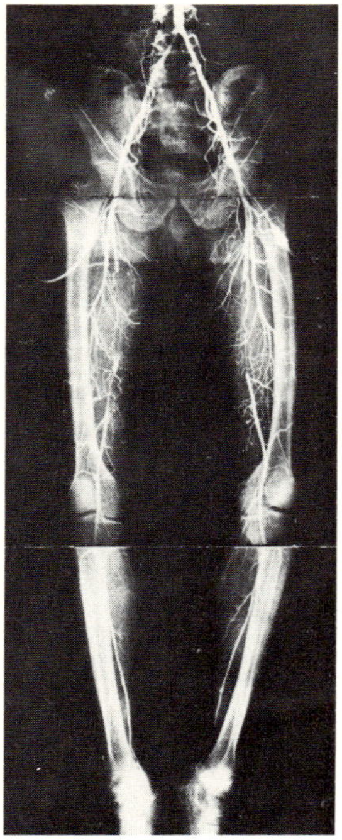

Fig. 1. Multi foci changes in the arteries of a lower limb arteriosclerotic patient

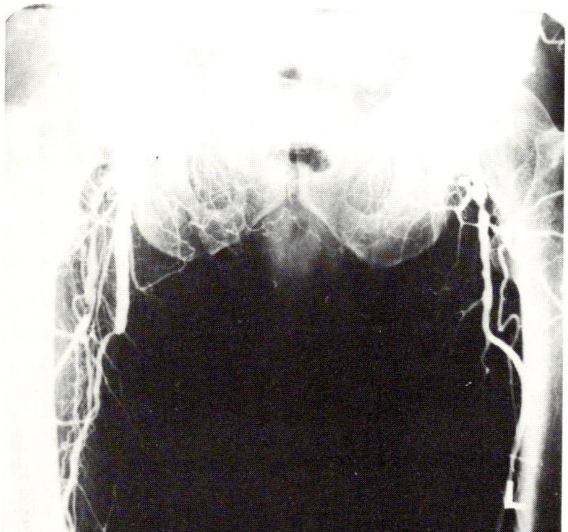

Fig. 2. Severe occlusive changes in arteries of both legs in a diabetic amputee. *L*, left

3.7 Double Amputation

Among our aged one-leg amputees, 24 (23.5%) had developed ischemia of the other leg, which had to be amputated in 2 years time. Only one of these could be rehabilitated with double limb prosthesis.

4 Conclusion

Concomitant disease, brain failure and poor supply to the other leg hindered the rehabilitation of the elderly amputees. One-third of them were satisfactorily rehabilitated in wheelchairs and one-fourth with a prosthesis. Only 48% of those who went home with a prosthesis are still using it. They constitute less than 12% of the total number of our amputees.

In view of the fact that only 11.6% of our patients could be considered successfully rehabilitated with prostheses, and in light of the effort and expense [5] involved in prosthetic rehabilitation, we advocate a special selective approach.

References

1. Miller MB (1979) Advanced occlusion arterial disease (gang.) in the aged and decision for amputation. J Am Geriatr Soc 22: 321
2. Devas MB (1976) Surgery for the aged. Ann R Coll Surg Engl 58: 15–24
3. Brocklehurst JC (1978) Geriatric medicine and gerontology. 2nd edn. Churchill Livingstone, Edinburgh, p 558

The Effect of Legal Settlement on Work Disability Following Compensable Injury

G. Mendelson*

1 Introduction

There is a widely held belief, shared by many lawyers and by some medical practitioners, that following compensable injuries litigants improve and return to gainful employment within a relatively short time of the settlement of their claim, irrespective of the legal outcome.

There is a fairly large body of literature on this topic, and the various terms used to describe the injured person reflect some of the contradictory views of the origin of the disability shown by the claimant, such as 'litigation neurosis,' 'compensation neurosis,' and 'accident neurosis.' These terms imply that the so-called neurosis is etiologically related to the process of litigation and its possible outcome of monetary compensation. Indeed, compensation neurosis has been defined by Kennedy as "a state of mind, born out of fear, kept alive by avarice, stimulated by lawyers and cured by verdict" [1].

The view that patients are "cured by verdict" was forcefully supported by the late Henry Miller, who reported a series of 50 patients who were, with one exception, symptom-free when followed up 2 years after settlement of their claim [2]. A similar observation was reported by Culpan and Taylor, who stated that of eight patients who had not resumed work at the time of settlement of personal injury claims, "it appeared" that all but one were back at work within a year or so [3]. Both these studies describe patients referred for assessment by lawyers or insurance companies: in Miller's case for a neurological opinion, and in that of Culpan and Taylor for psychiatric evaluation. A different picture of the outcome of personal injury claims is presented by Thompson. His report on 500 cases of posttraumatic psychoneurosis includes 190 patients interviewed after the conclusion of all litigation: 15% of these reported that "they were better after litigation had been terminated" [4].

A report on patients treated by a family practitioner following industrial or automobile accidents includes specific information on occupational disability. Of a total of 82 patients described by Balla and Moraitis, 42 were not working at the time of settlement. Of these 42 patients, 31 remained unemployed after an average period of 25 months following the settlement of their claim [5]. A more recent study performed for the Workers' Compensation Board in New South Wales showed that of 175 litigants who were younger than the statutory retirement age when surveyed, 62 (35%) were not working after a minimum period of 3 years from the finalization of their claim [6].

* Sister Nanete Fitzgibbon provided valuable assistance during the follow-up phase of this study

While it can be argued that occupational disability is perhaps not the most sensitive criterion of physical and emotional well-being, it is a convenient measure, as it can be easily ascertained during an interview as distinct from complex assessment that would be required to quantify pain, anxiety, depression, and other symptoms. In this study, work disability has been used as the criterion of outcome in a group of litigants referred to the author for psychiatric treatment or psychiatric assessment for legal purposes.

2 Patients and Methods

The files of 262 patients who were involved in litigation following personal injury sustained during industrial or automobile accidents were reviewed; the patients were personally assessed by the author during a 4-year period. After establishing whether or not the patient's claim had been settled, those patients whose litigation had concluded were contacted and asked whether they were continuing to receive medical treatment, whether they continued to experience symptoms, and whether they had resumed work either prior to settlement or since.

Statistical analysis was carried out of variables of personal data such as sex, age, marital status, occupation, type of accident, source of referral, nature of physical injury and psychiatric diagnosis, whether or not surgery had been performed, duration of litigation, and the time elapsed from settlement to follow-up. The patient's country of birth was also recorded.

Follow-up was by telephone, letter, or personal interview; a trained nursing sister with prior experience in epidemiological research assisted in the study.

3 Results

In 161 cases legal proceedings were continuing, thus leaving 101 patient files for analysis. The patients whose claims had been settled included 61 men and 40 women; 59 of these patients had been injured in industrial accidents and 42 in automobile accidents. Some clinical details on these patients are shown in Table 1.

Table 1. Clinical details of patients surveyed

		AA ($n=42$)	WC ($n=59$)
Men ($n=61$)		19	42
Women ($n=40$)		23	17
Age (years)	Mean	39.7	43.7
	SD	13.4	9.9
Duration of litigation (months):	Mean	31.7	36.3
	SD	14.2	15.7
Australian-born		17	14
Immigrants		25	45
Professional, clerical, and sales personnel		16	7
Skilled and semiskilled laborers		26	52

AA, automobile accident; *WC*, workers' compensation

The mean age of the group at time of settlement was 42.1 years (SD 11.6; range 20–68 years); the mean interval between injury and settlement was 34.7 months (SD 15.1; range 12–81 months).

Among the 101 patients there were 31 Australian-born and 70 born elsewhere. The main groups of foreign-born patients came from Greece (16%), Turkey (14%), Italy (8%), Egypt (7%), and Yugoslavia (5%) (see Table 2).

The range of occupations is shown in Table 3. There was a significant difference in the distribution of occupational groups, with professional, technical, and clerical workers overrepresented among litigants following automobile accidents, whereas tradesmen, production workers, and laborers were overrepresented among those seeking compensation following industrial accidents.

Table 2. Country of birth according to type of accident

	AA	WC
Australia	17	14
Greece	6	10
Turkey	2	12
Italy	1	7
Egypt	3	4
Yugoslavia	2	3
United Kingdom	3	1
Latvia	1	2
Poland	3	0
Czechoslovakia	1	1
Germany	2	0
Lebanon	1	1
Malta	0	2
Austria	0	1
Rumania	0	1

Table 3. Occupation[a] according to sex and type of accident

	AA		WC	
	M	F	M	F
Professional, technical and related workers	6	3	1	0
Administrative and managerial	0	0	1	0
Clerical	1	4	1	1
Sales	0	2	1	1
Farm, forest and related	1	0	1	0
Transport and communication	0	0	2	1
Tradesmen, production workers and laborers	7	7	31	12
Service and recreation	5	6	4	2

[a] Occupations are coded according to the Australian Bureau of Statistics Classification of Occupations, issued for the 1976 population census

$\chi^2 = 25.8$; $P < 0.001$ (Analysis of occupation × accident type)

There were 36 patients referred for treatment either by a family doctor or by another specialist; 53 patients were referred for psychiatric assessment by a lawyer acting on the patient's behalf, while 12 patients were referred for assessment on behalf of the insurance company (Table 4).

Table 4. Sources of referral of patients surveyed, according to type of accident

	A (n=42)	A (n=59)
Family doctor	16	13
Medical specialist	2	5
Litigant's lawyer	22	31
Insurer's lawyer	2	10

Although there was no difference between those injured in work-related accidents and those injured in automobile accidents in the proportion of different psychiatric conditions diagnosed (Table 5), there was a significant difference in the pattern of

Table 5. Psychiatric diagnosis according to type of accident

	AA (n=42)	WC (n=59)
Generalized anxiety disorder	14	16
Reactive depression	5	1
Mixed depression/anxiety	16	30
Conversion reaction	1	3
Schizophrenic reaction	0	1
Psychosomatic illness	0	2
Posttraumatic anxiety	5	2
None	1	4

Table 6. Nature of injury according to type of accident

	AA (n=42)	WC (n=59)
Fractured facial bones	2	0
Fractured pelvis	3	1
Fractured upper limbs	0	1
Fractured lower limbs	2	0
Cervical sprain/strain	16	5
Lower back sprain/strain	5	19
Sprain/strain, not to lower back or neck	0	6
Lower back disc prolapse	1	7
Chest injury	2	0
Abdominal injury	1	3
Lacerations/contusions to face or head	6	5
Lacerations/contusions, not to face or head	4	6
Other injuries	0	1
No physical injury	0	5

$\chi^2 = 37.6$; $P < 0.001$

physical injury. There was an overrepresentation of cervical sprain patients among those injured in automobile accidents, and an overrepresentation of lower back injury and "other sprains" in the industrial accident group (Table 6).
Thirty-five patients resumed work prior to the finalization of their claim. Patients were much more likely to return to work if they had been injured in an automobile accident than in an industrial accident; this difference was statistically significant (Table 7).

Table 7. Comparison of patients employed at settlement with those not employed

		Employed ($n=35$)	Not employed ($n=66$)
Men		21	40
Women		14	26
Age (years)	Mean	39.1	43.6
	SD	12.0	11.1
AA*		25	17
WC*		10	49

$\chi^2_{(YC)}=17.8$; $P<0.001$
YC, Yates' correction

Table 8. Comparison of patients lost to follow-up with those traced

		Lost ($n=13$)	Traced ($n=53$)
Men		7	34
Women		6	19
Age (years)	Mean	37.2[a]	45.2[a]
	SD	11.0	10.7
Duration of litigation (months)	Mean	33.9	36.7
	SD	19.5	14.7
AA		4	13
WC		9	40

[a] $t=2.38$; $P<0.05$

Among the 66 patients who were not gainfully employed at the time of settlement, 13 could not be traced during follow-up. These were compared with the other patients unemployed at the time of final settlement of their claim, and some details of the comparison are set out in Table 8. The mean age of the patients lost to follow-up was significantly lower than that of the group succesfully traced during follow-up. During the follow-up period, nine of 53 patients were employed (17%). The employed group were significantly younger than those not working, as shown in

Table 9. Comparison of patients employed at follow-up with those not employed

		Employed	Not employed
Men		5	29
Women		4	15
Age (years)	Mean	33.9[a]	47.5[a]
	SD	9.7	9.4
Duration of litigation (months)	Mean	42.7[b]	35.5[b]
	SD	21.2	12.9
Duration of follow-up (months)	Mean	12.1[b]	15.7[b]
	SD	10.1	9.9
AA		2	11
WC		7	33

[a] $t = 3.87$; $p < 0.001$
[b] No significant difference

Table 9. No other variable significantly differentiated between the working and nonworking groups, including origin of referral, physical injury, psychiatric diagnosis, occupation, or duration of litigation.

4 Discussion

The result of this study is in agreement with that of Balla and Moraitis, and with the review prepared for the Workers' Compensation Board in New South Wales, to the effect that a very significant proportion of compensation claimants do not return to gainful employment after their cases are settled; the frequently expressed expectation that the patient will be "cured by a verdict" is very often incorrect.

In this study, the only significant difference between patients who did return to work after settlement of their case, and those who did not, was in respect of age. The fact that the group of patients who could not be traced was also significantly younger introduced the possibility of an error in the final results. However, even if it is assumed that all patients in the group lost to follow-up were working, the final result is that 44 of 66 patients remained unemployed after a mean period of 15.7 months from settlement. This would indicate that 67% of litigants were unemployed during follow-up, as compared with 35% in the New South Wales study and 74% in the series reported by Balla and Moraitis. An inverse relationship between age and likelihood of return to work was also noted in the Compensation Board study, although in that series the trend did not reach statistical significance. Somewhat surprisingly, duration of litigation was not significantly associated with outcome in respect of occupational disability in this group of patients.

Given the finding that factors other than the prospect of financial gain are responsible for work disability that persists after legal settlement, the nature of these factors needs to be considered. There is a growing body of evidence pointing to the fact that they are related to the altered self-concept and body image of the injured person, and to the altered status of the patient both within the family and within his or her social milieu.

The notion of 'body image' refers to the individual's awareness of bodily integrity – or the awareness of having sustained an injury with the subsequent disruption of that integrity. The 'body image' includes emotional and symbolic associations with certain body regions, and forms part of the 'core' of the personality.

Described in these terms, 'body image' is to be differentiated from 'self-concept', which is a psychological construct embracing a perception of the individual's relationships to others of importance, and self-awareness along multiple dimensions of normal functioning, including the dimension of health – sickness. The victim of accidental injury very frequently suffers damage both to his body image and self-concept which is disproportionate to the actual physical injury. This is particularly the case for migrant workers, who usually have no specific skills, come from a rural background, and speak only basic English, if any at all. Their self-concept is heavily reliant on their role as hard-working providers for their families, usually in unskilled or semiskilled manual jobs that are traditionally performed by the most recently arrived group of immigrants. To sustain an injury in this setting is a profoundly distressing and demoralizing experience, and the subsequent job insecurity and all to frequent loss of employment, together with an adversary legal process when compensation is pursued, all contribute to a change in self-concept and lowering of self-esteem.

At the same time the status of the injured person within the family alters, and the newly acquired 'patient' status is validated and care-eliciting behavior reinforced [7]. This is strongly influenced by cultural factors, with other family members not infrequently having an emotional investment in maintaining the injured person in a passive and dependent role. This is often combined with the loss of status as the family 'provider' – an important component of the male role in our society. All these factors interact, and a frequent result is the establishment of a new homeostasis that endures after the physical injury has been resolved, with the injured person maintained in a perpetual 'patient' role.

Using the psychodynamic frame of reference, these factors operate at an unconscious level. They have to be distinguished from malingering, which in psychiatric terminology refers to conscious lying and simulation of disability.

Although the treatment of this group of patients is outside the scope of this paper, it must be acknowledged that this is a difficult and frequently unrewarding task. It has been suggested that the doctor–patient relationship is of crucial importance in determining the course of the functional mental disorder which may develop. To minimize the possible iatrogenic contribution to continuing disability, a thorough biopsychosocial assessment is necessary as a prerequisite for optimal treatment directed at the patient's needs, whether they be medical, social, or psychological [8, 9].

References

1. Kennedy F (1946) Mind of injured worker: its effect on disability neurosis. Compensation Medicine 1: 19
2. Miller H (1961) Accident neurosis. Br Med J I: 919–925
3. Culpan R; Taylor C (1973) Psychiatric disorders following road traffic and industrial injuries. Aust NZ J Psychiatry 7: 32–39
4. Thompson GN (1965) Post-traumatic psychoneurosis – a statistical survey. Am J Psychiatry 121: 1043–1048

5. Balla JI; Moraitis S (1970) Knights in armour: a follow-up study of injuries after legal settlement. Med J Aust 2: 355–361
6. Encel S; Johnston CE (1978) Compensation and rehabilitation. A survey of workers' compensation cases involving back injuries and lump-sum settlements. New South Wales University Press, Sydney
7. Henderson S (1974) Care-eliciting behavior in man. J Nerv Ment Dis 159: 172–181
8. Nemiah JC (1963) Psychological complications in industrial injuries. Arch Environ Health 7: 481–486
9. Raskin HA (1976) Mental disorder following industrial injury – iatrogenic factors. Leg Med 415–423

IV. Medicolegal Aspects

Medicolegal Criteria for Post-traumatic Psycho Syndrome

M. Sigal

1 Introduction

A Chinese proverb states: "When a piece of paper blows into a court of law, it may take a yoke of oxen to drag it out" [1].

Compensation suits are even more complicated because of the generally low reliability of current psychiatric diagnostic procedures [2]. Quite often, such litigation causes professional embarassment, one distinguished psychiatrist explaining that the claimant is ill and disabled following an accident and another insisting that he is not.

The attorney has to call upon the psychiatrist to "legitimize" his client's disability, i.e., to ascertain that the patient's subjective distress has a medical reality which must be considered in the disability determination. Attorneys and insurance companies also request an estimate of the degree of disability [3].

Yet, more often than not, the attorney does not trust the psychiatrist's diagnosis or his assessment of the claimant's disability. He prefers his client to go to court only when the permanent disability is clear and maximum medical rehabilitation has been achieved. Thus, medical procedures are prolonged and it may take years before a case is settled.

During this time, the patient is more or less led to believe that activity may aggravate his cerebral damage as well as lead to the loss of financial compensation in spite of persisting disability. The resulting inactivity, the tension accompanying the various medical examinations the patient has to go through, and the prolonged legal procedures themselves aggravate his disability, becoming a vicious circle [4].

The object of this paper is to find sufficiently validated criteria for medicolegal assessment of the post-traumatic psychosyndrome. To do this I began to look for diagnostic criteria for the syndrome itself [5], making a comprehensive review of the literature, and screening 250 patients hospitalized over a period of 14 years at Ness-Ziona Government Hospital [6].

The post-traumatic psychosyndrome represents a wide spectrum ranging from patients with symptoms resulting mainly from brain injury (post-concussion syndrome, change of personality and dementia) to patients whose symptoms are clearly psychogenic (neurotic reaction and compensation demand) [7].

The next stage in the study was reexamination of 40 claims referred by The National Welfare Institute and The Veteran Army Security Department for medical opinion:

1. The four syndromes composing the psychiatric sequelae of head injury on the basis of our precedent work [6] were diagnosed.

2. The etiological factor in each of those syndromes was isolated, since a constellation of factors contribute to enduring psychiatric disability. These are brain damage [8], emotional response to intellectual impairment [9], emotional repercussions of injury [10], specific neurotic conditions of the premorbid personality [11], a climate favorable to litigation for compensation [12], old and new environmental difficulties [13], and iatrogenic factors [14].
3. The causal relationship between the accident and the etiological factor (causation or aggravation) was examined.
4. Psychiatric impairment in each syndrome was evaluated and rated, based on the guides to the evaluation of permanent impairment of the committee on rating of mental and physical impairment of the American Medical Association [15].
5. We looked into the overall work status [16] of the claimants, considering (a) the motivation to return to work, doing the same job and/or at the same place; (b) the ability to angage in activities of daily life; and (c) whether the claimant is sick and cannot work, or weak and will not work.

To complete the psychiatric disability assessment we examined all factors, other than impairment, that affected the claimant's engagement in gainful activity: age, sex, education, socioeconomic status, personal motivation, and the surrounding type of society with its juridical possibilities [17, 18]. The medicolegal criteria were formulated on the basis of this overall assessment.

2 Criteria for Evaluating Psychiatric Impairment and Disability

For the diagnosis of post-traumatic psychosyndrome at least three of the following syndrome criteria are required: (a) the postconcussional syndrome, (b) the change of personality, (c) the post-traumatic neurotic reaction, (d) the compensation demand reaction. Impairment is a purely medical condition encompassing any anatomic or functional abnormality or loss after maximal medical rehabilitation has been achieved whereas disability is a condition in which the patient's actual or presumed ability to engage in gainful activity is reduced or absent because of "impairment," combined or not with other factors.

2.1 Postconcussional Syndrome

This is a subjective syndrome following a head concussion, lasting at least 2 months, but with a lack of commonly accepted neurologic signs. The most frequent symptoms are headache, dizziness, impairment of concentration, irritability, sensitivity to noise, high tolerance to analgesics and tranquilizers.

2.1.1 Causal Relationship Between Accident and Impairment

The etiology can be a brain concussion with lack of consciousness, even of a momentary nature, a whiplash injury of the neck without sensorium defect, or an injury to the audiovestibular apparatus; the medicolegal implication is therefore causation.

2.1.2 Criteria for Evaluating Impairment

Class 1: 0%–15%. The rating is according to the duration and severity of symptoms.

2.2 *Personality Changes and Dementia*

The changes of personality are characterized by a sharpening, sometimes a caricaturization of the preexisting personality structure. In the case of a sensitive or quarrelsome premorbid personality the patient's reaction may become paranoid. The process of change is slow, requiring about 2 years. The personality change is often but one aspect of the dementia which ensues, and cognitive defects are evident to some degree.

2.2.1 Causal Relationship Between Accident and Impairment

The etiological factoris brain damage, and the medicolegal implication causation.

2.2.2 Criteria for Evaluating Impairment

Class 1: 0%–15%. There is a striking change of personality with negative traits more prominent than before, along with difficulties in adapting to stress or frustration.

Class 2: 20%–45%. The subdivisions of this class are: (a) changes in personality with loss of self-control and inability to learn from experience, with a tendency to endanger self or others. Peripheral function (everything that may be learned and that is formed by life and environment) becomes partially ineffective and exposes the nucleus of the personality (all the tendencies contained in the individual's genetic inheritance); (b) a paranoid syndrome with definite difficulties in understanding the meaning of personal surroundings, and definite but mild disturbances in behavior; and (c) cognitive defects, requiring some supervision and direction to carry out most daily activities.

Class 3: 50–95%. This involves dementia (not including hysterical pseudodementia) with severe cognitive defect, requiring supervision and direct care in a confined environment.

2.3 Post-traumatic Neurotic Reaction

The neurotic reaction is mostly hysteria with one of its subtype forms (conversion, dissociation, pseudodementia or Ganser's syndrome). It may also take the form of anxiety, depression, and/or hypochondriasis. Truly basic predisposing factors must have been present before the trauma (either a premorbid neurotic personality or a pretrauma neurotic decompensation).

2.3.1 Causal Relationship Between Accident and Impairment

The link between trauma and neurosis has varying explanations according to the different schools. The accident is only one of a number of etiological factors in the neurotic reaction. Therefore, the medico-legal implication is aggravation. In addition, there is a controversy as to the role of the accident: It may either act as a trigger, causing aggravation of the constitutional state, or be the direct cause according to the principle of the "soft skull" (the trauma is beyond the capacity of the weak ego).

2.3.2 Criteria for Evaluating Impairment

Class 1: 0%–5%. The subject employs neurotic ego-protecting mechanisms in adapting to everyday stress, but without substantial loss of personal or social efficiency. The great majority of individuals in this class should be rated at either 0% or 1% impairment.

Class 2: 10%–45%: Neurotic syndromes are evident that cause disturbances in daily activities, last several weeks or longer, and require treatment. There is continued ability to take care of personal hygiene and other self-care activities.

Class 3: 50%–95%. Here are seen neurotic syndromes that cause permanent regressive states with or without tissue-organ pathology. Most individuals who fit the criteria of class 3 should be rated in the lower percentages of the range.

2.4 Demand for Compensation Reaction

Here there is a tendency to maintain symptoms or to aggravate them, as a defense against losing the secondary gains derived from disability "benefits." These gains may be material (money, better housing, better work conditions) or emotional (a change in patient's relationship with his family). This tendency appears mostly after a physical injury and disappears after the benefit is gained, provided that the disappearance of symptoms will not reverse the benefit.

2.4.1 Causal Relationship Between Accident and Impairment

In a certain sociopersonal context, the accident gives the individual the right and the opportunity to improve his or her status through litigation. Whether or not this reaction is conscious is controversial. Some jurists demand a clear distinction between the simulator (conscious) and the sick person (subconscious). This distinction is difficult because of the continuity between the conscious and the subconscious.

2.4.2 Criteria for Evaluating Impairment

There is no impairment in the sense of a mental or a physical defect.

2.4.3 Criteria for Evaluating Disability

The disability to engage in gainful activity is not caused by "impairment." It is correlated to the sociopersonal context prior to the accident, to the type of juridical possibilities in a welfare society, and to personal motivation.

3 Summary

Post-traumatic psychosyndrome, mainly neurotic; post-traumatic psychosyndrome, mainly demand for compensation; and post-traumatic psychosyndrome with changes of personality are possible diagnoses. The trauma itself may be either an aggravation of a preexisting syndrome or a cause. In case of different conclusions regarding the various parts of the syndrome the claimant will be given the benefit of the doubt. Impairment ratings overlap among the several aspects of the syndrome and combine with other impairments (orthopedic, auditory, etc.). The disability to engage in gainful activity is affected by age, sex, education, sicioeconomic status, juridical possibilities, the social environment, and personal motivation.

References

1. Critchley MD (1969) Introduction. In: Walker AE, Caveness WF, Critchley MD (eds). The late effects of head unjury. Thomas Springfield, pp 3–13
2. Spitzer RL, Endicott J, Robins E (1978) Research diagnostic criteria; rationale and reliability. Arch Gen Psychiatry 35: 773–782
3. Heimann EM, Shanfield SB (1978) Psychiatric disability assessment: clarification of problems. Compr Psychiatry 19: 449–454
4. Silfverskiöld BP (1969) The post concussion syndrome and its treatment. In: Walker AE, Caveness WF, Critchley MD (eds) The late effects of head injury. Thomas, Springfield, pp 135–137
5. Mifka P (1971) Post-traumatic psychiatric disturbances. In: Winken P, Bruyn GW (eds) Handbook of clinical neurology, vol 24, part II, North-Holland, Amsterdam, pp 531–574
6. Sigal M, Mozes T (tobe published) Post-traumatic psychosyndrome: A statistical survey
7. Peterson GC (1975) Organic brain syndromes associated with brain trauma. In: Freedman AM, Kaplan HI, Sadock BI (eds) Comprehensive textbook of psychiatry, Vol. I, Williams and Wilkins, Baltimore, pp 1093–1108

8. Lishman WA (1968) Brain damage in relation to psychiatric disability after head injury. Br J Psychiatry 114: 373–410
9. Goldstein K (1952) The effect of brain damage on the personality. Psychiatry 15: 245–260
10. Lishman WA (1973) The psychiatric sequelae of head injury: a review. Psychol Med 3: 304–318
11. Denker SJ (1958) A follow-up study of 128 closed head injuries in twins using co-twins as controls. Acta Psychiatrica Scand 33, Suppl 123
12. Miller H (1966) Mental aftereffects of head injury. Proc R Soc Med 59: 257–261
13. Fallik A, Sigal M (1973) Psychosocial factors in the development of the post-traumatic syndrome after head injuries. Harefuah 84: 16–19
14. Kelly R (1975) The post-traumatic syndrome: an iatrogenic disease. Forensic sci Int 6: 17–24
15. Committee on rating of mental and physical impairment of American Medical Association (1966) Guides to the evaluation of permanent impairment: mental illness. JAMA 198: 146–168
16. Dresser AC, Meirowski AM, Weiss GH et al. (1973) Gainful employment following head injury – prognostic factors. Arch Neurol 29: 111–116
17. Denny-Brown DE (1945) Disability arising from closed head injury. JAMA 127: 429–436
18. Cronholm B (1972) Evaluation of mental disturbances after head injury. Social J Rehab Med 4: 35–38

Informed Consent by Mentally Disabled Persons

H. Schünemann

1 The Physician's Duty to Cure and the Patient's Right of Self-determination

In the history of mankind, medical science has never made such great progress as during the last 150 yeats. Many human diseases which for thousands of years simply had to be endured can today be cured or at least palliated. At the same time, a process of development which began during the Age of Enlightenment has led to absolute recognition of the individual's freedom to arrange his or her own life. These courses of development, at first sight independent, soon collided. Due to their improved possibilities of treatment, physicians were able to do their duty according to the principle *salus aegroti suprema lex* [1] to an extent formerly quite unknown. On the other hand, however, the patients' freedom of decision ultimately had to enable them to reject medical treatment which was objectively useful, perhaps even absolutely necessary to maintain life. If restoration of the patient's well-being is the highest duty of the physician, the patient's own will does not count [2]; however if the patient's will has to be considered at all costs, there will be some cases where the physician is impeded by this very will in taking the steps necessary for the patient's well-being. Correctly, in resolving this conflict the patient's self-determination was placed before the patient's well-being. As early as the turn of the century the Supreme Court of the German Reich definitely stated the priority of the patient's right of self-determination over the physician's duty to cure. When passing down a penal judgement in 1894 [3] and a civil judgement in 1906 [4] – both concerning operations on children without the parents' consent having been sought – the Supreme Court declared, "There is no professional law by virtue of which the physician is permitted to interfere medically with another person's bodily integrity without or even against this person's very will" [5]. Only in this way could justice be done to human dignity. Had a different decision been made, the preservation and function of the human body would have gained clear priority over the free will which raises man above the animals. Man would be a mere object of medical science [6].

Today the primacy of the patient's decision over optimal medical care is generally acknowledged in Germany. It is based on Article 2 of the *Grundgesetz* (basic constitutional law), which guarantees the so-called right of self-determination [7]. As a matter of principle, no medical treatment may be performed without the patient having given his or her consent, and this consent is only legally valid if the patient realizes – through the physician – the consequences of his decision [8].

2 Consent by Mentally Disabled Persons

2.1 Ability to Consent

The rather simple principle of informed consent presents difficulties when it has to be applied to certain groups of patients, e. g., the mentally sick, who are in the center of interest in this context. Consideration of the kind of disease which often affects the mental activity of the patient immediately raises the question of the basis of the patients' consent, namely the ability to consent. This can only be clarified by gaining insight into the authority to consent and thus into the right of self-determination. Looking at the purpose of consent i. e., granting permission for the physician's actions, it is obvious that consent is an act of the party as an act of volition, with legal consequences [9]. The conclusion drawn from Section 105 of the German Civil Code is that a valid act requires the party to have contractual capacity. Applying this rule to consent, the patient would have to be capable of contracting in order to render consent valid [10]. This would simplify the classification and further [11] legal uniformity, but solving the problem this way would leave a certain feeling of uneasiness. Consenting to an operation is basically different from entering into a contract to purchase a new car. An operation affects a person infinitely more, since the decision falls within his or her individual sphere of life – it can even be called strictly personal. Thus, locating the authority to consent in the center of the right to one's individual sphere of life prevents equating ability to consent with contractual capacity. This justifies judging the ability to consent individually in each case, without consideration of the patient's ability to make a contract or of legal uniformity. The Federal High Court of Justice [12] is right in refusing to equate ability to consent with contractual capacity. In the court's opinion, the consent to medical treatment can a be regarded as an "authorization to perform acts which interfere with the individual sphere of the person who gives the permission" [13]. The ability to consent depends solely on whether the patient is able to understand the significance and impact of a proposed therapeutic measure.

This conception has practical consequences. If the ability to consent were equated with contractual capacity, a person deprived of his legal capacity would be unable to consent at all [14]. In my opinion the ability to consent is not out of the question in such cases and must be ascertained by individual examination of every patient. Vice versa, the inability to consent need not necessarily lead to deprivation of legal capacity. Such a step interferes with the patient's right to his individual sphere of life [15] and for this reason must not be undertaken lightly. Stating the inability to consent should not be combined with the deprivation of legal capacity, as the same examination might give a different result a short time later, in another situation, or when another kind of treatment [16] is planned. Although the examination of the ability to consent individually in each case is advantageous to the patient, the physician runs the risk of performing medical treatment without valid consent. A case can be made for diminishing these elements of uncertainty by having a physician not involved in the medical treatment of the patient in question establish the ability to consent. The burden of responsibility would then be shared. On the other hand, such a procedure would have disadvantages; in cases of emergency it would be impracticable, and an examination carried out by an unknown physician might confuse the patient. Finally, the attending physician can best judge the condition of his patient, and should therefore conduct the examination himself. In order to guarantee the safety of the patient and to protect themselves in cases of doubt, physicians should be obliged to enter their reasons for the final decision, as well as the basic facts of the case, into the treatment records [17]. The Federal High Court of Justice [18] has ruled that the criteria by which the ability to consent should be determined fall within the medical field. However, the courts must be entitled to review the essential aspects of the physician's decision, as it has legal consequences for the patient. The basic reason for limitating medical discretion is rooted in the patient's right to his or her individual sphere of life. An arbitrary decision on the part of the physician would violate the patient's legal position.

Besides, the patient's right to his individual sphere of life turns out to be a barrier to medical discretion. In cases of doubt the physician should not give priority to safety and declare the patient unable to consent, but should decide in favor of the patient's right of self-determination. In doing so any circumstances which – in case of possible inability to consent – suggest an exception should be emphasized, for instance, a so-called incidence interval or even the mere fact that the recommended treatment refers to a disease which is not related to the patient's basic sickness. Moreover, the patient's reaction to the information provided by the attending physician, for example the asking of specific, reasonable questions, may indicate ability to consent.

2.2 *Refusal of Consent*

Another particularly complicated problem is that of observing the patient's right of self-determination if he or she rejects medically indicated treatment; such a refusal poses difficulties enough when expressed by persons of sound mind. Often physicians have no understanding for such a reaction, and sometimes a refusal even gives rise to doubts about the patient's ability to consent [19]. As almost all patients do undergo medically indicated treatment [20], a refusal is considered abnormal. Nevertheless, the primacy of the right of self-determination, over what is medically desirable only becomes apparent in the act of refusal. This means that the refusal of a conscious, competent adult patient must basically be accepted [21]. The roots of such a decision, which often cannot be understood by others, may be found for example in religion or Weltanschauung, in tradition, in the family, or simply in the patient's stubbornness; refusal need not necessarily indicate mental illness [22]. In some mental diseases, however, the very nature of the disease [23] increases the probability of refusal of absolutely necessary medical care [24]. The patients either cannot wiegh the pros and cons or cannot make the right decision. Reasons for this inability range from mental incompetence to indefinable fear of any medical or surgical procedure. Nevertheless, the possibility cannot be excluded that a mentally disabled person declines necessary medical care for the same reasons as a person of sound mind. In this case the right of self-determination must be observed to the same extent as with patients of sound mind [25]. If a member of a religious group which prohibits blood transfusion rejects such a measure, whether or not he is mentally ill will not be relevant to the observance of his refusal [26].

When treating such patients, the greatest problem consists in stating their ability to consent. The physician is particularly responsible because he or she has to decide whether the patient's refusal is caused by the disease, and is thus irrelevant, or is independent of the disease, and therefore must be observed. In this context it is very important not to confuse the problem of ability to consent with the refusal of medical care. The physician should state the patient's ability to consent independent of whether consent is given, and should not – for reasons of safety – deny the ability to consent when confronted with a patient's objection. If he finds a patient able to consent, he should obtain a second opinion. If the colleague comes to the same conclusion, this should be entered in the treatment records and the patient's refusal should finally be respected.

Accepting a refusal expressed by a patient unable to consent poses even more problems. In these cases the physician is advised to get a guardian appointed or in case of emergency to be content with assumed consent [27]. In most cases this is a proper course of action, but it may, in some instances, curtail the patient's right of self-determination. One may well imagine the case of a member of a religious sect opposed to blood transfusion who develops a mental illness and in this state of mind needs a transfusion. If the patient were of sound mind a refusal of this treatment would be generally binding to every physician [28], but under the very circumstances of the case the physician may ask for the appointment of a guardian who will decide objectively on the basis of the patient's best interests. In cases od emergency, the physician is usually advised to assume that the patient's probable interests favor life saving [29]. In both proceedings, the basic decision in favor of the patient's right of self-determination is turned upside down. With mentally disabled patients, one generally decides in favor of the medically necessary measures [30]. Nevertheless, a patient unable to consent should at least be given a chance to reject treatment. In order to determine the patient's true will, for example, it may be useful to take recourse to a living will [31], written while the patient was sane. Here the problem of currentness of living wills emerges. The standard to be applied is: Would the patient uphold his former decision under the given circumstances? Nobody can really answer that question, but one should not hasten to neglect the patients will merely because it is not current. If all clues indicate that the patient would object to treatment if he were sane, this conclusion may not simply be disregarded [32]. The concept of assumed consent does not apply here, since the probable will [33] is directed towards refusal of the recommended treatment, not to consent. With guardianship, the physician is obliged to inform the guardian of the considerations speaking for a refusal so that these may be included in the evaluation of the patient's best interest.

As a general rule, we may say that if there are no indications of a negative decision by the patient, or if the clues are ambiguous, the physician may and must do the medically necessary on the basis of the guardian's consent or presumed consent. But if there are clear signs of a contrary will on the part of the patient, attention must be paid to them, and in exceptional cases this may even require acceptance of the patient's refusal [34]. In order to avoid abuse, careful medical documentation of the decision-making process is necessary [35].

3 Informing Mentally Disabled Persons

3.1 Basis of Duty of Information

Another unsolved legal problem in treating the mentally ill lies in the issue of information on the benefit-risk ratio involved in the proposed treatment. Typically, the physician is obliged to inform his patient fully in order to provide a basis for the patient's consent [36]; consent without prior information is generally invalid and can give rise to an action for unauthorized medical treatment [37]. From this we may conclude that the duty of information represents only a by-product of the consent requirement. Taking this a step further, one might believe that there is no need for information when the patient is unable to consent. For many mentally disabled patients this would mean not telling them what is happening to them. In my opinion, such an attitude is unacceptable. In order to avoid the patient being degraded to a mere object of medical activity, he must be informed eben if he is unable to render a legally valid consent. It is not only a rule of medical ethics [38] to give information on the planned course of medical treatment; the physician has the *legal duty* to inform, regardless of the patient's ability to consent [39]. This duty is grounded in the principle of human dignity [40].

3.2 Scope of Information

It is an entirely different question to what extent the physician has to inform his patient. As a principle, medical information should enable the patient to weigh the pros and cons of a given course of treatment [41]. This goes for both the mentally sound patient and the mentally ill patient who is able to consent. With regard to the latter, a restriction of the legally acquired scope of information may be appropriate in spite of his ability to render a valid consent. The rationale for this limitation [42] lies in the danger that the mentally ill patient's condition might deteriorate as a consequence of excessive information. The advantage of fully informing the patient has to be weighed against probable deterioration of the patient's state of mind. The evaluation of the possible risks is a medical question [43]. It involves factors such as the type of suffering or treatment [44] and the personality of the patient. If the physician in such a case therefore narrows the scope of information, he makes use of a therapeutic privilege [45] that is a legally permissible exception to the duty to inform. It is controversial whether the therapeutic privilege constitutes a privilege for the physician [46], with the duty to inform seen as the burden of information [47], or for the relieving him of possibly dangerous medical information. Probably there is an advantage to both sides, making the controversy superfluous.

As far as I know, the scope of information with regard to mentally disabled patients has not yet been explored. The patient's ability to understand must serve as starting point. This ability may well equal that of a mentally sound person if, for example, the patient lacks only the ability to evaluate the issues at stake. The patient must then be given the full information necessary for a valid consent. On the other hand, medical information may be completely omitted if there is no possibility of the patient understanding. The typical case will fall between these two extremes and some reduced amount of information will seem appropriate. Moreover, therapeutic aspects must be observed. If the therapeutic privilege would apply to a patient of sound mind it must also be considered with a patient of unsound mind. Finally, the type of proposed treatment should be considered. Thus, it is possible that medical information on treatment regarding the mental illness may be deemed inappropriate, while medical information regarding other unrelated conditions should be provided in full. Finally, the extent of information depends on the attending physician's evaluation of the individual case.

4 Summary

To summarize, my three main points are:

1. Incapacity and the inability to consent to medical treatment should not automatically be equated.
2. The refusal of medical treatment by a medically disabled person may have to be respected, provided that it is not conditioned by the mental disease.
3. The patient must be informed about the planned treatment even in those cases where he or she is deemed unable to render a legally valid consent to treatment.

References

1. Laufs A (1978) Arztrecht 2nd edn, No. 64. Beck, Munich
2. Deutsch E (1980) Das therapeutische Privileg des Arztes: Nichtaufklärung zugunsten des Patienten, NJW 1980: 1306, calls this a paternalistic view of physicians
3. RGSt 25, pp 375 ff
4. RGZ 68, pp 431 ff
5. RGZ 68, p 434
6. Dürig in Mainz-Dürig, Grundgesetz, Art. 1, note 28
7. BGHZ 29, pp 46 (49); pp 176 (179); Dürig, GG, Art. 2, Abs. 2, note 36
8. BGH NJW 56, 1107; BGHZ 29, p 50; Laufs, loc. cit. Nr. 65; Bockelmann p (1968) Strafrecht des Arztes. Thieme, Stuttgart, p 50
9. RG JW 1911, 748, Enneccerus-Nipperdey, Allgemeiner Teil, Band II, § 151 II 1 e
10. Münch.-Komm.-Gitter, Vor. § 104, note 98, considers § 104 BGB as applicable, mutatis mutandis. The contrary view is voiced by Landgericht München I, published in NJW 1980, p 646
11. Münchener-Kommentar-Gitter, Vor. § 104, note 95
12 BGHZ 29, pp 33 relying on BGHSt 4, 88; Staudinger-Dilcher, § 107, note 27; Larenz (1977) Schuldrecht, Besonderer Teil, 11th edn. Beck, Munich, § 71 I c; Engisch K (1958) Die rechtliche Bedeutung der ärztlichen Operation. In: Fehler und Gefahren bei chirurgischen Operationen. Jena 1530
13. BGHZ 29, 36
14. Münchener-Kommentar-Gitter, Vor. § 104, note 95
15. Müller G (1956) Behandlungspflicht des Arztes und ärztliche Aufklärungspflicht in der Sicht des Arztes und des Juristen. NJW 56: 1099
16. Helmchen H, Aufklärung und Einwilligung bei psychisch Kranken, p 4, proposes multiple examinations of the ability ot consent.
17. BGH NJW 78, p. 2339, stated a duty of documentation. Lilie H (1980) Ärztliche Dokumentation und Informationsrechte des Patienten. Lang, Frankfurt p 129
18. BGHZ 29, p 51
19. Criticizing this approach is Dunz W (1960) Grundrecht und Bevormundung. JZ 60: 477

20. Bockelmann loc. cit., Strafrecht des Arztes, p 56, proposes to ignore a patient's refusal when the treatment is necessary
21. RGZ 151, p 354; BGH VersR 54, 99; Göppinger H (1956) Die Aufklärung und Einwilligung bei der ärztlichen, besonders der psychiatrischen Behandlung. In: Fortschritte der Neurologie, Psychiatrie. Stuttgart, p 98; Münchener-Kommentar-Mertens, § 823, note 452. An exception should be made during pregnancy when the unborn child is in danger
22. Laufs loc. cit., No. 84 provides for an example, as well as the Chad-Green case in the United States of America (Newsweek April 17, 1978)
23. Göppinger, loc. cit. note 21, p 100
24. German law provides for one important exception to these principles: if the patient has been institutionalized on a court order initiated by a state agency, the physician is allowed to provide treatment for the mental disease even without the patient's consent. Here the patient's reight of self-determination is restricted by law. However, measures which involve a substantial risk to the patient's life, or health or which could change his personality, require the patient's consent. Further details: Göppinger H: Betrachtungen zur Unterbringung psychisch Kranker. FamRZ 80: 858
25. Of a different opinion is Hallermann (1971) Ärztliche Aufklärungspflicht aus medizinischer Sicht. In: Mergen A (ed) Die juristische Problematik in der Medizin II. Goldmann, Munich, p 44
26. Roß H (1959) Hindert Art. 104 GG eine ausreichende Fürsorge für psychisch Kranke? NJW 59: 2284
27. BGHZ 29, p 52; Laufs, loc. cit., No. 84
28. Laufs, loc. cit., No. 84
29. Göppinger, loc. cit. note 21, pp 88 and 101 gives the physician in these cases a right to treat the patient derived from extrastatutory necessity
30. Bockelmann, loc. cit.
31. Deutsche E (1979) Der Zeitpunkt der ärztlichen Aufklärung und die antizipierte Einwilligung des Patienten. NJW 79: 1907, discusses the anticipated consent of a patient to nontreatment in the terminal state of an illness given in a so-called living will
32. Deutsch, loc. cit. 31, p 1908, believes that an essential change in the patient's constitution is sufficient to remove the physician's duty to respect the patient's refusal.
33. The objectively determined interest of the patient in his convalescence is not sufficient. Larenz, Schuldrecht BT, § 57 I; Engisch, loc. cit. p 1530, is of a different opinion.
34. The exception for institutionalized patients is mentioned in note 23
35. Göppinger, loc. cit. note 23, p 97, holds the physician liable for documentation in these cases.
36. BGHZ 29, p 53; p 181; BGH VersR 71, p 930; BGH VersR 74, p 753; Staudinger-Schäfer § 823, note 399
37. RGZ 68, p 431; BGH VersR 76, p 293; Deutsch E (1965) Schutzbereich und Tatbestand des unerlaubten Heileingriffs im Zivilrecht. NJW 65; 1985; Münch.-Komm.-Mertens, § 823, note 456
38. BGH NJW 56: 1107; Deutsch E (1981) Theorie der Aufklärungspflicht des Arztes. VersR 81: 293
39. Göppinger, loc. cit. note 23, p 860
40. Dürig, loc. cit., Art. 1 Abs. 1, note 20
41. Jurisdiction as mentioned in note 36. Laufs, loc. cit., No. 65; Münch.-Komm.-Mertens, § 823, note 426
42. BGHZ 29, pp 176 (185); pp 46 (56); Deutsch, (fn. 2); Münch.-Komm.-Mertens, § 823, note 437; of different opinion is Giesen D (1981) Grundzüge der zivilrechtlichen Arzthaftung. Jura 81: 18
43. Göppinger, loc. cit. note 21, 103
44. Differentiating in a similar way: § 26, Abs. 2, PsychKG NRW; § 26 Abs. 2 Nds. PsychKG.
45. Deutsch, loc. cit. note 2
46. Deutsch, ibid.
47. Deutsch, loc. cit. note 38
48. Helmchen, loc. cit., p 3

Confidentiality: The Moral/Legal/Treatment Conflict

S. Schneider

1 Introduction

One of the most difficult areas of the psychotherapeutic process is the issue of confidentiality. Here we have the interface between the mental health professional, the client, and a third party. It is this third party – who comes in a variety of guises – that complicates our innate desires for privacy. Some professionals even dismiss the notion that there can ever be absolute protection: "We can no longer take for granted that our privacy will be respected or protected" [24]. In a certain Kafkaesque way, we can never escape the various agencies, institutions, governmental bodies, etc. that may intrude into the private lives of our clients [19]. More dangerous, can we avoid someone obtaining information from files which may now be accessible via computer technology [29]?

This paper focuses on the conflict inherent in the psychotherapeutic process with respect to the issue of confidentiality. The emphasis is on the psychiatric component – understanding the interface between client and mental health professional; how reports and progress notes should be written; how the therapist should handle the issue of client and third parties; and which is more important, the individual or society. The paper is written from the vantage point of a mental health professional and not from a legalist's viewpoint.

The inherent conflict is built into the interaction between the professional and society. While the conflict cannot be mitigated, it can be worked with. It is to this point that the paper will address itself. The conflict will be explored from a moral, a legal, and a treatment point of view.

2 The Moral Issue

Somehow it seems that the issue of confidentiality only grew out of proportion recently. Over the past 15 years state and federal courts have split hairs over who should be protected. While Hippocrates is credited with starting it all with his oath over 2500 years ago, it took modern man, with his strong sense of democracy and justice, to wreak havoc on the therapeutic system. Nonetheless, the psychoanalysts intensified the conflict, not because they were wrong in anything they did therapeutically, but because they consistently did the opposite in protecting confidences to the extreme. Stanton and Schwartz described this in their study of the mental hospital:

> Probably the psychoanalytic training institute contributed to the sharpness of the conflict. Its psychoanalytic practice was to use great care in protecting confidence . . . on the general principle that only the patient was to decide who might know what he had said. This was one of several ways in which psychoanalytic tradition seemed almost like a chronically irritating foreign body in the mental hospital structure [26].

The moral dilemma grows as "legislation determines what must be recorded and how privacy must be maintained in certain settings, and as massive computerized data bank systems compile private information on hundreds of thousands of individuals" [32].

Levy, in discussing confidentiality in the social worker-client relationship, states that "the social worker is obliged to maintain inviolate any confidence or information affecting his client that can, by the most minimal of criteria, be regarded as secret, personal, or private" [12]. However, what happens when the conflict pits ethical responsibilities for keeping clients' communications confidential against legal or dangerous consequences? Who is to decide whether (and how much) information should be divulged? The moral dilemma of the mental health professional creates inner turmoil and can damage the therapeutic alliance. The burden of guilt falls on the therapist, not on the third party.

Where confidential information must be given to a third party, Levy builds in certain safeguards: "The social worker is bound to divulge only the data necessary to safeguard manifestly threatened life or well-being and only to the extent that responsibility for their protection may be reasonably attributed to the social worker" [12].

The mental health professional should not have to bargain with third parties or negotiate over what material needs to be divulged. If anything, the therapist should question whether anything at all should be shared [24]. There must be justification for release of information if the moral dilemma is to be resolved.

Some writers have taken the other side of the moral position. Sometimes professionals are ethically and legally required to reveal confidential information [25]. Here the moral problem is between the therapist and client. Take the case of a client who describes in treatment how he intends to harm someone. What becomes the role of the therapist? Who is to be protected, the client (i.e., through his confidential relationship with the therapist) or society (the person who may be harmed)? This moral conflict is easier to solve because the dyad of therapist and client can work out this moral issue. The problems are compounded when a third party intervenes. Here the control is no longer contained in the therapeutic dyadic alliance. It is very difficult for the therapist to rationalize that the divulging of information is for the purpose of helping the client, unless he really believes it. The moral pains are stronger when the therapist fears that this breach of confidence may hurt the client. In a recent American Psychiatric Association publication, it was stated that "a breach of confidence will make the professional liable for damages in a tort action for invasion of privacy or defamation" [20, cf. 2].

Nonetheless, if a professional feels that a client may be a danger to himself or others, "he is obligated to take the necessary action to protect the individual, including committing him to a mental institution, even though he may have to reveal information given in confidence. Although the professional must give primary consideration to the patient, he must also consider the welfare and safety of others" [20].

The moral issue is clarified by Levy who connects the client's need for professional help with the therapist's inability to service that need without absolute confidence on the part of the client that his or her personal data will not be divulged. "Confidentiality ... is an ethical and at times a legal duty that is enforced to protect the client in view of the position he is placed in by his need for and recourse to the social worker's service" [12].

3 The Legal Issue

Wigmore listed four criteria that have been universally accepted for judging privileged communication [30]:

1. The communication must originate in the confidence that it will not be disclosed.
2. The element of confidentiality must be essential to the full and satisfactory maintenance of the relationship between the parties.
3. The relation must be one which, in the opinion of the community, ought to be sedulously fostered.
4. The injury to the relation that would be caused by disclosure of the communication must be greater than the benefit thereby gained for the correct disposal of the litigation.

Various professional groups have produced position paper statements on the issue of confidentiality and release of information [1–4, 10, 13, 14, 19]. The fear for the clients' well-being vis-à-vis third-party requests for confidential information is compounded by the fear of malpractice suits and the possible violation of the privacy of the individual [17].

The legalists have tried to differentiate between an absolute confidentiality (where nothing is ever divulged) and relative confidentiality [31]. In essence, there is very little of the former and plenty of the latter.

If we try to understand privileged communication, the essential fact is that "privilege belongs to the consumer" [24]. However, another legalism requires informed consent. This means that "the individual should have the right to consent to the sharing of any information about himself beyond the provider to whom he has voluntarily given the information" [24]. This consent should be time limited [19] for the protection in the client. In addition, the therapist who has to obtain the consent from the client naturally has influence over the client. Thus, how the therapist feels about the request for information will, in a large part, determine whether the client will give his consent [15].

In the United States in 1979, the State of Illinois enacted the Mental Health and Developmental Disabilities Confidentiality Act [6, 7, 22]. This act has been suggested as a model for the drafting of similar confidentiality codes for other states.

One of the issues clarified by the Illinois statute was the definition of "record," what constitutes records that are kept on clients and what information has to be revealed – the entire record or perhaps only a section. The statute states:

> Record does not include the therapist's personal notes if such notes are kept in the therapist's sole possession for his own personal use and are not disclosed to any other person, except the therapist's supervisor, consulting therapist or attorney (Sec. 2 [7]).

This, in effect, allows the use of process recordings for psychology, social work, and psychiatric students and interns. These recordings become part of the teaching-supervisory process [32] and are not considered confidential information that is shared with a third party. In essence, the supervisors are part of the dyadic alliance and not adjunct to it.

Many of the legal problems that arise in the mental health system of confidentiality relate to alcohol and drug abuse [8]. This is probably related to the stigma and possible legal repercussions that may result from disclosure [28]. Nye feels very strongly about the latest moves, some politically motivated, that have begun to violate a person's right to privacy:

> The issue of personal privacy has acquired new significance in the wake of two significant factors: the rise of computer technology and the experience of Watergate. It has become increasingly apparent that personal privacy and confidentiality of personal information may well be a thing of the past ... Health information, and particularly mental health information, is particularly vulnerable to misuse. The cases of Senator Eagleton and Daniel Ellsberg are poignant examples [16].

There are many articles that have been written relating to the whole issue of health records. The armed forces, industries with sensitive materials, licensing bureaus, etc. quite routinely request health records on potential applicants [14, 23]. Even if this is with the knowledge of the applicant, a usually overabundant amount of information is received. Once information has been requested, there are few ways to stop the flow [24].

One legal issue that has received widespread attention is the release of court records on juveniles. While this may not fit directly into the theme of this paper – confidentiality in the psychotherapeutic process – it has many implications for the stigmatization of the child and adolescent. In effect, it has secondary ramifications that impinge on the mental health of the child and adolescent. As the period of adolescence is a difficult time in terms of developing an identity and a self-image, issues of trouble with the law must be resolved before the adolescent can further grow emotionally.

In a New York City Domestic Relations Court Memorandum, this position was stated by the legalists:

> It is universally agreed that the period of adolescence is the most difficult time of life ... If a child becomes entangled with the law and is aware that the records of his misdeeds are forever open to public inspection he could very well arrive at the conclusion that Society has branded him with a "Scarlet Letter" for anyone to see who cared to look, and hence, he "belonged" with the *criminal* element, and would probably seek the company of those who had a *common* cause. He would consider himself an enemy of society, take pleasure in the "hero" worship of gangsters, and consecrate his life to crime and his ultimate self-destruction [27]).

The purpose of "closing" the record of a juvenile was clear: to remove any suggestion, or implication of criminality.

> The policy behind these provisions is clear and unmistakable, viz., to avoid the perpetual stigma of conviction as to persons who in early life have run afoul of the law. In cases of offenses by juveniles there was to be a type of amnesty by oblivion (matter of *Adler* v. *Lang,* 21 A.D. 2nd 107, 109 [1st Dept., 1964], quoted in [27]).

When an adolescent comes of age and either wants to enlist in the armed forces, or is counseled in that direction by his therapist, a still "open" criminal record may prevent his induction. Eli Ginzberg describes the problem:

> Rejection for military service represents still another failure along the road for these young people. They have not succeeded in school, they have been unable to find a place in the civilian world of work, and now they are shunted aside by the military. It would be difficult even for a person with a very strong ego to take these successive rebuffs and absorb them without hitting back [8].

Since we are dealing with adolescents who do not have strong egos, it is clear what damage an "open" record can cause.

Sussman [27] discusses various state laws in the United States that have differing provisions on handling juvenile court records. Some states "close" or "seal" the record; this means that the record can only be reopened by court order. Some states "destroy" or "obliterate" the record. Other states allow the juvenile, upon reaching a certain age of majority (this age varies from state to state), to request his record to be "destroyed". All of the above can take place if the juvenile has reached a certain age and has not committed any further crimes.

The legal issue has slowly moved in the direction of protecting the child and adolescent in order to allow him to grow emotionally. This cognizance on the part of the legalists has created a merger between the legal profession and the psychiatric profession [11, 17, 18, 21].

4 The Treatment Issue

One of the major treatment issues regarding confidentiality concerns the access that a client may have to his psychiatric records. Up to this point we have discussed the inherent conflict as built into the interface between the professional and society. We have defined a dyadic therapeutic alliance with the "intruder" as a third party. Now we shall deal with the client's desire to gain access to his own psychiatric record.

In writing psychiatric reports (we will employ this phrase to refer to mental health records written by mental health professionals) that clients may at some point be able to gain access to, should care be taken to delete serious diagnoses, in order to avoid possible legal recriminations? Should two sets of reports be kept, those for internal use and those for external consumption? Can proper psychiatric treatment be given with the "threat" of legal repercussions hanging in the air? As a tangential issue, should professionals writing recommendations for applicants to graduate schools be careful how and what they write if the applicant has not waived his right to access?

In the United States, the Federal Privacy Act of 1974 (referred to as Public Law 93–579, 93rd Congress, December 31, 1974) required that the client (referred to as the "consumer") have access to his records. The law was passed because of the concern that clients were not adequately informed of the information being kept on them. At present "the act pertains to federally funded and administered programs only, though some nonfederal programs receiving federal grant monies may have to abide by the regulations in the cases of consumers receiving services through such monies" [31].

If a client who has been or is being treated has the possibility of seeing his record, is able to challenge the diagnoses, is able to correct or amend his record as he feels necessary in order to render it accurate, etc., can the mental health professional be totally honest in keeping his records? The professional will undoubtedly be very careful about what he or she puts into print, being aware that it could lead to a lawsuit [9].

This does not mean that the client should not be protected. If a third party is involved, informed consent is a necessary and important requirement to protect the privacy of the client. The part of the act that allows the client to "find out what records are being maintained on him and how they are used or disseminated . . ." [31] might be legitimate. However, the issue that must be debated is that part which allows the client the right to question, challenge, and amend. If we are to avoid two sets of records and diagnoses, part of the contractual arrangement between client and therapist must allow for professional freedom with professional accountability.

Wilson lists certain arguments for restricting client access to records. To name a few:

1. Psychological damage to client
2. Adverse client reaction to professional diagnostic material
3. Material from outside sources unsuitable for client's perusal
4. Client lawsuit against the social worker
5. "Practitioners know best"
6. Secrecy of records "essential to professional effectiveness"
7. Availability of unsuitable material to significant others [31]

Gordon and Barnard present a frightening list of possible repercussions that may occur if a patient is able to have a copy of the record in his possession [9].

What seems clear is that the issue is unclear. While there may be arguments in favor of not allowing the client total access and all of the rights the Federal Act of 1974 gives to him, there nonetheless has to be a mechanism that allows a type of access that can protect both client and professional. Also, if the professional is aware that his written record may be seen by the client, he may take more care and be more accurate [11, 13]. This is an issue that is being worked on by all the professional mental health organizations and the legalists. Hopefully a solution that is fair to both sides can be developed; no one wants the frightening possibility of an unbalanced client gaining access and suing his therapist. Nor do we want an abuse of the clients' rights, however so a compromise solution will have to be worked out.

Another area of confidentiality in psychotherapeutic situations concerns confidentiality in group therapy and family therapy contexts. Schuchman writes that: "While information shared in the presence of a third person is not legally confidential, that which is shared by one family member alone with the provider should be so treated in contacts with other family members" [24]. This implies that confidentiality in the dyadic therapeutic alliance is stronger than confidentiality in group and family therapeutic situations ("not legally confidential").

The Illinois statute that we discussed previously tries to correct this. Communication is now extended by law to include group and family therapy.

> "Confidential communication" or "communication" means any communication made by a recipient or other person to a therapist or to or in the presence of other persons during or in connection with providing mental health or developmental disability services to a recipient (Sec. 2 [1]).

This allows information gained from group or family therapy to be treated the same as confidential information obtained from individual therapy sessions.

The issue of confidentiality in group therapy contexts is not all that simple. "Not only must the group leader keep the confidences of members, he or she must also get the group members to keep one another's confidences" [5]. This involves repeating and emphasizing "the importance of confidentiality at various stages of the group's evolution" [5].

It may be difficult for group members to discern what is confidential, and therefore, to avoid "leaking" information to outsiders. A case in point concerns a very disturbed girl who had difficulty in understanding the boundaries of reality. When Nancy spoke to her individual therapist about an incident that occurred in her group therapy session, she felt she was violating the contract that the group had established regarding confidentiality. The issue she raised with her therapist was the shooting of John Lennon. She felt that since the group discussed Lennon's murder it was a confidential issue not to be raised outside the confines of the group. While this clinical vignette may be an exaggeration, the point is made that confidentiality in group therapy contexts is not as "easy" to handle as individual therapy situations.

5 Summary

The issue of confidentiality is one of those areas in the psychotherapeutic process that is not able to be fully defined. This means that not every possible situation can be covered and that there are inherent conflicts built into the system.

This paper has attempted to review three major issues in the area of confidentiality as it applies in the psychotherapeutic process: the issues of morality, legality, and treatment.

It is clear that more work has to be done in this area. A little more democracy has to be brought into the psychotherapeutic system taken out of the legal system.

References

1. American Association of Social Workers (1946) Principles of confidentiality in social work. AASW District of Columbia
2. American Psychiatric Association (1978) Principles of medical ethics, with annotations especially applicable to psychiatry. Am Psych Assoc, Washington, DC

3. American Psychological Association. (1979) Ethical standards of psychologists (revision). Am Psychological Assoc, Washington, DC
4. British Association of Social Workers (1971) Confidentiality in social work, Discussion Paper No. 1. BASW, London
5. Corey G, Corey MS (1977) Groups: process and practice. Brooks/Cole, Monterey
6. Foster L (1974) Illinois: a pioneer in the law of mental health privileged communications. Illinois Bar Journal 62: 668–670
7. Foster LM (1980) State confidentiality laws: the Illinois act as model for new legislation in other states. Am J Orthopsychiatry 50: 659–665
8. Ginzberg E (1966) The social order and delinquency. In: Report of the president's commission on crime in the District of Columbia. U.S. Printing Office, Washington, DC
9. Gordon RE, Barnard GW (1974) Why a patient should never get a copy of his psychiatric report. Consultant 14: 110–111
10. Group for the Advancement of Psychiatry (1960) Confidentiality and privileged communications in the practice of psychiatry, report no. 45. Group Adv Psychiatry, New York
11. Katz J, Goldstein J, Derschowitz A (1967) Psychotherapy, psychoanalysis and the law. Free, New York
12. Levy CS (1979) Social work ethics. Human Sciences, New York
13. National Association of Social Workers (1979) Code of ethics. NASW, Washington, DC
14. National Commission on Confidentiality of Health Records (1978) Health records. Law and practice. Nat Comm on confidientiality of Health Records
15. Noll T (1976) The psychotherapist and informed consent. Am J Psychiatry 133: 1451–1453
16. Nye SG (1980) Patient confidentiality and privacy: the federal initiative. Am J Orthopsychiatry 50: 649–658
17. Perr I (1971) Problems of confidentiality and privileged communications in psychiatry. Leg Med 327–360
18. Popiel DJ (1980) Confidentiality in the context of court referrals to mental health professionals. Am J Orthopsychiatry 50: 678–685
19. Privacy Protection Study Commission (1977) Personal privacy in an information society. GPO, Washington, DC
20. Reynolds M (1976) Threats to confidentiality. Social Work 21: 108–113
21. Rubin B (1975) Psychiatry and the law. In: Arieti S (ed) American handbook of psychiatry, 2nd edn, vol 5. Basic, New York
22. Schlensky R (1977) Informed consent and confidentiality: proposed new approaches in Illinois. Am J Psychiatry 134: 1418
23. Schuchman H (1975) On confidentiality of health records. Am J Orthopsychiatry 45: 732–733
24. Schuchman H (1980) Confidentiality: practice issues in new legislation. Am J Orthopsychiatry 50: 641–648
25. Slovenko R, Usdin GL (1961) The psychiatrist and privileged communication. Arch Gen Psychiatry 4: 436
26. Stanton AH, Schwartz MS (1954) The mental hospital. Basic, New York
27. Sussman A (1971) The confidentiality of family court records. Social Service Rev 45: 455–481
28. Szasz T (1967) The psychiatrist as double agent. Transaction 1: 16–24
29. Westin A (1976) Computers, health records and citizens rights. U.S. Dept. of Commerce, Washington DC
30. Wigamore JH (1961) Code of the rules of evidence in trials at law, vol 8. Little, Brown, Boston
31. Wilson SJ (1978) Confidentiality in social work. Free, New York
32. Wilson SJ (1980) Recording: guidelines for social workers. Free, New York

Disability, Medical Intervention, and Individual Freedom

J. K. M. Gevers

In a recent authoritative work on the welfare state it is claimed that the emphasis on citizens' rights and the almost total omission of citizens' duties are conspicuous features of the contemporary social climate [1]. To redress the balance "the rights of citizens to the benefits of the welfare state must be accompanied by reciprocal duties" [1]. This statement may be correct in a very general way, but for the student of welfare law it is not difficult to find numerous exceptions to it. Even where the law of social welfare did not grow up on "the theory that welfare is a gratuity furnished by the state, and thus may be made subject to whatever conditions the state sees fit to impose" [2], it contains many obligations for citizens as conditions of their entitlement to benefits, and the fact that interpretations of these obligations by administrators often go unchallenged allows for wide administrative discretion in their enforcement. As a reacting to this, and in the wake of the general revival of interest in fundamental rights, the substantive and procedural rights of individual beneficiaries are recognized to a growing extent as creating important legal issues, deserving more attention than has been paid to them before [2].

One of the areas where the public interest and the efficient implementation of welfare law may come into conflict with individual rights is the field of disability. Disability – or longterm incapacity for work resulting from handicap or disease – imposes a considerable financial burden on society. Following the extension and improvement of social security schemes, the prevention of disability has become a definite goal of public policy, together with the protection of funds against unjustified claims and the exclusion from benefit of those who remain incapacitated as a result of their own conduct. In pursuing these policies, society relies to a large degree on medicine: medical checkups on hidden handicaps and diseases, in order to start treatment in good time or to protect other persons; medical examinations to assess the degree of disability and the entitlement to benefits; medical treatment to stabilize the process of health deterioration or to restore the capacity for work.

This extensive use of medicine is reflected in the labor and social security legislation of most modern legal systems. In the majority of Western industrial countries legal provisions oblige employees and claimants of disability benefits to submit to medical examinations or treatment. It is here that a conflict with the fundamental rights of the individual may arise: the duty to undergo examination or treatment may encroach – directly or indirectly – upon the right to self-determination, i. e., the right to dispose over one's own body and to decide on one's own physical and mental well-being.

Since this conflict cannot always be avoided, the question is by what substantive and procedural provisions law can contribute to its adjustment, safeguarding to an extent individual freedom and providing room for a certain degree of medical intervention. In addressing myself to this question, I will refer mainly to Dutch welfare law, but use it merely as an example of the question of principle which, in more or less the same form, applies to other countries as well. In the following pages I will discuss first the duty to submit to medical supervision in the phase of prevention of disablement, then medical examinations to assess eligition of disablement, then medical examinations to assess eligibility for benefits, and finally the obligation to comply with medical directives in the phase of treatment.

1 Medical Supervision of Employees

Involuntary medical checkups, intended for the prevention of accidents and other causes of disablement, can be found in several fields of social life, such as the widespread but very limited medical checkups of candidates for drivers' licenses. The single most important area where various forms of involuntary preventive medical supervision are concentrated is that of work; I will therefore limit myself to medical supervision at work. Two types of obligations can be distinguished here. The first consists of those provisions that are directed at the prevention of accidents and diseases in society at large. An example is the obligatory initial and periodical medical checkups for personnel of ships and aircraft that exist in all countries. Very common are comparable obligations for drivers of motor coaches, personnel of public waterworks, teaching staff at schools, etc. The second type concerns a much larger part of the working population, and in some countries even all of them. It consists of provisions that have as their primary objective the protection of fellow employees against diseases or accidents, the timely detection of handicaps and diseases, and the tracing of harmful agents in the working environment.

In the Netherlands, the new law on health and safety at work (*Arbeidsomstandighedenwet* 1980) allows for the imposition of far-reaching obligations; it gives wide competences both to the district head of the labor inspectorate (who may require any examination he thinks desirable) and to the minister of labor (who may enact regulations obliging all workers to submit themselves to periodical medical supervision). Up to now, these regulations have not been enacted, and the labor inspectorate makes a rather restricted use of the powers conferred upon it by the law. In practice, obligations to submit to medical checkups are predominantly found in collective labor contracts as a result of demands by the labor unions.

In several countries, however, comprehensive legislation does exist on compulsory medical supervision of individual workers, e.g., in Italy (cf. the decree of 1953, No. 303, on industrial hygiene) and in France (cf. the decree of 1979, No. 231, on occupational health services, which provides for initial and periodical checkups for all employees). Over the last 10 years, there has been an increase in the number of national provisions of this kind; the same holds for the development of international labor standards, such as the EEC recommendation relating to medical checkups for employees exposed to special hazards (Official Journal 1966, C 151) and the ILO conventions of 1971 (on benzene) and 1974 (on occupational cancer). Recently, the need for legislation of this kind has grown still further, as many countries have begun to set standards concerning admissible concentrations of dangerous substances at the work place (see also the EEC directive on the protection of workers from chemical, physical, and biological agents at work, Official Journal 1980, L. 327). Some of these standards relate to concentration of substances (e.g., lead) in the human body; periodical medical examinations are then necessary in order to monitor the concentrations and enforce the standards.

The compulsory character of both types of obligations results not merely from the fact that they are formally binding, but primarily from the way they are enforced. The obligations of the first type – and often also those of the second – are enforced by means of a prohibition of access to work. Compliance with the requirements is then a necessary condition for having or keeping the job. In some cases employment depends not only on submitting to the examination, but also on its outcome. Even where the obligation is not laid down under statutory regulation, but in collective labor contracts, noncompliance may be followed by dismissal.

Although in the majority of cases compulsory examination also serves the interests of the individual employee, his obligation to submit to it may conflict with the fundamental right to dispose over his own body. This becomes more probable insofar as the outcome of medical investigations is decisive for his employment, and insofar as such investigations are more intensive and do interfere more with his physical and mental integrity. By which substantive or procedural rules can this conflict be adjusted? How can individual freedom be balanced against the demands of public policy with respect to the prevention of disability? In my opinion, medical action based on legal obligation must generally answer four criteria (for a comparable approach see [3]):

1. It must have specific objectives that can be justified in terms of public policy.
2. It should in each individual case be necessary to fulfill these objectives.
3. It must be reasonable, e.g., without excessive risks, relatively painless, and taking into account personal circumstances.
4. There must be sufficient procedural safeguards (e.g., previous information about its purpose, the right to appeal against undue compulsion, information about the outcome, the right to reexamination in case of a negative outcome which threatens personal interests).

What do these criteria imply for the medical supervision of employees? As to the first of them, obligatory medical examinations would seem to be justified when they serve the purpose of protecting other people – be it fellow workers or society at large – from the potential risks caused by the persons on whom the obligation is imposed. According to J. S. Mill, the prevention of harm to others is the only reason for legally compelling someone to do something he would not otherwise do [4]. Risk to others can be included in the definition of actions or qualities affecting others that can be considered for restriction or control by the state. This does not mean that there is no case for legal obligations that are primarily directed to the protection of the individuals subjected to examination. As long as this protection is necessary in the public interest it can be justified as essentially affecting others. As it has been put by Weale [5], "... we should also include in the other-regarding category legislation and policies to promote public goods [sic] ... where private and social costs typically diverge." Legislation to prevent disablement constitutes such a case whenever the costs of disablement are for a large part shouldered by society.

Medical examinations of candidates for a job often serve other purposes as well: it is in the interest of the employer to select the person who is medically most fit for the job and offers the lowest risk of absenteeism due to ill health. This role of medicine does not go undebated, however, with respect either to the possible contribution of medicine to the "positive" selection of applicants, or to its acceptability in terms of professional ethics. Also, if one accepts this type of medical examination as fully legitimate, the selection of the "best" candidate should not become the objective of legally compulsory examinations, since this objective cannot be justified as a goal of public policy. This leaves us with two legitimate goals for obligatory check ups for workers: the health and safety of others, and the health and safety of the examined themselves insofar as the protection of social security funds calls for it.

The second and third criteria regard the recourse to medical checkups in specific cases and the way they are carried out. It is hard to specify these criteria further, apart from the concrete situation in which they must be applied. So far there are no judicial decisions – at least in the Netherlands – that deal with the limits of the legal duty of employees to submit to medical examination. As we will see later, there are such decisions with regard to compulsory examinations in disability law, and from these one might infer more specific guidelines for the medical supervision of workers.

The fourth criterion appears to be especially relevant, since exhaustive regulation by means of substantive rules is impossible. Adequate procedural provisions can make up for the lack of substantive provisions that are sufficiently clear and determinate. Dutch legislation provides for a right to reexamination in case of prohibition to work on the basis of the outcome of an obligatory examination. It does not contain explicit provisions on the preliminary information of employees or on the disclosure of the examination results to them, though the right to information prior to and following medical intervention in general is recognized by all writers (although they are not unanimous on the ways it should be realized in practice). Up to now, the conflict between individual freedom and medical supervision at work has not been a definite legal issue. However, as the legal obligations relating to medical checkups for employees are extended, and as submitting to medical acts becomes less self-evident and more a matter of critical choice, the need for protection from undue compulsion can be expected to increase.

2 Medical Examination of Disability Benefit Claimants

Provisions for disabled persons in different countries vary to such an extent, and operate within such heterogeneous statutory frameworks, that international comparisons are difficult. The wide differences between the various countries' statutory definition of invalidity alone renders any comparison of dubious value [6]. Yet various systems of social security law with respect to disability seem to have at least one aspect in common: they rely on medical examinations to establish incapacity for work, or the degree of incapacity. Nevertheless, there may be disparities between different systems as to the extent to which they employ medicine for purposes of control and certification. In countries where the threshold to disability benefits is relatively low (like in Netherlands, where benefit is paid for any incapacity in excess of 15% [for employees] or 25% [for the population in general]) and where an elaborate classification of degrees of disability exists (again like the Netherlands, where seven [for employees] or six [for the general population] classes of invalidity exist, each with a corresponding benefit level) presumably more use will be made of examinations and reexaminations than in countries like Belgium, France, and Italy, where the minimum percentage of invalidity is 67% and where a further differentiation in degrees of disability is nonexistent or less elaborate (see [7], pp. 53–64).

The two Dutch disability laws (the *Wet op de Arbeidsongeschikthiedsverzekering* of 1967 covering employees, and the *Algemene Arbeidsongeschiktheidswet* of 1976 covering the population at large) oblige the claimant to cooperate with medical investigations, consisting either of a mere examination or of a hospital stay for observation. If the claimant does not submit, the professional associations administering the law may refuse or withdraw the benefit, partially or completely and on a temporary or permanent basis. These decisions of the social security administration are subject to judicial review by social security tribunals *(Raden van Beroep)*. It is the claimant's duty to cooperate, unless he has – according to the law – "a valid ground for refusal." Parallel provisions can be found in other countries, for example in Great Britain, where the claimant may be disqualified from benefit for a maximum period of 6 weeks if he fails "without good cause to comply with a notice in writing . . . requiring him to attend for and to submit himself to medical or other examination . . ." [Stat. Instr. 1975/564, Reg. 12(1) (b)].

Before discussing how these sorts of obligations must be interpreted in the light of the four criteria for compulsory medical examinations mentioned before, I want to touch on a point in passing which is also relevant to the obligatory checkups for employees discussed earlier, i. e., the question of why refusal to cooperate cannot be met with direct phsyical compulsion. The argument against direct coercion may run as follows. While loss of work or loss of benefit constitute serious sanctions on noncompliance, they leave the employee or claimant still free to decide to submit or not, so the right to self-determination is safeguarded, at least to some extent. Physical constraints would override this right. Such a drastic disregard of fundamental rights would only seem to be acceptable in cases where there is an urgent necessity to protect public health and safety against immediate and serious threats, and where the interference with the physical integrity of individuals constitutes the only means to cope with these threats, e. g., in the case of serious contagious disease or mental illness. Furthermore, legality demands that in such cases the exercise of physical coercion is expressly allowed under formal statutes. Medical examinations of workers and of recipients of disability benefits obviously do not meet these requirements. Besides, a further argument against direct constraints can be found in the fact that labor and social security laws already provide for serious sanctions in case of noncompliance. If obligatory medical examinations of disability benefit claimants can be accepted in principle (provided that no direct coercion is used), the issue is by which substantive and procedural rules they should be governed. According to the first criterion, mentioned earlier, they must serve specific objectives that can be justified in terms of public policy. This demand is satisfied as long as the purpose is to protect social security funds against unjustified or fraudulent claims, or to assess the degree of disability which gives rise to a specific level of benefit.

As to the second criterion, Dutch tribunals have several times underlined its relevance: the examinations must be absolutely necessary to realize this aim [8].

Third, the examination must be reasonable. What makes it unreasonable, or constitutes a "good cause" (Great Britain) or "valid ground" (Holland) for refusal to cooperate? According to Ogus and Barendt [9], in English social security law, beside illness or physical disability preventing the claimant from attending the examination, a "good cause" exists when the claimant satisfies the authorities on the conviction of his beliefs which prevent him from compliance. The claimant must prove that it is his personal conviction which compels him to do so, and not only the abstract tenets of his religion.

Dutch tribunals have accepted the refusal of claimants who were not supposed to be able to make well-considered decisions on cooperation or noncooperation; they likewise accepted the refusal of a claimant who would have suffered serious financial loss in case of commitment to a hospital for observation, and of another claimant who had already been subjected to the same medical examination. They dismissed the claim of a beneficiary who had simply refused to submit to a lumbar puncture [8].

It is also defensible for the claimant to refuse when the examination entails unreasonable risks or pain. One can base this rule on the principle that burdens placed on a person should not exceed, but be proportional to the goals. There seems to be virtually no case in which the protection of social security funds would allow for individuals to incur serious health risks, at least not involuntarily.

Obviously, an assessment of what constitutes good cause for refusal must be made in each individual case. This calls for procedural provisions laying down the right to full information with respect to the objective and character of the examination, the right of appeal in case of (imminent) sanctions, and the right to reexamination when compulsory examination results in the witholding or withdrawal of benefits. In the Netherlands the right to information is – as mentioned before – not explicitly recognized under labor or social security law, but is acknowledged in juridical writings. Special procedures in case of refusal to submit to medical examinations do not exist; a case of withdrawal of benefit on the basis of the result of a compulsory examination or because of lack of cooperation is subject to the general proceedings laid down by the social security acts. To improve protection against undue compulsion, a special procedure of appeal has been suggested in case of obligations in social security law that may constitute an infringement on the claimant's right to physical integrity.

3 Medical Treatment of Recipients of Disability Benefits

The risk of a serious conflict between individual freedom and obligatory medical intervention increases when the claimant is required to submit to treatment, instead of only to examination. As a rule, treatment will interfere more with the physical integrity of the individual than a mere examination (although this need not always be the case). Because the average treatment encroaches more on the right to self-determination, there would seem to be even more grounds for protective rules.

On the other hand, one should realize that the conditional duty to undergo treatment in order to restrict damage also applies to the victim of an accident under civil or common law. Who ever sues for damages takes it upon himself to do everything that can be reasonably expected to recover; if he does not, he may forfeit part of the compensation.

Thus, the obligation to submit to medical treatment as a condition for compensation is not altogether new. What is new about it is that what previously was only a legal duty toward a private party has now become a duty toward society at large, represented by the social security administration. As such, it is an example of the general tendency of the moral duty to protect or regain one's own health to change, at least partly, into a legal one. Both in recent traffic legislation and in occupational health and safety legislation, one can find several examples of these obligations of self-protection (cf. the legislation on safety belts in motor traffic, and the obligation for the self-employed – in recent English and Dutch acts – to comply with industrial safety legislation). While the legislature cares less now about the "moral good" of the citizen (cf. the liberalization of laws on public morality, abortion, euthanasia), it is interfering more and more with his "physical good" to safeguard more tangible societal interests [10].

The obligation to submit to medical treatment is contained in both of the Dutch disability laws; if the beneficiary does not comply with the directives relating to his treatment issued by the social security administration or its experts he may lose his benefit, unless there is "valid ground" for noncooperation. The same rule is stipulated by English social security law, where a ground for disqualification arises if the claimant "fails without good cause to attend for, or to submit himself to medical or other treatment" (Stat. Instr. 1975/564, Reg. 12(1) (c)).

The principles governing compulsory treatment are identical to the four criteria governing medical examinations discussed earlier. As far as the first (legitimacy of objectives), second (necessity in the light of objectives), and fourth (procedural safeguards) principles are concerned, reference should therefore be made to the preceding section. As to the third principle (reasonableness of the obligation to submit to treatment), something more should be said, if only because it has to some extent been the subject of public debate. Which steps in recovery might be reasonably required of an individual? Ogus and Barendt [9] describe the discussion of this question at the committee stage of the National Insurance Act of 1911:

> "On the one hand, it was argued that to compel a person to be vaccinated or to undergo an operation interfered with a fundamental liberty, and in many cases would involve a risk greater than that inherent in avoiding the treatment. The opposing view was that the contributors to the Fund ought not to support for a number of years a man who refused to undergo on wholly inadequate grounds an operation which was necessary for his health and which could not possible endanger his life. A compromise solution was reached, and the amendment so formulated has been incorporated in the legislation ever since. In its present form it provides that the 'disqualification shall not apply to any failure to attend for or to submit to vaccination or inocculation of any kind or to a surgical operation, unless the failure is a failure to attend for or submit to a surgical operation of a minor character and is unreasonable.'

How should "unreasonable" be interpreted here, and how should one distinguish between "major" and "minor" operations? According to Ogus and Barendt "both the policy inherent in the provision and the currency of medical usage, suggest that a 'minor' operation is one which, in ordinary circumstances, does not involve a risk to life." This interpretation does not leave much room for noncompliance.

Dutch tribunals seem to be somewhat more liberal in their approach. They have accepted refusals to run "unreasonable" risks, and to submit again to a new operation for the same disease; the refusal of a foreigner to undergo treatment in a hospital because of his completely different mental and cultural background; and the refusal of a person with an allegedly "neurotic personality structure" who was not considered to be accountable for his decision not to cooperate. These examples bear witness to the diversity of circumstances taken into consideration by Dutch tribunals (cf [8] 1976, pp. 766–767).

Again, it seems difficult to resolve the conflict between fundamental liberty and medical intervention by means of substantive rules alone. Adequate procedural provisions are necessary to maintain an acceptable balance between individual and societal interests. In this respect medical intervention to prevent, to assess, and to cure disability seems to share a common characteristic feature of many medicolegal problems: since they evade detailed regulation their satisfactory solution depends ultimately on the expansion of legal participation through adequate procedures.

References

1. Robson WA (1976) Welfare state and welfare society; illusion and reality. Allen and Unwin, London, pp 38, 174
2. Reich CA (1964–65) Individual rights and social welfare: the emerging legal issue, Yale Law J 74: 1245–1257
3. Roscam-Abbing HDC (1978) Dwang en drang in de sociale verzekeringswetgeving (Compulsion and impulsion in social security legislation), Tijdschrift voor sociale geneeskunde 56: 694–699
4. Mill JS (1976) On liberty (Acton HB ed), Dent, London, pp 65 ff
5. Weale A (1978) Paternalism and social policy. J Social Policy 157–172
6. Kaim-Caudle PR (1973) Comparative social policy and social security; a ten-country study. Robertson, London, pp 191–193
7. Commission of the European Communities (1978) Comparative tables of the social security systems in the member-states of the EC, 10th edn., CEC, Brussels
8. Martens HJO (1976) De medewerkingsplicht bij een geneeskundig onderzoek of een geneeskundige behandeling in het sociale verzekeringsrecht (The duty to cooperate with medical examinations or treatment under social security law). Sociaal Maandblad Arbeid 35: 763–769
9. Ogus AI, Barendt EM (1978) The law of social security. Butterworths, London, pp 160–161
10. Tak PJP (1978) Leven en laten leven; over paternatistische strafwetgeving (Live and let live; on paternalistic criminal legislation). Kluwer, Deventer, p 14

Medicolegal Aspects of Sterilization for Mentally Disabled Persons

B. L. Gonzales

A lawsuit was recently filed on behalf of four patients who had been sterilized when they were teenaged residents in the state of Virginia. The class-action suit, filed with the help of the American Civil Liberties Union (ACLU) asks that Virginia officials notify each of the estimated 7200 men and women who had been sterilized at state mental institutions between 1924 and 1973 that they had undergone a surgical procedure which would permanently prevent childbearing or fatherhood.

The lawsuit also asks that state hospitals be barred from performing such sterilizations in the future, except under the narrowest of circumstances, and demands that the state pay for operations to reverse the procedure among the more than 2000 patients who are still young enough to have children.

These surgical procedures were done legally under a statute that deemed sterilizations of some institutionalized persons to be in the best interest of society. The Association for Voluntary Sterilization (AVS) believes that some of the 7200 persons may indeed have welcomed permanent birth control as an advantage, but that they were given no choice in the matter is a tragedy for all the people involved. AVS is supporting the ACLU suit because practices like this must never be repeated.

These few facts affect a great many people – doctors, socialworkers, psychiatrists, family planning counselors, legislators, and judges – who are currently agonizing over the fate and future of thousands of mentally disabled persons.

Surley a way can be found to fully protect the rights and interests of those who are mentally retarded without depriving them of the options for contraception available to the rest of the community.

Civil libertarians and other conservatives interested solely with protection against involuntary sterilization would argue that a mentally incompetent person is incapable of ever giving an informed consent. On the other hand, liberal thinkers, and those who are interested in reproductive freedom for all sexually mature persons, would argue that no group of people should be categorically denied the benefits of sterilization.

The laws tend to confuse, rather than clarify, the issue. In most countries, legislation pertaining to voluntary sterilization is either non existent or non specific. Where laws exist, they appear to fall into three groups:

1. One group permits consent for surgical treatment to be given by the parents or guardians of incompetent persons (without apparent regard for the wishes of the individual); Grenada and Yugoslavia have such laws [4].
2. Another group considers eugenic sterilization to be legal; Egypt, Panama, Saudi Arabia, and Sweden take this stand [4].

3. The third group takes into account the probability that there is serious limitation of the capacity of the person concerned to care for a child. This is considered grounds for sterilization in Finland, Iceland, Norway, and South Africa [4].

In the United States of America, 24 states[1] have laws providing for some form of sterilization of persons suffering from mental disorders [6]. The statutes vary in their provisions, some distinguishing between mental illness and mental retardation, others failing to do so. Some laws allow relatives, guardians, physicians, welfare boards, or others to initiate the sterilization proceedings. Only one state[2] permits the mentally retarded person to petition for his or her own sterilization.

Many of these laws were written with institutionalized persons in mind. Some were written earlier in this century, when public policy was rooted in the idea – now discredited – that mental retardation is invariably hereditary. Laws sought to control the occurrence of retardation by preventing retarded persons from reproducing, thereby "protecting" society. Today, with increased knowledge and recognition of the need to protect the rights of mentally incompetent persons, the underlying rationale for these old laws is no longer valid. All laws permitting compulsory sterilization should be declared null and void.

From the legal aspect, the most pressing issue is how to ensure that any decision to be sterilized is one which is informed and unpressured. The assessment of the client's capacity to understand that information is one of the basic responsibilities of those who provide voluntary sterilization services. Few family planning counselors or service providers are willing to take the risk of assessing persons who have an impaired capacity to understand. It is much easier to say they cannot serve any mentally retarded clients, or that it is "against the law."

The United States Department of Health and Human Services was not able to come to satisfactory terms with the difficult question of sterilization for mentally incompetent persons. In spite of the fact that the agency observed that there was indeed a class of people whose continued fertility may be against the best interests of the individual and society, the Department was not willing to establish a mechanism which would permit some sterilizations under proper safeguards. They feared that they would be unable to enforce compliance with any such rules, and that monitoring (or "policing") program activities would be extremely difficult. The Department chose instead to ban all federal funds from programs or projects which would provide sterilization for a mentally incompetent individual [5]. They defined this as "a person who has been declared mentally incompetent" by a court. A loophole was built into this definition; it continues, "... unless he or she has been declared competent for purposes which include the ability to consent to sterilization."

The Department should be commended for having had the foresight to recognize that although some individuals who have been declared incompetent cannot handle some of their affairs – for example, their financial responsibilities – they could nonetheless be perfectly capable of making decisions regarding their own health or contraceptive needs.

---

1 Arizona, Arkansas, California, Colorado, Connecticut, Delaware, Georgia, Idaho, Iowa, Maine, Minnesota, Mississippi, Montana, New Hampshire, North Carolina, Ohio, Oklahoma, Oregon, South Carolina, Utah, Vermont, Virginia, West Virginia, Wisconsin

2 Colorado

The intention of the Department was to protect persons from involuntary sterilizations, but the unintended effect is that access to sterilization is also denied to others. Those who are not dependent upon financial assistance programs are free to seek sterilization unaffected by the government's ban. But their indigent counterparts are subject to discrimination and exposed to substantial unnecessary suffering as a result of this restriction.

The regulations have another unintended effect upon people who have limited capacity to understand, but who have not legally been declared incompetent. Although the regulations only address the matter of adjudicated mental incompetence, the providers of service, especially surgeons and hospitals, are reluctant to sterilize any mentally handicapped individuals, because they fear possible liability claims. Service is being withheld categorically, even though individual counseling would reveal that many persons are fully capable of understanding the nature and consequences of sterilization, and because they are aware of their limited capabilities want to exercise their right to be sterilized.

For more than a decade, the Association for Voluntary Sterilization has gathered and studied material relating to U.S. sterilization statutes. Many of these laws leave unanswered questions and, in effect, create inequalities by their omissions. The Association has recently prepared a model voluntary sterilization act and will make it available to those who have determined that there is a need for such legislation in their particular jurisdiction.

The purpose and effect of a voluntary sterilization law should be to permit sterilization to be used by all adults who are capable of giving informed consent, and who request such a procedure as a permanent form of contraception. The central legal issue is one of consent; the AVS model statute authorizes only voluntary sterilization.

This model act permits sterilization after the person requesting it has received counseling and has given consent in writing. Where the person requesting sterilization is retarded or mentally impaired, his or her ability to give informed consent must be determined. Under this act, a person whose ability to comprehend the meaning of such a request or whose capacity to give informed consent may be questioned receives counseling, the assistance of and representation by a patient advocate, and review by a special committee.

Because the voluntary nature of an institutionalized person's consent is uniquely difficult to ensure, the AVS model act does not include such persons. Because AVS is an organization concerned only with voluntary sterilization, this model bill also does not address the issue of sterilization for those persons who are too impaired to be able to comprehend the implications of sterilization. Yet, it is from parents or guardians of persons in this category that pleas for guidance and assistance come. Support for any development of a statute which would accept the consent of parent or guardian as a substitute for that of a profoundly retarded person will probably come from groups dealing specifically with retardation, rather than from family planning groups.

It is obvious that individuals without a capacity to give informed consent are particularly vulnerable to sterilization against their will or without their knowledge, possibly for the convenience of parents, guardians, or other custodians. But, it is also true that severe hardships could result for some from continued fertility. Individual cases often present unique and painfully difficult circumstances in which the benefits of sterilization could far outweigh its risk. These would include some who are unable to use other forms of contraception and who may be totally incapable of caring responsibly for any children.

Prior to the 1974 federal court decision which placed a moratorium on sterilization of mentally incompetent persons dependent upon U.S. federal funds, a study [3] had been in process at Case Western Reserve University School of Medicine in Cleveland, Ohio. Twenty mentally retarded children were sterilized between the ages of 10.5 and 19.5; nine by tubal ligation, one by vasectomy, and ten by hysterectomy. Follow-up showed that the patients were able to assume greater social independence. School attendance improved for the hysterectomy group because previously they had been excluded from school several days each month while they were unable to cope with menstrual hygiene independently. No adverse personality changes were observed. Even two who had preoperatively expressed a desire to "have babies" did not become depressed postoperatively.

The subject of elective hysterectomy raises a set of separate controversies. The story of Camille Whitney, as told by her mother, illustrates some of the problems [7].

Camille was an adolescent with Down's syndrome who could not understand menstruation and was frightened by the sight of blood despite the mother's attempt to bring some understanding to her bewildered child. Mrs. Whitney, who was a nurse, broached the idea of hysterectomy to several surgeons. Not one would commit himself; not one would become involved. Some probably refused because of religious beliefs. Others claimed they had never heard of the practice, and apparently did not want to hear of it now, either. Others said Camille's problems were not sufficient reason for surgery.

Eventually, Mrs. Whitney found a doctor who believed a hysterectomy was appropriate for Camille, and who performed one. But Mrs. Whitney asks, "How many mothers will fight for the liberation of their retarded girls?" These girls, too, deserve the chance to be like Camille – a happy little girl, free of that "bodily function which they will never understand, which confuses and terrifies, dulls and tires, and for some, hurts terribly".

If hysterectomy may be the procedure of choice in such cases why would surgeons refuse to perform it? It is the opinion of Dr. Warren H. Pearse, executive director of the Amiercan College of Obstetrics and Gynecology (ACOG), that there are increasing difficulties in doing what both the physician and family believe is best. "Medical audit or concurrent peer review would certainly 'flag' such a hysterectomy as outside the norm of practice, exposing the physician to censure and the family to denial of insurance benefits" [1].

The case of Camille has medical, legal, social, and cultural implications, and well captures the frustrations parents of mentally retarded adolescents often experience because of a present-day cultural trend that is caught up in 'protecting individual rights' to the exlusion of common sense. By not having a hysterectomy, Camille would have the 'right' to continued anxiety and tears throughout her life. Social workers are suggesting we should also pay attention to the rights of the parents and the rights both of the unborn child and the community which may have the responsibility of caring for the potential child.

Many retarded individuals understand that they are emotionally unable to cope with the responsibilities of rearing children, and in their limited capacity, are forced to consider economic as well as genetic realities. Most of those who support themselves in the community have minimal incomes at best. If they marry, it is seldom to anyone above their own level of intelligence and earning power. The birth of a child poses increased financial burdens that can only cause further deprivation. If the offspring is retarded, with concomitant medical problems, the impact is often unmanageable. Various social agencies must intervene, and any concept of independent living is destroyed.

The philosopher Robert Neville, writing in a publication of the Institute of Society, Ethics, and the Life Sciences [8], argues that it can be morally permissible to sterilize some mildly retarded people without their understanding consent if that would foster their membership in the "moral community." He admits that such a stand is tantamount to regarding these persons as unqualified for full membership in the moral community. But he believes that full membership requires what the retarded lack – a complete personality structure that makes a person responsible for his actions.

Neville argues that sterilization "acknowledges real incapacities and neutralizes their effect, thereby enabling other capacities to be realized." However, the price society has made the retarded pay for their incapacity to be parents is the sacrifice of their capacities for affection, sexuality, personal freedom, even marriage, all of which could be developed with freedom from childbearing.

The AVS does not encourage sterilization for minors, believing that with additional years of development (which hopefully include sex education) the retarded person will be better prepared to take an active part in making any decision regarding contraception. One reason to delay the decision is that with improved methods of training and teaching, it is no longer possible to predict accurately what level of functioning a young retarded person will eventually attain.

Another reason for delaying the decision is that some persons who are labeled retarded are suffering instead from emotional or physical disabilities which hinder learning. Additional years may provide enough time for their problems to be identified and successfully treated, freeing them of the 'retarded' label.

Conclusion

Until our ever-growing knowledge of the etiology of retardation becomes more refined, and until other methods of birth control become more practical, voluntary sterilization can be the wisest choice for many who want to lead reasonably normal and responsible lives. People who suffer from mental retardation have the right to live the most satisfactory, socially productive lives possible. Barriers to this end must be surmounted.

The Association for Voluntary Sterilization believes a step toward the solution of the problem of whether or not voluntary sterilization is an appropriate component of rehabilitation services for sexually mature retarded persons lies in the acceptance of guidelines which would make sterilization available to all, and imposed upon none.

References

1. Editorial (1976) Hysterectomy was a solution: Was it the right one? R. N. Magazine, Oradell, NJ, December, pp 45–46
2. Pallister PD, Perry RM (1973) Reflections on marriage for the retarded: The case for voluntary sterilization. Hosp Community Psychiatry 24 (No. 3): 172–174
3. Perrin JC, Sands CR, Tinker DE, Dominguez BC, Dingle JT, Thomas MJ (1976) A considered approach to sterilization of mentally retarded youth. Am J Dis Child 130: 288–290
4. United Nations Fund for Population Activities (1979) Survey of laws on fertility control. UN, New York
5. US Department of Health, Education and Welfare (1978) Federal register, Nov. 8, vol 43. US DHEW, Washington, DC, p 217
6. US Department of Health, Education and Welfare (1978) Family planning, contraception, voluntary sterilization and abortion: An analysis of laws and policies. USGPO, Washington, DC pp 38–44
7. Whitney RP (1976) I dared to seek surgery for my retarded daughter. R. N. Magazine, Oradell, NJ, December pp 38–44
8. Willard G, Thompson T, Neville R, Bayles M (1978) Sterilization of the retarded: In whose interest? Hastings Cent Rept 8 (3): 28–41

V. Epilogue

The Eighties: Decade of Handicapped People

B. Posner*

In the stories of two early leaders of the black people of the United States of America lie the past, present, and future of the handicapped people of the world. Both lived a hundred years ago, in the years after the civil war which brought an end to black slavery.

Booker T. Washington was one of them – strong-willed, absolutely sure of what was best for the black people of the USA, pragmatic to the point of being willing to sacrifice principles for programs. In a speech made in Atlanta – to which the entire US government paid close attention – he proposed that the blacks would be willing to give up all claims to equality, to political power, to civil rights, in exchange for a national programm of decent vocational education, through which they could begin to finds jobs in crafts and industry, and leave the back-breaking work of the fields.

W. E. B. Du Bois, on the other hand, would strike no bargains. He proclaimed that equality was equality; there were no degrees. And equality meant taking control of one's own life, making one's own decisions, for better or for worse. Let him tell of his own beginnings, in his own words:

> I was born by a golden river in the shadow of two great hills (in a town in New Hampshire) ... The schools were simple but good. I started in one school and continued there until I was graduated. The colored people were not set aside [1, p. 61].

But then he wanted to attend college – Harvard or Yale – and was informed in no uncertain terms by the townspeople that black folks went to black colleges. "Thenceforth," he said, "I knew I was a Negro" [1].

He was an uncompromising black, urging his people to speak out for themselves. Halfway measures, as proposed by Booker T. Washington, were unacceptable. He said: "So far as Booker T. Washington apologizes for injustice, I must oppose him."

Booker T. Washington and W. E. B. Du Bois symbolize two diverse directions the world has been taking in pursuing better lives for handicapped people. Within the context of its own time and place neither approach is completely right, yet neither is completely wrong.

The Washington approach – the experts know what is best for the people they serve – has been around for a long time, and is still strong in many places. It is rooted in a kind of paternalism: "We know more about the needs of these clients, these patients, than they themselves know, and we tell them what kinds of careers to pre-

* Executive Director, President's Committee on Employment of the Handicapped, Washington, D.C.

pare for. what kind of rehabilitation to undertake, what to do with their lives." For example, it is still somewhat the practice here and there to place handicapped people in sheltered workshops, because the professionals think they are not capable of handling regular jobs.

For years, the handicapped went along with having their destinies made by others; there was not much that they could do about it. Many of them actually took their cues from society, and considered themselves not quite as good as other people, somehow imperfect.

An articulate, sensitive young man in England wrote of his impressions in the matter. Here are the team of professionals, he says – social workers, counselors, rehabilitation people, others – joining forces, planning strategies, swooping down upon the poor unsuspecting handicapped persons, taking over their lives, capturing their souls.

The W. E. B. Du Bois approach is newer, dating to the past decade and not much before that. It is rooted in a basic yearning for equality and nothing less. It is impatient, militant. It wants to take over decision-making, taking it out of the hands of well-meaning professionals, the providers of services.

This approach is becoming more prevalent as we enter the decade of the 1980s, not just in the United States, but in a growing number of nations. Israel's own handicapped consumers' movement has just recently gotten off the ground. The approach is bound to grow and proliferate in the decade ahead. To understand why, it might be useful to look back at the 1970s and examine some of the international roots of this approach.

First there was the 1971 United Nations Declaration on the Rights of Mentally Retarded Persons, not benefits, not welfare, but rights. These are rights that imply self-determination, taking control of their own lives, rights to education, to rehabilitation, to training, enabling them to develop to their fullest.

Second came the 1975 United Declaration on the Rights of Disabled Persons, both the physically and the mentally handicapped. Here are the words that count: "Disabled persons have the inherent right to respect for their human dignity. This implies first and foremost the right to enjoy a decent life as normal and full as possible."

Third, there is the report of a task group of the International League of Societies for the Mentally Retarded – a report applying to all disabled persons – pointing out that resolutions are not enough. They must serve as the underpinnings of laws enacted by individual countries, legal cases settled by judges around the globe.

Finally, there is the most recent UN Declaration establishing 1981 as the International Year of Disabled Persons. This is a recognition that even laws alone are not enough. There must be a galvanized public awareness. There must be the positive shaping of world public opinion. There must be a revived self-awareness of handicapped people themselves. This was the meaning of the Year; it was a year in which the key words were "full participation" and "full equality."

With those strong international roots, it is quite evident that the Du Bois approach – self-determination, full equality – will be dominant in the 1980s.

Obviously, this does not mean we are approaching Utopia or anything like it. This approach brings with it an entirely new set of vexing problems. It is an approach which does not spread equally, like a blanket, over the whole world; different countries make progress at different rates, but the direction is that of Du Bois, toward fuller rights. It implies several things.

First, the movement brings with it a new, positive self-concept of disabled people.

For too long their self-concept was imposed from outside: they were disabled; could not possibly be on a par with those who were not. But now disabled people are beginning to realize that their handicaps are nothing to be ashamed of. They need not think of themselves as "inferior," as "incomplete," as "deficient" because of disabilities. Their disabilities are rather a fact of their lives.

This is sometimes difficult for the rest of the world to understand, difficult for professionals as well. When regulations were being written for a law passed in the United States, the question arose: "How can handicapped people be identified?" A solution was proposed: "Let them get doctors' certificates." Handicapped people protested loudly, and the approach did not prevail.

This new self-concept of handicapped people – that they are just as good, just as able, just as "normal" as all others – leads to a second point. Handicapped people are now beginning to organize – not in social clubs, not in recreation societies, but in organizations intent on exercising political power. They are becoming a visible, viable bloc in several countries, to be reckoned with by lawmakers and government leaders. In some countries, the United States and Israel for example, these organizations are in the nature of coalitions, a bringing together under a single umbrella of many groups made up of handicapped people or their advocates. These newly emerging organizations of the handicapped speak in a sense for all handicapped people of a city or nation. Lawmakers are well aware of this; they listen carefully and respond when they can.

In the United States, organizations of disabled people played a key part in the enactment of laws in 1973, requiring most employers in the U.S.A. to give equal opportunities to disabled workers. In Israel, the new umbrella organization of diability groups was the key to enactment of the new accessibility law, requiring that Israel's public buildings, new and old, be made accessible to disabled people. This kind of organized political action could not have taken place without the positive self-image disabled people have been developing in recent years.

A third point is that a new public concept of the "wholeness" that of diabled people seems to be developing. We are beginning to realize that we cannot compartmentalize them, that we cannot think of them two-dimensionally. We are beginning to be concerned with their total lives – work, school, recreation, daily living, transportation, accessibility, marriage, parenthood, and everything else that goes into the creation of total people.

This growing concept of "wholeness" can lead to a breakdown of the sterotypes society has held about handicapped people. It is rather hard to retain a sterotype in one's mind when confronted with the totality of human existence. All of a sudden, these people about whom one has held stereotyped ideas appear in the flesh, in their humanness. They are people, and stereotypes start to melt away.

Some of us specialize in certain areas – employment, or housing, or rehabilitation, or whatever. We, too, have to retain our awareness of the "wholeness" of people, and not get carried away by our own little piece of the whole.

Another point is that as disabled people begin to come across as total people, some facts begin to emerge, and society seems to be accepting those facts quite naturally. There is the fact that some disabled people need special considerations to retain their "wholeness." Those with ambulatory problems need accessible buildings and transportation. Those who are deaf need interpreter services in many places – at meetings, on television, at the theater. Those who are blind may need some of the remarkable equipment which enables them to "read" words.

There is also the fact that many of these special considerations – curb cuts, ramps, reading machines – cost money, but we are beginning to experience a surprising degree of social willingness to bear the costs. Why? Perhaps because we already are accustomed to bearing costs for other special groups in our society. Or perhaps because we have a sort of positivism about handicapped people, or because many of these costs are one-time-only. We also see that some of these adaptations benefit all and not just a few; we all prefer ramps to steep stairs.

Whatever the reasons, society bears the cost willingly, and disabled people begin to appear everywhere, to enjoy broadened options of life, to get the chance to grow as other people do. Ramps and all the rest become symbols of people who are in society, not apart from it.

The final point relates to employment. Some important changes have been occurring in the employment of handicapped people around the world. Slowly, some countries seem to be getting away from purely voluntary systems of employment whereby a firm can hire disabled people or refuse, as it prefers. Laws are being enacted requiring their employment. Some European countries and Japan have instituted quota systems. In the USA a law has been enacted which ends the voluntary system of hiring handicapped people; discrimination has been declared illegal.

These laws have come about mainly because handicapped people themselves have used their new-found political power to advocate them. But not only handicapped people, other segments of society, too, have helped to forge these laws and to make them work. In other words, handicapped groups do not work alone. They join with other forces of society, such as labor and management, and deep-rooted progress takes place.

The laws barring discrimination or setting up quotes are far from perfect. They are difficult to enforce and present frustrations for employers, for labor unions, for rehabilitation, and for disabled persons themselves. But the laws exist and are symbols of the rising aspirations, the increasing visibility and sense of self-worth of disabled people.

Will the 1980s be a decade of disabled people? Who can tell? All we know is that disabled people will be more in evidence than they were in decades past.

We part company from Booker T. Washington and find ourselves following the proud and demanding footsteps of W. E. B. Du Bois. His way leads over rough terrain, with heartbreak and frustration, but there is no turning back. In fact, we would not turn back even if we could.

References

Du Bois WEB (1968) Autobiography: A soliloquy on viewing my life from the last decade of its first century, 1st edn. International Publishers, Inc.

Subject Index

accident insurance 87
accomodation 45
amputees 193
architectural barriers 53
assessment – disability 84

brain injured 191

chronic pain 106
compensation neurosis 198
competence 16
– measurement 23
confidentiality 222
consent, – ability to – 216
– assumed 218
– patient's 135
– refusal 217
court cases 51, 58, 63, 75, 81, 92, 106
credibility 72

declarations, international 3
dependent adults act 16
dignity, protectin of 168
disability 7, 84
– assessment 84
– behavioral aspects 119
– economic 96, 116
– environmental aspects 117
– functional 13
– housewife 95
– insurance 79
– medical 12, 90
– occupational 93
– pension 11, 97
– policymaking 77
– programs 76
– psychological 147
– psychosocial aspects 115, 117
– self concepts measures 147
– social aspects 101, 120
– sociocultural 116
– tabular grading 86
– work 198
disabled newborn 181
d-, sterilization 238
discrimination 46
drug addiction 188

economic disability 96
–, constraints 75
educational institutions 50
elderly amputees 193
employment 41, 76
euthanasia 182

family and the invalid 141

guardianship 17, 37, 240
– mentally ill 218

handicap 7, 41, 45, 247
handicapped offenders 58
health definition 85
heroin addicts 188
housewife's disability 94
hyperactive 58

impairment 7
incapacity 11
income, loss of 99
individual freedom 230
industrial injuries 89
informed consent 20, 28, 135, 183, 215
integration 4
invalid and family 141
involuntary medical intervention 230
isolation 4

judges, emotional reactions 68
judicial self-awareness 63, 70

learning disabilities 58
legal settlement 198
legislation 75
–, rehabilitation 159
loss of income 99

malpractice 128
–, causalty 132
–, evidence 131

medical malpractice 128
memory 71
mental disabled, sterilization 238
– incompetency 17, 80
– retardation 18, 80
mentally ill, informed consent 215, 238
methadone treatment 188

national insurance law 11
newborn, disabled 181

occupational disability 93

pain, chronic 106
perception 70
post traumatic psycho syndrom 209
prostheses 193
psycho post traumatic syndrom 209
psychoanalytic, countertransference 63
psychosocial issues 108

refusal to medical treatment 235
rehabilitation 60, 79, 141, 159
– brain injuries 191
– definitions 159
– drug addicts 188
– elderly amputees 195
– international 5
– psychosocial 125
– teeth 125
rehabilitative medicine 5
rheumatoid arthritis 147

settlement, legal 198
sickness benefit 94
social disability 101
statistics 3, 6, 41, 42, 58
sterilization compulsory 238, 239
– voluntary 240
stigma 168

testimony 59, 63, 70, 75
transference 64

United Nations 3, 41

work disability 198
workers' compensation 106

Medicolegal Library

Editor: **A. Carmi**

Volume 1

Child Abuse

Editors: **A. Carmi, H. Zimrin**
With contributions by numerous experts

1984. 39 figures. Approx. 224 pages
ISBN 3-540-12471-3

Contents: The Phenomenon. – Child Abuse and the Law. – Child Abuse and Psychiatry. – The Sexually Abused Child. – Child Abuse and Pathology. – Subject Index.

Child Abuse is the first volume in Springer-Verlag's important new series **Medicolegal Library.** An interdisciplinary approach to one of modern society's most appalling phenomena, it shows that child abuse is not the result of uniform behavior patterns, but rather has many causes requiring many different types of treatment. The contributions focus on legal, pathologic, sexual, psychiatric, and familial aspects of the problem and show how they are dealt with in various Western countries.

Volume 2

Euthanasia

Editor: **A. Carmi**
With contributions by numerous experts

1984. Approx. 160 pages
ISBN 3-540-13251-1

Contents: Introduction. – The Duty to Live and the Right to Die. – Law, Culture, and Euthanasia. – The Doctor and Euthanasia. – The Patient and Euthanasia. – Active and Passive Euthanasia. – Epilogue: The Serene Voyage to Death. – Subject Index.

The second volume in the Medicolegal Library, **Euthanasia** provides a cross-cultural view of the dignity of life and the right to die. The authors trace the phenomena of euthanasia from its earliest recorded instances to the present and consider it from the points of view of law medicine, psychology, sociology, philosophy, and religion.

Springer-Verlag
Berlin
Heidelberg
New York
Tokyo